LEGAL WORDS
YOU SHOULD
KNOW

Over **1,000 Essential Terms** to Understand
Contracts, Wills, and the Legal System

LEGAL WORDS YOU SHOULD KNOW

COREY SANDLER AND **JANICE KEEFE,**
bestselling authors of *Performance Appraisal Phrase Book*

Avon, Massachusetts

Published by
Adams Media, a division of F+W Media, Inc.
57 Littlefield Street, Avon, MA 02322. U.S.A.
www.adamsmedia.com

ISBN 10: 1-59869-865-6
ISBN 13: 978-1-59869-865-7

Printed in the United States of America.

J   I   H   G   F   E   D   C   B   A

Library of Congress Cataloging-in-Publication Data
is available from the publisher.

This publication is designed to provide accurate and authoritative information with regard to the subject matter covered. It is sold with the understanding that the publisher is not engaged in rendering legal, accounting, or other
professional advice. If legal advice or other expert assistance is required, the
services of a competent professional person should be sought.
  —From a *Declaration of Principles* jointly adopted by a Committee of the
American Bar Association and a Committee of Publishers and Associations

Many of the designations used by manufacturers and sellers to distinguish
their product are claimed as trademarks. Where those designations appear
in this book and Adams Media was aware of a trademark claim, the designations have been printed with initial capital letters.

This book is available at quantity discounts for bulk purchases.
For information, please call 1-800-289-0963.

DEDICATION

To our in-laws

ACKNOWLEDGMENTS

THIS BOOK BEARS TWO NAMES AS AUTHOR, BUT IT WOULD not be in your hands without the assistance and encouragement of many others. Thanks to Andrea Norville at Adams Media. Thanks, too, to our legal eagle Ed Claflin who minds the *p*s and *q*s.

INTRODUCTION

WE LIVE IN A WORLD OF LAWS AND LEGALITIES, SWIMMING IN a sea of legalese.

Do you have a mortgage or a lease? Is there a credit card or two in your wallet or purse? How many checking, banking, or investment accounts do you have? Are you an addicted fan of *CSI* or *Law and Order* or the latest paperback legal thriller?

Or, do you have some legal problems of your own— from traffic misdemeanors to estate issues to criminal charges? You would be *non compos mentis* to attempt to mount a legal defense without some level of understanding of the words that exist in the agreements we are asked to sign, the legal documents we are presented, the demands of an attorney or court.

We are not lawyers, and nearly all of the readers of this book have not gone to law school either. As professional writers, though, our goal is to provide a translation between the essential words of the law and finance into terms you can understand. The best use of this book is as a guide to learning the questions to ask as you try to navigate that sea of laws.

1040, *noun*

The standard form issued annually by the Internal Revenue Service for individuals to use in filing an income tax return.

*Form **1040** includes provisions for taxpayers to list itemized deductions and take advantage of various tax credits.*

See also: 1040EZ

1040EZ, *noun*

An Internal Revenue Service form, similar to the 1040, simplified for use by taxpayers with lower income.

*The IRS **1040EZ** form is intended for taxpayers who do not make use of itemized deductions or other elements that require more detailed reporting of information.*

See also: 1040

1099, *noun*

An Internal Revenue Service form used to report various types of income other than wages.

*Many taxpayers receive a **1099**-DIV form from companies or brokerages that have paid them dividends in the prior tax year. An SSA-1099 is a form issued by the Social Security Administration reporting benefits paid to individuals.*

A

ABA number, *noun*

As developed by the American Banking Association, a routing code imprinted on checks and deposit slips that is used to direct electronic transfer of funds to and from accounts.

*To enable direct deposit of a paycheck, the employer requires the **ABA number** for your bank as well as your account number at the bank.*

See also: Routing transit number

Abandonment, *noun, verb*

To give up control of something, such as real or personal property. Or to give up responsibility for a person, such as leaving a spouse or a child.

*Depending on the circumstances, in some situations the **abandonment** of a child may rise to the level of a crime.*

See also: Desertion

Abate (ah-BATE), *verb*

To end a problem.

*State regulators reached an agreement with the company to **abate** the discharge of untreated waste into the municipal wastewater system through the installation of a private treatment plant at the factory.*

See also: Abatement

Abatement (ah-BATE-mint), *noun*

(1) A reduction or end to a particular tax or fee. (2) Also, to lessen or mitigate the burden of a regulation on a person or business.

*(1) The state legislature approved a bill giving tax **abatements** to businesses that build new facilities or add new jobs within the state. (2) The parties agreed to an **abatement** of the zoning violation that called for the gradual reduction in the usage of the land for manufacturing and a change to use for offices, over a period of five years.*

See also: Abate

Abduction (ab-DUK-shun), *noun*

(1) The act of forcibly taking a person away. (2) Also applies to acts that allow someone to take a person away against their will through improper persuasion or fraud.

*(1) Schilling was accused of the forcible **abduction** of the woman from the bar where they met. (2) The prosecutor alleged that Gerschwin committed the crime of **abduction** when he misled the man into thinking he had to come to the collection agency or face arrest.*

See also: Kidnap

Abet (uh-BET), *verb*

To encourage, incite, or assist someone to commit a crime, violate a law, or perform an illegal act.

*If you aid and **abet** someone in committing a crime or an illegal act, you could put yourself in legal jeopardy.*

See also: Accessory, Accomplice

Abeyance (a-BAY-ince), *noun*

(1) A condition of being temporarily unenforced, or (2) of being undetermined.

*(1) The judge held enforcement of the law in **abeyance** pending review by a higher court. (2) Issuance of the title to ownership of the land was held in **abeyance** while issues related to the estate were resolved.*

See also: Stay

Abrogate (AB-ro-gate), *verb*

(1) To make null, or to repeal a law. (2) Also to revoke or withdraw an element of a contract.

*(1) The legislature **abrogated** the court case when it repealed the law against sale of widgets on Sunday. (2) By mutual agreement, the parties **abrogated** the section of the contract that called for the use of virgin plastic components in the manufacture of widgets and substituted a clause that encouraged the use of recycled plastic wherever practical and possible.*

See also: Null, Void

Abscond (ab-SKOND), *verb*

(1) To leave a place or jurisdiction to avoid being served with legal papers or to avoid arrest. (2) Also, to leave with stolen property.

*(2) According to the prosecutor, the defendant attempted to **abscond** from the county before she could be served with the subpoena. (2) The lawsuit claimed the defendant had **absconded** with a large sum of cash from the day's receipts.*

Absolute, *adjective*

Complete and without limitation or conditions. Also known as an absolute privilege.

*The U.S. Constitution includes an **absolute** right against double jeopardy, where someone is tried twice for the same crime.*

Abstract of Title, *noun*

A summary of the details of the history of ownership and conveyances of a property that is intended to prove the true owner of a piece of land as well as the owner's right to sell or otherwise dispose of the land.

*The buyer's attorney required a current **Abstract of Title** for the property, as well as a title insurance policy to protect against any undisclosed flaws or impairments to the transfer.*

See also: Title, Title insurance policy

A

Abuse, *noun*

(1) Mistreatment of a person including physical, psychological, or sexual cruelty. (2) Also, the improper exercise of a right or power.

*(1) The defendant was charged with **abuse** of her children by not providing a safe and healthy place for them to live. (2) The sheriff was accused of **abuse** of the powers of his office for selective traffic arrests of persons who disagreed with his policies.*

Abuse of discretion, *noun*

Courts and government agencies are sometimes allowed to exercise discretion in certain matters such as application of particular laws or regulations or determination of sentences, penalties, or fines. A higher court or an administrative body may find that such a decision was an abuse of that discretion.

*The appeals court found that the county court's pattern of dismissing charges against all first offenders in misdemeanor cases to be an **abuse of discretion** and directed that state judicial guidelines be followed.*

Abuse of process, *noun*

The use of the judicial process for an improper purpose such as a means of extortion or as a means to gain an advantage unrelated to the intended purpose of the lawsuit.

*The judge threw out the lawsuit filed by Consolidated Intergalactic, calling it an **abuse of process** because the matter could have been settled by negotiation rather than by the threat of an expensive and time-consuming court process.*

See also: Frivolous suit, Vexatious

Abutting (uh-BUTT-ing), *verb*

Something that touches upon or borders a piece of land, including other land, a structure, or a road.

*The zoning code requires persons seeking exemptions from town regulations to notify owners of all **abutting** properties at least thirty days before the board holds a hearing on the request.*

See also: Zoning

Accelerated depreciation, *noun*

In financial accounting and taxation matters, a schedule for lowering the value of certain assets faster than the ordinary period of time. If a piece of equipment is depreciated in this way a company may be able to reduce its taxes, although it will also reduce reported income on financial statements.

Accelerated depreciation is sometimes employed to write off (remove from the books) the value of major pieces of equipment that are likely to be replaced after a short period of use, including computers and other technologies that rapidly become obsolete.

See also: Depreciation

Accelerate, Acceleration, *verb, noun*
To move forward the due date on a loan or contract, or to move forward the time when ownership of property is transferred.

The promissory note gives the lender the right to **accelerate** *the due date of the full amount of principal and accrued interest if the borrower falls more than forty-five days behind scheduled payments.*

See also: Call

Accessory, *noun*
A person who provides assistance in the commission of a crime without direct involvement.

The defendant's wife was charged with being an **accessory** *to the crime for serving as the driver of the getaway vehicle. Although he was not a participant in the fraud, Cain was convicted of being an* **accessory** *in the commission of the crime because he provided confidential information about the company's financial practices.*

See also: Accomplice, Abet

Accommodation (uh-COM-uh-day-shun), *noun*
Something that is done as a favor, without the exchange of payment or other consideration.

Although we feel that the failure of your product was not our fault, as a special **accommodation** *to a valued customer we have decided to repair or replace the item.*

Accomplice, *noun*
Someone who assists in the commission of the crime.

The indictment also named Dowd as an **accomplice** *in the act, alleging that he was a full participant in the robbery.*

See also: Accessory, Abet

Accord (uh-CORD), *noun*

An agreement between two parties to settle a claim, either ending a lawsuit or avoiding the filing of a suit.

*The two sides reached an **accord** before the case came to trial and the lawsuit was dismissed.*

See also: Settlement

Accounting, *noun*

A system for recording and summarizing how an individual, business, or estate has acquired, managed, or disposed of assets.

*The agreement calls for a full **accounting** of all of the business activities of both corporations for the period covering the past five fiscal years before the merger is finalized.*

See also: Calendar year, Fiscal year

Accounts payable, *noun*

(1) Money that is owed by a company or professional to another party. (2) Also, a department at a business that is responsible for keeping track of obligations owed and for paying them when due.

*(1) The auditor reported that the company averaged about $600,000 in **accounts payable** each month. (2) The **accounts payable** department asked all creditors to provide necessary information to permit electronic payment of all bills.*

See also: Accounts receivable

Accounts receivable, *noun*

(1) Money owed to a business by customers or clients. (2) Also, a department at a business that is responsible for keeping track of and collecting money owed.

*(1) The analysis showed the company had **accounts receivable** totaling $1.2 million. (2) The request for payment was made by the **accounts receivable** department.*

See also: Accounts payable

Accretion (uh-CREE-shun), *noun*

The increase in the size of a piece of property caused by the deposit of soil on the shoreline of a river, lake, or the sea.

*On one side of the island of Nantucket, property is seeing gradual **accretion** caused by tides and storms, while at the other side miles of beachfront has been eroded by the same forces.*

See also: Erosion

Accrue (uh-CREW), *verb*

(1) To grow or accumulate, such as the effect of interest applied to a debt or an investment. (2) Also, to come into existence or become able.

*(1) Under terms of the agreement, the security deposit given the landlord will **accrue** interest at 5 percent annually. (2) Under terms of the contract, the right to sue for damages only **accrues** after all reasonable attempts at reaching an accord have been made.*

Accrued interest (uh-CRUDE interest), *noun*

The amount of interest that has accumulated on the unpaid principal balance of a loan.

*In most loans, the **accrued interest** is calculated daily, based on the outstanding balance of principal plus any unpaid interest that has been added to the principal.*

A

Accuse, accused, *verb, noun*

(1) To formally charge with a crime. (2) When someone is officially charged with a crime by a police officer, prosecutor, or grand jury; the person is referred to as the accused.

*(1) Police **accused** Sam Ochs of robbing the convenience store. (2) The **accused** burglar was apprehended inside the store. The court ordered the **accused** held on $100,000 cash bail until trial.*

See also: Charge, Indict, Defendant, Plaintiff

Acknowledge (ack-NAW-lidj), *verb*

Acceptance by an individual of legal responsibility.

*I **acknowledge** that the statement of facts in this document is accurate and true.*

Acknowledgment (ack-NAW-lidj-ment), *noun*

In a civil case, an admission by an individual or an entity that a particular statement is true or factual.

*In a contract or other legal document, the **acknowledgment** is the section at the end where a notary public verifies or witnesses the signing of a document.*

Acquiring bank, *noun*

In a credit card or debit card transaction, the financial institution that accepts payment on behalf of a merchant or service provider.

*When a retailer accepts a credit card in payment for a purchase, the processing of the transaction and the transfer of funds is handled by the **acquiring bank** with which it has contracted.*

See also: Credit card

Acquit (a-QUIT), *verb*

To find a defendant not guilty of a charge in the course of a criminal trial or at its conclusion.

*The jury voted to **acquit** Wolf of all charges of bank fraud and the judge ordered his immediate release from custody.*

See also: Verdict, Not guilty, Convict, Conviction

A

Act of God, *noun*

A natural catastrophe beyond the ability of humans to prevent, such as an earthquake, a hurricane, a tornado, or a volcanic eruption.

*The company is not responsible for delays or damage caused by **acts of God**.*

Action, *noun*

A civil lawsuit.

*The plaintiff initiated an **action** against the manufacturer, seeking compensatory and punitive damages as the result of the collapse of the storage shed.*

See also: Lawsuit

Actionable, *adjective*

A situation where a party feels it has sufficient reason to file a lawsuit. In general, a judge will decide if the facts recited in the suit or complaint meet the legal requirements to bring a matter before the court.

*The company's counsel advised the board of directors that the breakdown of the contract had reached the point where it was **actionable**, and he advised filing a lawsuit.*

See also: Cause of action

Ad hoc (ADD hock), *adjective*
A Latin phrase meaning, "for this purpose only."
*The county commissioner convened an **ad hoc** committee to study the unexpected impact of the new shopping mall.*

Ad litem (ad-LI-tem), *adjective*
A Latin phrase meaning "for this purpose only." It is generally used in situations such as the appointment of a legal guardian for a minor or an adult who is incapable of making decisions or making appearances in court.
*The court appointed the child's aunt as guardian **ad litem** and allowed her to manage finances and make medical decisions.*
See also: Guardian

Ad valorem (ad-ve-LOR-em), *adjective*
A Latin phrase meaning "to the value." An ad valorem tax is a levy that is based on a percentage of the value of property.
*Some states impose an excise or **ad valorem** tax on real property such as land and homes, or on certain types of personal property such as automobiles; the tax is calculated as a percentage of the assessed value or assumed value.*
See also: Excise tax, Property tax, Sales tax

Addendum (a-DEN-dum), *noun*
A clause or term added to a standard contract or to an insurance policy. Also called a rider.
*The employment contract included an **addendum** that required Jones not to participate in dangerous sports such as hang-gliding, skydiving, or bungee-jumping.*
See also: Rider

Additur (ad-di-TUR), *noun*
(1) A power given to a trial judge in some jurisdictions to increase the amount of an award for damages made by a jury. (2) This might be done because the judge finds the amount awarded to be inadequate, or as a condition of an agreement with the defendant that denies a motion for a new trial.
*(1) The judge, finding that the jury's award of damages was inadequate and unreasonable, increased the amount with an order of **additur**. (2)*

*The defendant agreed to an **additur** to the damages awarded by the jury as a condition for the denial of the plaintiff's motion for a new trial.*

Adeem (ah-DEEM), *verb*
To effectively revoke a gift made in a will by giving it away, destroying it, or other disposing of the item during the lifetime of the person writing the will. For example, if the will states that a person is to receive a valuable work of art from the testator but before death the art is sold or given to someone else, the writer of the will has adeemed the gift.
*Mr. Adelie **adeemed** his bequest of his collection of rare stamps when he donated them to charity two years before his death.*
See also: Ademption, Bequest, Testator

Ademption, *noun*
The reduction in the value of an estate as the result of funds, investments, or property that have been sold, given away, or otherwise disposed of before the death of the testator.
*Because of a pattern of **ademption** over the years, the value of Mr. Buckley's estate was near zero by the time of his death.*
See also: Adeem

A

Adjournment, *noun*
The postponement of a court session or the temporary stoppage of a meeting of a public agency until another time and date.
*The judge granted an **adjournment** of the proceedings until the results of DNA testing were received and entered into evidence.*
See also: Continuance

Adjudicate (a-JU-dih-kate), *verb*
(1) The act of submitting a case for decision by a court, or (2) the act of a judge or administrative agency in making a ruling on a case.
*(1) The parties were unable to resolve their differences and chose to **adjudicate** their dispute. (2) The agency **adjudicated** the matter to a hearing officer who ruled that the company had violated state regulations.*

Adjustable rate mortgage, *noun*
A mortgage with an interest rate that can vary over time. Adjustable Rate Mortgages (called ARMs by some lenders) are usually linked to published interest rates such as the prime rate or an interbank lending rate.

Depending on the language of the mortgage, the rate can be adjusted every month, once a year, or after any other specified period of time.

*Some financial advisors recommend taking out an **adjustable rate mortgage** if interest rates are higher than recent patterns and seem likely to decline over time.*

See also: Fixed-rate mortgage

Adjusted basis, *noun*

In accounting, recalculating the value of an asset by including the costs of improvements and deducting depreciation, damage, and other things that would reduce its value.

*On an **adjusted basis**, the value of the home was calculated at $750,000.*

See also: Basis

Administrator, *noun*

A person appointed by a court to administer the estate of someone who died intestate (without having a valid will).

*The court appointed Sam Jones as **administrator** of the Williams estate.*

See also: Intestate, Estate

Admissible, *noun*

Evidence or testimony allowed to be heard or entered into a court case. Certain types of evidence are otherwise inadmissible or immaterial.

*The judge ruled that the grand jury testimony of the defendant was **admissible** as evidence in the trial and could be used in the examination by the prosecutor.*

See also: Material, Inadmissible, Immaterial

Admission, *noun*

A statement made by a party to a lawsuit, or the defendant in a criminal case.

*The prosecution entered into evidence an **admission** by the defendant to some of the facts of the case.*

Adoption (uh-DOP-shun), *noun*

The legal process that gives an adult or a married couple the rights, responsibilities, and status of a parent to a child who is not a natural offspring.

*Each state has its own laws and procedures for the **adoption** of a child.*

Advancement, *noun*

An advance payment or transfer from a testator (the author of a will) to an heir. This is intended as a substitute for the gift or transfer that would otherwise take place after the testator's death.

> *Mr. Beckett made an **advancement** of part of his estate to his daughter.*

Adversarial (ad-ver-SAIR-ee-al), *adjective*

The nature of a legal proceeding in which each side of a dispute has the responsibility to present or refute evidence so that the judge, acting as the finder of fact, can make a decision.

> *In a lawsuit, the plaintiff and defendant engage in an **adversarial** contesting of the facts of the case.*

Adverse possession, *noun*

Under certain conditions, the acquisition of property by someone who is not the owner, by continuous and open possession over time. As an example, a trespasser who occupies a property or premises without being challenged could receive title. Similarly, if an abutter places a road or fence on property and is not challenged, they could claim adverse possession of the property.

> *The neighbor claimed title to a portion of the property under **adverse possession** because he had installed and maintained a road that crossed over the property line for more than twenty years.*

See also: Squatter, Tacking

Affidavit (af-ih-DAY-vit), *noun*

A written statement, made under oath before a notary public or an officer of the court, in which the signer swears that the contents of the document are true. An affidavit may be used in a legal process or entered into evidence in a court.

> *Venutti was asked to answer a series of questions in the form of a written **affidavit** regarding the facts of this case.*

Affirm (ah-FIRM), *verb*

(1) A solemn or formal declaration—without an oath—that statements on the record, or that will be made in testimony, are true. Although it is not given under oath, it has the same legal effect as if it were given under oath. (2) Also, in the legal system, when an appeals court or other higher-level court agrees with a lower court's ruling or finding.

*(1) I **affirm** that the statements I am about to give are true. (2) The appeals court **affirms** and upholds the circuit court's ruling.*
See also: Affirmation, Oath

Affirmation (ah-fir-MAY-shun), *noun*
A formal or solemn declaration of the truthfulness of a statement or testimony, given by someone who declines for reasons of conscience or religious belief to take an oath.
*I hereby give my **affirmation** that the testimony I am about to give is true.*
See also: Affirm, Oath

Affirmative action, *noun*
An effort by a business or a government agency to encourage or give special advantages to a protected class in an effort to make up for past discrimination against hiring, admission, or promotion.
*The corporation's employment office has an **affirmative action** program aimed at increasing the number of minorities and women in the workforce to numbers that are roughly equivalent to the percentage of such persons in the community.*

After-acquired property, *noun*
Personal or real property that is purchased or otherwise acquired by a debtor after agreeing to secure a loan with all existing property. In such a circumstance, the newly acquired property also becomes part of the collateral for the earlier loan.
*The lender sought to include the new second home of the borrower as **after-acquired property**, adding it to the secured collateral for the original loan.*
See also: Security, Collateral, Promissory note

Age of consent, *noun*
As set by individual states, the age at which a person is deemed to be legally able to consent to sexual intercourse, or to get married without parental consent.
*Jones was charged with statutory rape for having sex with a minor younger than the **age of consent**.*
See also: Consent, Statutory rape, Minor

Agent, *noun*
(1) Someone who is given permission to act on behalf of someone else or who performs a particular service for someone. (2) Also, certain types of government investigators or law enforcement officers.

*(1) Curry appointed Ives as his **agent** in negotiating for the rental of business space in Chicago. (2) The state police called in a special **agent** from the Federal Bureau of Investigation to assist in the processing of the crime scene.*

Aggravated, *adjective*
A crime that rises to a more serious level, generally because of the use of a deadly weapon or because of the infliction of serious injury.

*The prosecutor charged Rudin with **aggravated** assault because the crime involved the use of a gun.*
See also: Special circumstance, First degree, Mitigating circumstances

Agreement (uh-GREE-mint), *noun*
In legal usage, a legally binding understanding with all of the elements of a binding contract.

*This **agreement** covers all of the elements of the work to be performed.*
See also: Contract, Consideration

Alias (AY-lee-us), *noun*
A name other than someone's given, married, or court-recognized official name.

*In most situations it is permissible for someone to use an **alias** or a pseudonym or otherwise be "also known as" another name, as long as this is not done for the purposes of committing fraud or hiding a true identity.*
See also: Also known as, Pseudonym

Alibi (A-li-bye), *noun*
A Latin phrase that means "in another place" and as such, a defense by a criminal defendant that he or she was elsewhere when the crime occurred. In more broad terms, it is also sometimes used as any excuse that would tend to exculpate a person from a charge.

*Simpson's defense presented an **alibi** that placed him a thousand miles away at the time the prosecution says the crime was committed.*
See also: Exculpate

Alien, *noun*

In the United States, a person who is not a citizen.

*A resident **alien** is a foreign citizen who has registered with the government and received permission to live in the United States and engage in certain types of employment. An illegal **alien** is someone who has entered the country without permission, or who has overstayed a limit on permitted time in the United States.*

See also: Green card, Resident alien

Alienate (ALE-ee-an-ate), *verb*

The voluntary transfer, gift, or sale of real property to another person or organization.

*Jane chose to **alienate** her ownership of the painting by giving it as a gift to a friend.*

Alimony (A-le-moan-ey), *noun*

Monetary support, or occasionally payment in kind, paid by one former spouse to another as the result of a court order in a divorce proceeding.

*The judge ordered Mr. Algarve to make monthly **alimony** payments of $3,000 to his former wife for her housing and maintenance expenses.*

See also: Palimony, Maintenance

Allege, Allegation (uh-LEDGE), *verb, noun*

To make a claim of a fact or an action, usually as part of a lawsuit or criminal case.

*The prosecutor **alleges** that Ms. Goniff committed larceny when she removed the garden gnome from her neighbor's yard. Goniff vigorously denied the **allegation**.*

Allocution (al-oh-CUE-shun), *noun*

(1) In a criminal case in which a defendant pleads guilty, a judge or a prosecutor may engage in an allocution, in which the judge asks questions of the defendant to make certain that he or she understands the charges and the effect of making a plea of guilty. An allocution usually includes a request that the defendant acknowledge that the plea is being made in free will. (2) Also, a right given to a defendant to speak on his or own behalf before sentencing,

*(1) The judge conducted an **allocution** of the defendant after the guilty plea, seeking to make certain the defendant understood the consequences of*

the plea. *(2) Before sentencing, the defendant was given time for an **allocution** to the court about the circumstances of the case.*

Also known as, *noun*
A way to indicate that an individual has more than one identity. This could be because of a name change due to marriage or adoption, because of the use of a stage name or a pen name, or because a person is willfully attempting to hide a true identity.

*The indictment charged Donald Nixon, **also known as** Ronald Rix and Jerry Kennedy, with fraudulently obtaining several bank loans.*

See also: Alias, Pseudonym

Ambiguity (am-bih-GYU-ih-tee), *noun*
When a phrase or law has multiple meanings or cannot be precisely defined.

*There is a great deal of **ambiguity** when it comes to certain areas of the law, including claims of discrimination.*

Amend (uh-MEND), *verb*
The act of revising or correcting a legal document.

*I wish to **amend** our previous agreement to include my correct date of birth.*

Amicus curiae (ah-MEE-cuss KYUR-ee-eye), *noun*
A Latin phrase meaning "friend of the court," used when a party that is not part of a legal case is invited by the court or given permission by the court to submit an opinion.

*The Society for Prevention of Cruelty to Animals was invited by the court to submit an **amicus curiae** brief to inform the judge about the issues involved in the case. Earlier, the judge had rejected a request from the Vegan Liberation Army to present an argument as a friend of the court.*

Amnesty (AM-nis-tee), *noun*
An action by a government to forgive specific past offenses for an identified or specified group or class of people. Under an amnesty, charges or convictions or legal proceedings are wiped out.

*The city has declared a tax **amnesty** until December 31, permitting anyone owing back property taxes to pay them without penalty.*

See also: Clemency, Pardon, Parole, Reprieve

Amortization (ah-muhr-ti-ZAY-shun), *noun*
(1) To pay off a debt over time, in an arrangement where interest and a portion of the principal are included in each payment spread over a specific period. (2) Also, in tax terms, the process of writing off or deducting from income tax a portion of the cost of an asset over time.

*(1) The loan's **amortization** schedule calls for monthly payments of $150, continuing for forty-eight months at which point the principal and accrued interest will be fully paid. (2) Tax regulations allow **amortization** of the value of certain capital investments over time.*

Annual contribution, *noun*
A retirement or other similar fund that allows a certain amount of money or a certain percentage of income to be deposited per year, in an annual contribution.

*A traditional IRA fund allows workers to deposit money, up to a maximum amount, in an **annual contribution**.*
See also: Individual retirement account

Annual meeting, *noun*
A yearly meeting of shareholders, members of a cooperative, or other such groups usually called for the purpose of electing officers or meeting financial oversight requirements.

*The corporation's **annual meeting** includes the election of the board of directors, a presentation by the chief financial officer about the previous year's results, and other organizational matters.*

Annual report, *noun*
A document required to be filed once per calendar year or fiscal year for most corporations and certain other types of businesses.

*A company's **annual report** may be required to include details of its balance sheet and income statement for a publicly held company, or information about the names of the owners of a closely held corporation.*

Annual percentage rate, *noun*
The annual percentage rate (APR) is the effective interest rate that is charged to the borrower, incorporating any fees and converting daily, weekly, or monthly interest into an annualized number.

A

*The credit card company charges a daily periodic rate of 0.0356 percent which works out to an **annual percentage rate** of 12.99 percent.*
See also: Interest

Annuity (ah-NEW-it-ee), *noun*
(1) Regular income paid at specified income based on an investment or award, continuing for either a fixed period of time or (2) for the lifetime of the recipient.

*(1) The court settlement was made in the form of an **annuity** that pays $2,500 per month to the defendant for the remainder of his life. (2) He purchased an **annuity** from the life insurance company, paying $100,000 and receiving a guaranteed monthly income of $2,000 for the remainder of his life.*
See also: Pension

Annul, *verb*
To make null or overrule an order or judgment by a court. Other words to the same effect are negate or set aside.

*The appeals court **annulled** the lower court's order and sent it back for re-argument.*
See also: Negate, Quash, Set aside

Annulment (ah-NULL-ment), *noun*
A declaration or ruling by a court that something is legally invalid or void.

*The judge granted an **annulment** of the marriage, which for legal purposes makes it as if the marriage never occurred. The judge declared an **annulment** of the contract based on the escape clause agreed to by both parties.*
See also: Divorce, Escape clause

Answer, *noun*
A written response by the defendant to the plaintiff's charges in a lawsuit.

*In their **answer** to the lawsuit, the defendants denied the facts of the case point by point.*

Antitrust, *adjective*
The set of laws and government policies intended to prevent establishment of monopolies and cartels and otherwise promote free and fair competition.

The federal Department of Justice examines most proposals for major mergers to see if any **antitrust** *laws and regulations have been violated or are likely to be violated.*

See also: Monopoly

Appeal, *verb, noun*

A request made to a higher court to overturn (or reverse) the decision or trial result of a lower court.

We have decided to **appeal** *to the appellate division to overturn the district court's ruling.*

Appear, *verb*

An official appearance in a court by one of the parties or an attorney representing one of the parties.

The judge ordered the defendant to **appear** *in court at 9:00 A.M. on October 1 to answer the charges in preparation for a possible trial.*

Appearance, *noun*

Paperwork filed with the clerk of a court to indicate the name of an attorney who will represent a defendant, or to indicate that the defendant will appear without an attorney. Also, coming before the court to give notification of the appointment of an attorney or the summoning of a witness.

The defendant's attorney made an **appearance** *before the judge, seeking a continuance to permit the preparation of the case.*

Appellate court, *noun*

A court designated to hear appeals of decisions or rulings made by lower courts.

Immediately after the judge made his ruling, the defendant's attorney filed papers with the **appellate court** *seeking review of the decision.*

Appoint, *verb*

(1) To designate someone to be your representative. (2) Also, to designate the recipient of property under a power of appointment granted by the owner.

(1) Kristol decided to **appoint** *William Bryant to be his agent in disposing of real property. (2) Bryant chose to* **appoint** *Lawrence Simon to receive the property.*

A

Appraisal, *noun*

A professional determination of the value of real or personal property. An appraisal can be used as part of the process of selling property or to place a value on something for insurance or legal purposes.

*Before the bank would issue a mortgage, it required that an **appraisal** of the property be conducted by a professional.*

Appreciation, *noun*

Increase in the value of property or a building because of improvements in the market. Or, increase in the value of an investment because of the accrual of interest or improvements in the market. Appreciation does not include improvements or additions made to property or investments.

*The company's stockpile of precious metals showed an **appreciation** of 15 percent in the past year because of increases in the value of the commodities.*

Appropriate, Appropriation, *verb, noun*

(1) The taking of something. (2) In legislative terms, the act of setting aside funds for a specific use.

*(1) The sheriff chose to **appropriate** the disputed property until the courts can decide on its ownership. (2) The county commissioners made an **appropriation** of $100,000 for emergency repairs to the parking lot.*

Appurtenant, *adjective*

A right or restriction that is attached to a piece of land and would pass with the title to a new owner. For example, an easement allowing access across the land by neighbors or a utility company, or a covenant that puts certain restrictions on use of the land or the type of building that might be constructed on it.

*The certificate of title included an **appurtenant** easement that permits the town to install and maintain water and sewer lines that pass through the property.*

See also: Title, Easement

Arbitrage (ar-bi-TRAZH), *noun*

A financial tactic of buying and selling the same security in different markets and hoping to make a profit based on the usually small difference in price that exists.

*The trader specialized in **arbitrage** of commodity contracts, often making his profit on the tiny difference in price that exists for short periods of time in different marketplaces around the world.*

Arbitration (ar-be-TRAY-shun), *noun*

A process that seeks to resolve disputes without involving a court. The parties might agree to submit the dispute to a arbitrator or a panel of arbitrators. Some contracts require that the parties seek arbitration, using professional or certified private arbitrators. In some situations the parties agree to be bound by the decision of the arbitrator, in which case the process is called binding arbitration.

*As required by the contract, the parties submitted their dispute to an impartial third party for **arbitration**.*

See also: Binding arbitration, Mediation

Arm's length, *adjective*

A type of agreement by two or more unrelated parties, each with its own interests and without any special relationship.

*The two utilities agreed on an **arm's length** agreement to cooperate on the installation of an underwater cable that will carry electrical power, fiber optics, and other forms of communication. Each party will pay for its portion of the cost of the work and retain ownership of its share of the project.*

Arraign (uh-RAIN), *verb*

A

To bring a defendant before a court to answer a criminal charge. At an arraignment, the accused may enter a plea or ask for a continuance. A judge may choose to release a defendant pending trial, hold the defendant in custody, or set a bail that would have to be posted before the accused is released.

*Sheriff's deputies brought Ford to court on Monday morning to be **arraigned** on charges of driving while intoxicated.*

See also: Arraignment, Accused

Arraignment (uh-RAIN-mint), *noun*

The initial appearance of an accused before a judge at which the defendant answers charges and begins the process of defense.

*At the **arraignment**, when the defendant chose not to answer the charge, the judge entered a plea of "not guilty" on his behalf.*

See also: Arraign, Accused

Arrears (a-REARS), *noun*

Money that is overdue for payment.

*The arbitrator found that the defendant was six months in **arrears** on rent.*

Arrest, *verb*
To take someone into custody, under the legal authority granted a police officer or other official.

*Orbison was placed under **arrest** at the scene by a sheriff's deputy and transported to a detention center; he was scheduled to be arraigned the next morning in county court.*

See also: Custody, Detain

Arrest warrant, *noun*
An official authorization, granted by a court or other judicial agency, to arrest an individual charged with a crime.

*The police secured an **arrest warrant** from a magistrate before going to Mr. Smith's place of work to take him into custody.*

See also: Warrant

Arson, *noun*
The criminal act of intentionally setting fire to a building or other property.

*Weaver was accused of felony **arson** for starting a fire in a building he owned in an attempt to collect damages under an insurance policy. Additional charges of fraud are pending.*

Asportation (as-pour-TAY-shun), *noun*
Illegally removing items from a place. In some states, the crime of larceny requires that an object be removed from the place where it was taken.

*Woodzinski was charged with larceny by **asportation** for removing some twenty pounds of tomatoes from her neighbor's garden.*

See also: Larceny

Assault, *verb, noun*
(1) A threat or attempt to strike someone. (2) Also, the crime of threatening or attempting to strike someone.

*(1) Allison was charged with attempting to **assault** the police officer who was placing her husband under arrest for a traffic violation. (2) After a trial in county court, the defendant was found guilty of **assault** in the fight at a hockey game.*

See also: Assault and battery

Assault and battery, *noun*

The crime of threatening to strike someone as well as actually making physical contact with that person.

> *The defendant was charged with **assault and battery** for threatening and then hitting the doorman who blocked his entrance to the building.*

See also: Assault

Assess (uh-SESS), *verb*

(1) To determine the value of something, often for calculating property taxes. (2) Also, to impose a tax, duty, fine, damages, or other required payment.

> *(1) The county employs a professional appraiser to **assess** the value of homes, commercial buildings, and vacant land. (2) The commission **assessed** a fine of $10,000 for violation of shipping regulations.*

See also: Assessment, Assessed value

Assessed value, *noun*

The value of a piece of real property as determined by an assessor or other qualified evaluator. The assessed value is multiplied by the local tax rate for the particular type of property to calculate the amount of tax due.

> *The Hills challenged the **assessed value** placed upon their home by the town, saying that their land and home were overvalued by $500,000.*

See also: Assessment, Assess

Assessment, *noun*

(1) The determination of the value of a piece of real property by an assessor or other qualified evaluator, for property tax purposes. (2) Also, the dollar amount of a fine or tax, or the value of damages as determined in a court proceeding.

> *(1) The town conducts an **assessment** of all real property every two years; the total assessed value of all taxable property is then divided by the amount the state or county is seeking to raise to determine the tax rate. (2) To pay for the repaving project, the town imposed an **assessment** of $1,000 per residence with frontage on the road.*

See also: Assessed value, Assess

A

Asset (AH-set), *noun*

Something of value, including property, investments, financial instruments, accounts receivable, and intangible things such as intellectual property or good will.

> *The administrator of the estate drew up an accounting of the estate's **assets** and liabilities prior to determining the amount of money that might be made available to heirs.*

See also: Liability, Solvency

Assign, *verb, noun*

(1) To transfer to another person or business something of value, including real property, a contract, or a financial instrument such as a promissory note. Liabilities can also be assigned to another by a court, or as the result of an agreement between parties. (2) Also, the person, sometimes instead called an assignee, who receives something of value by transfer.

> *(1) As part of the agreement, the company **assigned** its interest in the promissory note to the buyer. (2) As the designated **assign**, Fern was given possession of the property as well as the outstanding tax liability assessed against it.*

See also: Assignment, Promissory note

A

Assignment, *noun*

The act of legally transferring a right, asset, property, or liability to another person.

> *Under terms of the **assignment**, the assignee was required to maintain and hold on to the property for a period of at least ten years.*

See also: Assign, Promissory note

Associate (a-SO-see-it), *noun*

(1) A judge who is a member of a group of justices but not in charge of the others. (2) Also, an attorney who is a salaried employee of a law firm, as opposed to a partner who receives a share of profits instead of or in addition to salary. (3) Also, a partner in an action or business. In criminal proceedings a defendant or an acquaintance may be described as being an associate of the accused.

> *(1) At the Supreme Court, the chief justice has supervisory assignments beyond those of the **associate** members of the court. (2) Ms. Baez is a young **associate** at the law firm, reporting to a partner. (3) The*

prosecutor alleged that Mr. Collins was a criminal **associate** of the defendant, although he was not charged in the same case.

Assume (a-SOOM), *verb*
To take on the liability for a debt.
> The buyer of the business **assumed** all of the former owner's debts and other liabilities as part of the deal.

Assumption, *noun*
The right of a buyer to take over an existing mortgage or promissory note and be liable for all of its terms and conditions.
> Some lenders permit the **assumption** of an existing mortgage by the new buyer; any money paid for the property above the amount of the mortgage is made directly to the seller.

See also: Mortgage

Asylum, *noun*
The promise of protection from extradition offered by the federal government to persons who are determined to have fled from certain other countries because of a credible claim that they would be politically persecuted.
> Shaheed sought political **asylum** in the United States, claiming that he would be imprisoned and abused because of his political beliefs if he was to be returned to his home country.

At will, *noun*
(1) A provision in state laws or in employment contracts that declares that an employee can be terminated at any time for any reason except for unlawful discrimination. (2) Also, a provision that allows the termination of a contract or other relationship for any reason.
> (1) Company policy provides that all salaried and temporary workers are employed on an **at-will** basis and can be terminated without cause if it suits the needs of the organization. (2) The contract includes a clause that allows either party to end the agreement **at will**, provided reasonable notice of not less than 30 days is given.

Attachment, *noun*
A legal seizure of property of funds, usually done prior to a final ruling in a case to protect assets that may be awarded to the other party.

A

*The court ordered an **attachment** of all bank accounts and investments held by the defendant to preserve funds in the event the plaintiff succeeded in his demand for damages.*

See also: Garnishment

Attest (uh-TEST), *verb*

A declaration or confirmation that a document is genuine, that a signature was witnessed, or that something is accurate or true.

*I hereby **attest** that I know Janice Keefe and witnessed her placing her signature on this document.*

Attorney-client privilege, *noun*

A privilege granted to clients that protects communication and exchange of documents with their legal counsel.

*The attorney refused to reveal comments made by his client in preparation for the trial, citing the **attorney-client privilege**.*

Attorney general, *noun*

In the federal government, the chief legal officer of the country; the AG oversees the enforcement of federal statutes and advises the President on official matters related to the law. Most states have an equivalent executive.

*The U.S. **Attorney General** is a member of the President's cabinet and advises the executive branch on legal matters and law enforcement; as defined by the U.S. Constitution, the judiciary branch is a separate and independent branch of the government and is overseen by the Chief Justice of the Supreme Court.*

Attorney-in-fact, *noun*

A person who acts on behalf of another, invoking rights given in a power of attorney document.

*She signed the contract as **attorney-in-fact** for her ailing father.*

See also: Power of attorney

Auction, *noun*

A sale of real or personal property to the highest bidder.

*The company conducted an **auction** of surplus vehicles, selling trucks and cars to any qualified bidder.*

Autopsy, *noun*

An examination by a coroner or medical examiner to determine the cause of death of a person.

*In many states, the law requires an **autopsy** be conducted on any person who dies in a place other than a hospital so that there can be assurance that the death occurred from natural causes.*

See also: Inquest, Post mortem, Coroner, Medical examiner

Bad debt (bad DETT), *noun*

A debt that is considered uncollectible. For accounting or tax reasons, a company may "write off" debts, declaring them as losses.

*In its latest annual report, the company included a balance sheet that showed it had nearly $1 million in **bad debt**.*

Bail, *noun*

(1) A system under which a person accused of a crime is released from custody before trial in return for posting money or something else of value as a guarantee to return for further court proceedings. If the accused fails to appear for a court hearing or trial, the court can confiscate the bail. (2) Also, money, other financial instruments, or property given to the custody of the court to secure the release of someone charged with a crime. The funds can come from the personal assets of the accused or may be posted by a bondsman or bond agency that may collect a fee from the defendant.

*(1) The prosecutor asked the judge to set a very high **bail** for the defendant, asserting that he was a risk to leave the jurisdiction. (2) The defendant was released on **bail**, posting a $100,000 cash bond.*

See also: Bond

Balance sheet, *noun*

A financial statement that lists the assets and liabilities of a business at a particular moment in time.

*The company's most recent **balance sheet** shows that it is deeply indebted, with its liabilities far exceeding assets including accounts receivable.*

See also: Book value

B

Balance transfer, *noun*
The act of transferring outstanding debt from one credit card to another.

> *The credit card company made a special offer to customers allowing them to make a **balance transfer** from another card and pay no interest on the borrowed funds for six months.*

Balloon mortgage, *noun*
A form of mortgage that provides for relatively small amounts due over the term of the loan with a final, significantly larger payment to discharge the debt.

> *The fifteen-year **balloon mortgage** calls for monthly payments of interest only, with the full amount of the principal due at the end of the loan.*

See also: Balloon payment

Balloon payment, *noun*
The final payment that closes out a balloon mortgage or other form of balloon loan. During the life of the note, borrowers pay only interest or interest plus some of the principal but not enough to fully amortize the loan.

> *The promissory note called for payment of interest plus a minimum amount of money to reduce the outstanding principal; at the end of the term, a final **balloon payment** is due to pay off the remaining principal.*

See also: Balloon mortgage

Bankruptcy (BAN-krupt-see), *noun*
A process by which an individual or a business unable to meet financial obligations can seek to have financial affairs placed under the control of the court or designated third party.

> *Fran and Zoe McClure have filed for **bankruptcy**, seeking the protection of the court as they attempt to restructure their personal finances.*

Barter, *noun*
An exchange of goods or services without cash payment.

> *The company agreed to a **barter** of $1 million in product in exchange for an equivalent amount of advertising time on television.*

See also: In kind

Basis, *noun*

In financial terms, the original cost of an asset plus any improvements made. For tax purposes, the basis of an asset is subtracted from the selling price to determine whether there is a profit or loss and to determine any tax (such as capital gains) due. In examining an investment in negotiable instruments such as shares of stock or bonds, the basis is the difference between the purchase price and its sales price, adjusted to also include stock splits, reinvested dividends, and other distributions.

*The building was purchased for $500,000 and sold for twice that amount, but its **basis** was $1.2 million when the cost of improvements was included.*

See also: Adjusted basis, Betterment

Battery, *noun*

(1) The act of intentionally striking someone. In some states, the battery must have been committed with an attempt to cause harm; other laws define battery as striking someone in an offensive way. (2) Battery can also be an actionable cause for a civil lawsuit seeking damages.

*(1) The defendant was charged with **battery** for pushing the parking meter attendant who was placing a ticket on his car. (2) The hotel doorman filed a civil lawsuit seeking damages for pain and suffering that resulted from an alleged **battery** by the defendant that occurred as the result of an argument between two guests hailing the same cab.*

See also: Assault, Assault and battery

B

Bear market, *noun*

An extended period of decline in the value of investments.

*Financial analysts said the economy was in a **bear market**, as bellwether stocks continued to decline and the general economy entered a recession.*

See also: Bull market

Bearer, *noun*

A person who has possession of a negotiable financial instrument, such as an endorsed check or promissory note.

*As **bearer** of the promissory note, she was entitled to collect payment of interest and principal when due.*

Bellwether, *noun*

Something that shows the way or is an indicator of future trends. The word is derived from a phrase that dates back to the 13th century: herders hung a bell around the neck of the wether, the male sheep that led the flock.

Analysts look to the performance of certain industries as **bellwethers** *for the general economy.*

Bench, *noun*

(1) A general term referring to the judicial system. Also, (2) the podium occupied by a judge; also used to indicate whether a judge has made a ruling in court or by filing papers from his office.

(1) Officers of the court, including attorneys, are expected to show appropriate deference and respect for the **bench** *at all times. (2) The judge returned to the courtroom to issue his ruling from the* **bench**.

See also: Chambers

Beneficial interest, *noun*

The right of an individual or business to receive benefits generated by assets held in another party's name.

Under terms of the agreement, the children of Allen and Ann Pedroia have a **beneficial interest** *in the proceeds of the trust.*

Beneficiary (ben-ih-FI-she-ary), *noun*

A person or a legal entity who is to receive assets or proceeds from an estate, insurance policy, or other instrument.

Mary is the **beneficiary** *of Ben's life insurance policy.*

Benefit, *noun*

A profit or a privilege, such as might be obtained in a contract.

As a **benefit** *of the contract, Ms. Myers was paid a $100,000 fee and given the use of the company's Fenway Park box seats for four games during the season.*

Bequeath (bih-KWEETH), *verb*

To leave personal property and other assets to a beneficiary under provisions of a will. (The term "devise" is used in reference to real property.)

I **bequeath** *my baseball card collection to my brother Neil.*

See also: Bequest, Escheat, Devise, Gift, Inheritance

Bequest (bih-KWEST), *noun*

The property and other assets left to a beneficiary under provisions of a will.

> *The local Little League acknowledged the* ***bequest*** *from the Remy estate and announced that the main field would be named in his honor.*

See also: Bequeath, Escheat, Devise, Gift, Inheritance, Dower

Betterment, *noun*

The increased value of a parcel of real property that is the result of improvements, other than ordinary upkeep, made to it after purchase.

> *The property was valued at $1.2 million, reflecting* ***betterment*** *of $200,000 for installation of water and sewer lines as well as the general increase in real estate values.*

See also: Basis

Beyond a reasonable doubt, *adjective*

A very stringent standard of proof in a criminal trial. In most jurisdictions this is the highest standard of proof required for conviction; a lesser standard in some courts is preponderance of evidence, and the lowest standard is clear and convincing evidence.

> *The judge instructed the jurors that they can only vote for conviction if they are convinced of the defendant's guilt* ***beyond a reasonable doubt***.

See also: Standard of proof, Preponderance of evidence, Clear and convincing evidence

Bias (BYE-iss), *noun*

An alleged or demonstrated predisposition by a party in a legal proceeding for or against one of the parties.

> *The filing with the court alleges that one of the jurors in the case has expressed a* ***bias*** *against the defendant.*

See also: Prejudice

Bid, *noun*

A specific amount of money offered to purchase an item or to sell a service.

> *The buyer made a* ***bid*** *of $150,000 for the surplus snowplows being offered by the town.*

Bifurcation, *noun*

A division of some of the issues in a trial so that one is decided before the other is considered. This is also called severance.

*The judge ordered a **bifurcation** of the issues in the trial so that the matter of whether the defendant was guilty of negligence would be decided before the matter of compensation was considered.*

See also: Severance

Bigamy (BIG-ah-mee), *noun*

Entering into a marriage while already married to another. Or, the state of being married to two persons at the same time.

*Amrey was found guilty of **bigamy** when it was proved he had married three different women in Boston, Austin, and San Diego.*

Bill of sale, *noun*

A written or printed and signed document that confirms the transfer of ownership of personal property from a seller to a buyer, or from a vendor to a reseller.

*In order to register a used vehicle with the state motor vehicles department, it is necessary to produce a **bill of sale** that shows the amount paid; in many states, the buyer must pay sales tax on the purchase.*

See also: Title

B

Binder, *noun*

A written and signed or certified summary of the main points of an agreement or an insurance policy that confirms a contract is in effect.

*The insurance agent issued a **binder** for the automobile coverage; the full policy will come from the company within two weeks.*

Binding arbitration (BIND-ing ar-be-TRAY-shun), *noun*

A form of arbitration in which both parties agree to resolve disputes without involving a court and accept the findings of the arbitrator.

*Under terms of the agreement, the dispute was submitted to **binding arbitration** conducted by a professional.*

See also: Arbitration, Mediation

Blackmail, *noun*

An attempt to force or extort someone (or an organization) to do something by threatening to reveal embarrassing, damaging, or private information.

The defendant is accused of attempting to **blackmail** *Mr. Jones by threatening to expose details of an illicit relationship.*
See also: Extortion

Blind trust, *noun*

An arrangement under which someone's assets are managed by an agent who does not disclose how they are invested. A blind trust is sometimes set up to shield a public official, a candidate for office, or certain jobholders in the private sector from potential or real conflicts of interest.

The candidate announced that he had placed all of his significant investments under the management of a **blind trust** *so that there would be no question of whether he would personally benefit from decisions made in office.*

Blockbusting, *noun, adjective*

An action to persuade someone to sell their home, or to make a change in the price of property by claiming that racial or ethnic minorities are moving to the area.

The real estate agent was indicted on charges of attempted **blockbusting** *for spreading rumors about purchases of neighborhood houses by Mexican families.*
See also: Redlining

B

Blue chip stock, *noun*

Shares in companies generally considered to be profitable and well run, with a good history of growth.

In general, buying shares of **blue chip stock** *is a relatively safe, conservative way to invest money.*
See also: Stock, Share

Board of Directors, *noun*

The governing body of a corporation, as elected by the vote of shareholders.

The **board of directors** *is intended to represent the voice of the investors in a publicly traded company, with the ability to hire and fire executive officers and make certain major decisions.*
See also: Chairman of the Board

Boilerplate, *adjective*

An informal or slang term for routine and commonly reused elements of a contract, form, or other legal document.

*The requirements for bidders are included in the **boilerplate** of the contract.*

Bona fide (BONE-ah-FIDE), *adjective*

A Latin phrase meaning "good faith." It can be used to indicate that a party to an agreement is honest and real, or that a document is real.

*We consider Mr. Jones to be a **bona fide** candidate to enter into the contract.*

Bond, *noun*

(1) A financial instrument issued by a company or a government that promises to pay a specific amount of money at a particular time. Some bonds are sold at a discount; for example a bond with a face value of $100 at maturity in five years may sell today for $80. (2) Also, a formal obligation to guarantee the performance of a specific act or the payment of money. For example, a vendor may be asked to post a financial bond or purchase a surety bond from a third party to guarantee performance as agreed to under a contract. (3) Also, an amount of money posted by a bonding agency to secure the release of an accused on bail. The agency or bondsman is obligated to pay the full amount of the bail if the defendant fails to appear for a hearing or trial.

*(1) The county offered an issue of **bonds** to pay for the new sewage plant. (2) The contract specified that the vendor must post a **bond** in the amount of $1 million or arrange for a surety bond in the same amount to protect the shopping center from losses that might arise if the paving project was not completed on time. (3) The agency posted a **bond** with the court to cover the release of the defendant on bail.*

See also: Bail

Book value, *noun*

(1) The net value of a company, calculated by totaling the stated value of tangible corporate assets (excluding intangible assets such as patents, trademarks, and good will) and then subtracting the sum of all liabilities. (2) Also, the current value of a specific asset, determined by subtracting depreciation from original cost.

*(1) The company's **book value** is $12 million, down from the previous year because of an increase in liabilities. (2) The **book value** of the corporate fleet of trucks declined to $3.2 million due to depreciation and the fact that no new vehicles were added in the previous year.*

See also: Balance sheet

Bound over, *noun*

The act of transferring a felony case to a trial court after a judge at a preliminary hearing finds that there is probable cause to believe that the accused committed a crime or after an accused person waives a preliminary hearing.

*At the preliminary hearing, the judge heard testimony from the arresting officer and determined there was sufficient probable cause to have the defendant **bound over** for trial.*

See also: Preliminary hearing

Boycott (BOY-kott), *noun, verb*

An organized effort to avoid purchase of products or the conduct of business with a company. Boycotts may be launched in an attempt to protest an action, influence a policy, or otherwise attract attention to a political, social, or economic cause.

*The committee voted to organize a **boycott** of Guilt Trip Jewelers because of the company's involvement in importation of diamonds from groups associated with African rebel groups.*

B

Breach (breech), *noun*

Breaking an agreement or law or failing to perform a duty.

*The failure to deliver the products on time is a **breach** of contract.*

Breach of contract, *noun*

A failure to perform any element of a contract, except when excused because of specific circumstances named in the contract or because of a release from an obligation given by the other party in the contract.

*When the swimming pool was unable to open because of improper maintenance, the town sued the service company for **breach of contract**.*

See also: Contract

Breach of warranty, *noun*

A claim or finding that a warranty made in relation to real property or personal property is untrue.

> *The lawsuit alleges that the seller of the painting did not have the right to dispose of it, a **breach of warranty** of the bill of sale.*

See also: Warranty

Break-in, *noun*

A forced or unapproved entry into a building or vehicle. In most laws, break-in also includes an attempt to commit a crime such as theft.

> *Merriam was charged with burglary for the **break-in** of the tool shed at the county park.*

See also: Breaking and entering, Burglary, Trespass

Breaking and entering, *noun*

The crime of entering a premises without permission by some measure of force; the force can be as little as pushing open a door or gate.

> *Pignanelli was arrested and charged with **breaking and entering** after he was found inside the storage shed at the high school; the door was closed but not latched.*

See also: Break-in, Burglary, Trespass

Bribery (BREYE-buh-ree), *noun*

The crime of giving money or anything of value to a public official in an attempt to influence them in the conduct of their duties. Also, the crime of accepting something of value for that purpose.

> *The contractor was convicted of attempted **bribery** for offering $10,000 to the town building inspector to overlook various infractions of the construction code. In a separate matter, a sheriff's deputy was charged with **bribery** for accepting $100 from a motorist who had been stopped for speeding; the incident was witnessed by a court officer.*

See also: Suborn

Brief, *noun*

A written summary of the facts, applicable laws or regulations, precedents, and their relation to a legal proceeding, as put forth by one side of a case.

> *The defendant's attorney filed a **brief** with the court arguing that the charges are not supported by the facts already on record in the case.*

Broker, *noun*

A person who is paid to act on behalf of another in certain transactions such as a real estate or securities purchase. Also, someone who acts as a middleman bringing together a buyer and seller.

> *The company employed a **broker** to locate facilities for its new sales office in Coshocton.*

See also: Agent

Bull market, *noun*

An extended period in which the value of investments rise faster than historical averages or expectations.

> *Financial advisors say they expect that the economy cannot sustain the current **bull market** for much longer, pointing to share prices that seem to be unrealistically high.*

See also: Bear market

Burden, *noun*

A legal restriction. Examples include an easement placed on a real estate deed, building or zoning codes, or a licensing fee placed on certain professions or types of business.

> *The fees and license requirements for transportation of hazardous materials are a significant **burden** on that industry.*

B

Burden of proof, *noun*

The requirement that a plaintiff (the party bringing a civil lawsuit) or a government entity prove their claim or charge to a particular defined standard.

> *In the civil suit against the company, the plaintiff has the **burden of proof** to show that the preponderance of evidence supports their claim.*

Burglary, *noun*

A forced or unapproved entry into a building or vehicle with the intent of committing a crime. In most states, a direct confrontation with another person for the purposes of stealing something is called robbery.

> *The teens were charged with **burglary** after they were found inside the unoccupied store after closing.*

See also: Break-in, Breaking and entering, Trespass, Robbery

Buy down, *noun, adjective*

A form of mortgage financing in which the interest rate is reduced for the first few years of the loan because of a payment made by the builder or seller of the property. It is in effect a discount.

> *The builder of the home offered sought to entice buyers by cooperating with a local bank that offered a mortgage with an initially lower interest rate because of a **buy-down** payment.*

See also: Mortgage, Adjustable rate mortgage, Fixed-rate mortgage

Buy-sell agreement, *noun*

An agreement amongst the owners of a privately held business that requires that if any shareholder chooses to dispose of shares they must be offered to the remaining owners of the enterprise at a set or calculated price. The same would apply if the shareholder were to die.

> *The three principals of the business entered into a **buy-sell agreement** at the time the company was established, to ensure that the founders could maintain control of their operations.*

Buyer's agent, *noun*

A real estate broker or an agent who represents only the buyer in the finding of real property and the negotiation of a deal.

> *In some circumstances, employing a **buyer's agent** for a real estate transaction may help the purchaser avoid conflicts of interest that occur in many common deals.*

See also: Agent, Broker, Seller's agent

Bylaw (BUY-law), *noun*

Rules established by an association, group, or organization to govern its operations. Bylaws are not part of any official document, such as articles of incorporation. In some forms of government, local ordinances are called bylaws.

> *The group's **bylaws** require that two-thirds of all members must approve any changes to fees.*

Calendar year, *noun*

The period of time between January 1 and December 31 of a particular year. Also, a period of year between a particular date in one year and the same date in the next year.

> For the **calendar year** of 2006, the company showed a profit of $11 billion. However, since the company states its results based on a fiscal year that runs from February 1 to January 31, the adjusted profit was a mere $10.2 billion.

See also: Fiscal year

Call, *noun*

A demand for payment or other financial action by the issuer of a bond or other instrument. Or a demand by a corporation that stockholders pay an assessment on shares. Also, in an option contract, the right to purchase a specified quantity of shares at a particular price during a period of time.

> The corporation issued a **call** for payment on its most recent series of bonds.

See also: Acceleration

Capacity, *noun*

Deemed legally able to perform an act that is binding or actionable, such as entering into a contract, getting married, or being a party to a lawsuit.

> The judge ruled that the minor did not have the **capacity** to sign and be bound by the contract and dismissed the lawsuit.

See also: Incapacity

Capital, *noun*

The basic assets of a company, including cash and property but not including inventory and intangible assets. Also, the amount of money and negotiable financial instruments owned by an individual.

> **Capital** is considered any form of asset that can be used in the production of more wealth.

See also: Capital assets, Capital expenditures

Capital assets, *noun*

Actual funds put into a business, including equipment and property purchased. Various special types of property or investments may be excluded by one or another special provision of local, state, or federal tax codes.

*The **capital assets** of the corporation are calculated and kept current by the company's internal accounting and auditing department as well as by outside firms that may be engaged to determine accounting.*

See also: Capital

Capital expenditures, *noun*

Spending by a business for basic capital assets including property and machinery, excluding operational costs such as payroll, benefits, and marketing.

*The company took advantage of tax breaks to increase its **capital expenditures** at its domestic factories.*

See also: Capital

Capital gain, *noun*

The difference between the purchase price and sale price of a capital asset, minus the cost of improvements. Also, the net gain or loss from the sale of a financial instrument. If there is a loss on a sale, it is called a capital loss.

*The company reported a **capital gain** of $5 million on the sale of its Lumberton property, taking into account various improvements and additions put into place over the years.*

Capital offense, *noun*

A crime punishable by the death penalty.

*In many states, premeditated homicide is a **capital offense**.*

See also: Capital punishment, Death penalty

Capital punishment, *noun*

An execution of a person by the government.

*Many nations do not engage in **capital punishment** of criminals, instead choosing to incarcerate for life those convicted of murder and other serious crimes.*

See also: Capital offense, Death penalty

Capital stock, *noun*

The total of the amount paid by investors to a corporation to purchase stock. Once the stock has been issued, it may trade at a price above or below its original price but this is not reflected in the value of capital stock.

*The company announced it would offer for sale an additional one million shares of stock at a price of $25 per share, raising the total of **capital stock** in the corporation to $50 million.*

Capricious (ke-PREE-shes), *adverb, adjective*

Arbitrary, unpredictable, or subject to whim. Also, a claim that a ruling by the court does not properly follow the law or procedure.

*The defense attorney argued that the judge's ruling was **capricious** and was not supported by the rules of the court or state law.*

Caption, *noun*

The title or description of a lawsuit or legal pleading.

*The **caption** of the Supreme Court case, Brown v. Board of Education of Topeka 347 U.S. 483, gives no hint of its landmark status in the ending of legalized segregation in the United States in 1954.*

Captive reinsurance, *noun*

An arrangement under which a lender or other financial institution assumes part of the risk involved in a transaction by purchasing insurance from a company it owns or with which it has other business relations. In most situations, the borrower must be notified that premiums being paid for insurance are not going to a third party but instead are being fully or partly retained by the lender.

*In a mortgage, if the lender has an affiliation with an insurance provider that is involved in the loan, the borrower must be notified of the existence of a **captive reinsurance** arrangement.*

Carnal knowledge, *noun*

Sexual intercourse between a male and a female.

*James was charged with unlawful **carnal knowledge** of a minor younger than the age of consent.*

See also: Age of consent, Statutory rape, Minor

Carryover, *noun*

In tax accounting, a situation where a previous year's financial events, including certain losses, credits, or deductions, is applied to a subsequent year's filing.

*The company was able to apply an unused tax credit from the previous year as a **carryover** for the current filing.*

Case, *noun*

The entirety of a lawsuit or claim filed with a court.

*The court deemed the plaintiff's **case** was not sufficient to proceed to trial.*

Cash advance, *noun*

A short-term loan. One form of cash advance is a paycheck advance, which provides money to someone who is due a paycheck. Another form of cash advance is to use a credit card to obtain cash, with the amount taken out considered a loan.

*A **cash advance** is usually made for a short period of time at what works out to be a very high interest rate if it were expressed as an annual percentage rate.*

Cashier's check, *noun*

A check issued by a bank to a specific payee; the name of the purchaser is also indicated.

*Some contracts require that payment be made only in the form of a **cashier's check** as a way to ensure that the draft has funds to cover the stated amount of money.*

See also: Check, Draft, Certified check

Casualty (KA-jul-tee), *noun*

(1) An accident, which by definition, could not have been foreseen or protected against. (2) Also, a person or thing injured, killed, or damaged as the result of an accident.

*(1) The barn collapsed as the result of an unexpected **casualty**. (2) Mr. Jones was one of six **casualties** of the fire.*

Catastrophic coverage, *noun*

An insurance policy that has a very high deductible before it takes effect.

*Some individuals choose to purchase health insurance or other types of policy where they agree to bear most of the risk with the policy provider paying only for **catastrophic coverage** above a certain high minimum amount.*

Causation (KAWZ-ay-shun), *noun*

A factual link between an action or event and a particular result.

*The lawsuit established a **causation** between the defendant's failure to properly maintain the machinery and the plaintiff's claim for damages because of its failure.*

See also: Cause

Cause, *verb, noun*

(1) To make something happen. (2) Also, the action or event that is the reason something has happened.

*(1) According to the prosecutor, the defendant **caused** the accident by reckless speed through thick fog. (2) The plaintiff's attorney argued that the **cause** of the foundering was negligence by the ship's captain.*

See also: Causation

Cause of action, *noun*

The basis or foundation of a lawsuit; that is, the facts and the law make a case actionable.

*The judge ruled that based on the preliminary filings that the plaintiff has a valid **cause of action** to proceed toward a trial on the lawsuit.*

See also: Actionable

Caveat (KAH-vee-at), *noun*

From the Latin phrase, "let him beware." A warning, or an indication that there may be a hidden problem in a situation.

*The attorney agreed to take on the case, with the **caveat** that it might prove to be difficult and expensive to prevail in a court of law.*

See also: Caveat emptor

Caveat emptor (KAH-vee-at EMPT-or), *noun*

From the Latin phrase, "let the buyer beware." An admonition that the buyer has a responsibility to determine if a product or service is appropriate or properly priced.

*Although modern law includes protections for the consumer including implied warranties of merchantability and lemon laws, the buyer is still well-advised to remember that **caveat emptor** still applies: the buyer must beware (or be aware) of the nature of an agreement.*

See also: Caveat

Cease and desist order, *noun*

An order from a court or government agency directing a person, business, or organization to stop from a particular action that has been deemed to be harmful or unlawful.

The judge issued a **cease and desist order** *against the defendants, ordering them to immediately stop distribution of the illegally imported and uncertified pharmaceuticals.*

Censure (SENT-shur), *noun, verb*

A formal condemnation issued by a government body or a professional organization against one of its own members for improper behavior.

The state legislature voted to **censure** *Assemblyman Matt Gomes for improperly diverting campaign funds to his personal use; Gomes was found guilty of the charges in a court proceeding.*

Census, *noun*

(1) The official count of the population of the United States, performed every ten years as required by the Constitution. (2) Also, any systematic count of people or items as required by a state or other government.

(1) The federal **Census** *is used as the basis for allocation of funds under many federal programs and in the determination of the number of members of the U.S. House of Representatives from each state. (2) The court ordered a* **census** *of the population of the county jail to see if it met the standards of health and safety mandated by state law.*

Certificate, *noun*

An official document attesting to the truth of a specific fact or confirming an act.

The building inspector issued a **certificate** *of occupancy, declaring that the contractor had met all of the requirements of local codes.*

Certificate of deposit, *noun*

A form of investment issued by a bank or other institution. A CD generally pays a fixed rate of interest for a specified period of time,

Marion purchased a six-month **certificate of deposit** *paying 6 percent interest.*

Certificate of title, *noun*

(1) A document issued in most states that identifies the registered owner of a motor vehicle. If the vehicle was purchased using a loan or was leased, the lender will usually place a lien (a security interest) on the vehicle to ensure that they receive their money if the car is sold or otherwise disposed of. (2) Also, a written opinion from a real estate attorney, title examiner, or title insurance company that states that the record indicates that a seller has proper title to a piece of land and is capable of authorizing its sale. The certificate is not a guarantee or insurance for the validity of the title.

> *(1) The **certificate of title** lists the vehicle identification number (VIN), details about the vehicle, the name of the person who has registered the vehicle, and the name of any person or company that has a security interest in it as a lender. (2) The title examiner issued an unqualified **certificate of title** for the land. On that basis, the seller was able to purchase title insurance to protect the buyer against future claims.*

See also: Title insurance policy

Certified check, *noun*

A check issued by a bank but drawn on the account held by the maker of the check; the bank guarantees that funds equal to the amount of the draft have been set aside so that there will be funds available to pay the check.

> *The automobile dealer required payment by **certified check** before it would release the vehicle to the purchaser.*

See also: Check, Draft, Cashier's check

Certify, *verb*

To make a written opinion or guarantee that something is true or authentic, or to attest to the fact that a particular act has been performed. Also, to issue a certificate of any sort.

> *Under powers granted me as a notary public, I hereby **certify** that I witnessed the signing of this document and verified the identity of the signers based on government-issued passports and driver's licenses.*

CFO (Chief Financial Officer), *noun*

An executive or senior manager of a company responsible for overseeing financial activities.

C

*The **CFO** is in charge of planning and executing the financial operations of a company.*

Chain of custody, *noun*

A documented record of the original location, subsequent locations, and the names of all persons who have had custody of a piece of physical evidence.

*The defense attorney challenged the validity of a piece of evidence, pointing to a gap in the **chain of custody** of several weeks during which time it could have become switched, tampered with, or altered.*

See also: Evidence

Chain of title, *noun*

A researched report of the history of all titles, conveyances, attachments, and other recorded information about a piece of property for as far back as is possible. The chain ends with information about how the current owner obtained possession.

*The real estate attorney discovered a flaw in the **chain of title** for the property and recommended against purchase of the land unless an unrestricted title insurance policy was provided by the seller.*

See also: Title, Title insurance policy

Chairman of the Board, *noun*

The chief officer of a corporation, elected by the board of directors, and given general responsibility for policy and the supervision of executive management.

*The board of directors, in a sharply divided split between factions of investors, voted to dismiss the **chairman of the board** and select a new chief officer from amongst its members.*

See also: Board of Directors

Challenge, *verb, noun*

(1) An objection by attorneys for either party to the eligibility or selection of a person to be a member of a jury for a specific reason. (2) Also, an objection to a claim of the truth of something put forth by the other party in a trial.

*(1) The defense counsel **challenged** a prospective juror, alleging an expressed bias against the defendant. (2) The prosecutor made a*

challenge *against evidence put forth by the defense attorney that tended to put into question his client's attendance at a particular meeting.*

See also: Peremptory challenge

Chambers, *noun*

The private offices and workspace for a judge. Under certain circumstances, a judge may invite counsel for both parties to meet in chambers for arguments or rulings conducted out of the hearing of the jury.

*The judge suspended the trial and asked the attorneys to meet with him in **chambers** to determine if proposed evidence was appropriate to be introduced or whether it would tend to improperly sway the jury.*

See also: Bench

Champerty (CHAM-per-tee), *noun*

A situation in which a third party, not involved in a dispute or representing a side in a lawsuit, agrees to finance the expenses of the court case in return for a share of any damages received. Today many civil trials are conducted on a contingency basis under which the plaintiff's attorney is fully or partly paid from the proceeds of a successful case.

*A **champerty** arrangement to finance a court proceeding was discouraged or made illegal in the past because it was thought to have encouraged frivolous lawsuits.*

Chapter 11 bankruptcy, *noun*

An element of federal law under which a business, given permission of the court, can continue to operate while a plan is developed to give the business more time to reduce its debt or extend the payment schedule for debts.

*The company filed for **Chapter 11 bankruptcy** protection, seeking time to restructure its debt.*

See also: Bankruptcy, Reorganization

Character witness, *noun*

A witness brought to the stand to testify about the character or reputation of a defendant or to vouch for another witness in the case.

*The defense called several former employees of the defendant to testify as **character witnesses**.*

Charge, *noun, verb*

(1) The specific nature of the crime a defendant is accused of committing. (2) Also, an accusation of a violation of law. (3) Also, the instructions given by a trial judge to the jury before they begin deliberations.

> *(1) Cain was arrested on a **charge** of vehicular homicide. (2) The district attorney **charged** Cain with reckless disregard for the safety of his passengers. (3) In his **charge** to the jury, the judge instructed jurors that they must be convinced of guilt beyond a reasonable doubt or else they must acquit the defendant.*

See also: Accuse, Indict

Chargeback, *noun*

In credit card transactions, where the cardholder disputes a transaction or there is an error in the processing of a charge, the acquiring bank issues a chargeback to the merchant to deduct the funds that had been transferred. Also known as a charge-off.

> *The Jacksons disputed the charge for the flowers, telling their credit card issuer they had never received the delivery; the issuer processed a **chargeback** to the merchant.*

Chattel, *noun*

Personal property or possessions, by definition items that are movable. Real property is land and buildings and other improvements made to the land.

> *Loans made to finance the purchase of **chattel** are usually at a higher interest rate than things considered permanent and unmovable, like real estate.*

See also: Personal property, Real property

Check, *noun*

A legally binding instrument, sometimes called a draft, where a person or business (the drawer) directs a bank or other financial institution (the drawee) to pay money to the person named as the payee.

> *Fern Whalen presented a **check** from her personal account at the bank to pay the amount due on the invoice.*

See also: Draft, Cashier's check, Certified check

Child support, *noun*

Payments from one person to another (a former spouse, a separated spouse, or sometimes the mother or father of a child in a situation where there never was a marriage) to pay for the basic and special needs of a child. The amount of child support is determined by a court.

> *The judge ordered the mother to pay $1,000 per month to her former husband, the custodial parent, as* **child support**.

See also: Alimony, Maintenance

Churn, churning, *verb, noun*

A practice, generally illegal, where a stockbroker or other financial advisor engages in excessive and unnecessary buying and selling of shares or other instruments.

> *The broker was accused of* **churning** *his clients' accounts to generate commissions rather than for the benefit of investors.*

Circuit court, *noun*

In some jurisdictions, a judge in a circuit court travels between various geographic regions to hear cases as necessary. In current usage, the term might also be used to describe a court that has jurisdiction over a wide area although it might meet in only one place.

> *The judge of the* **circuit court** *hears cases every three weeks in the local courthouse; in an emergency, a special session can be convened or a defendant can be transported to a different location for a hearing.*

Circumstantial evidence, *noun*

Evidence that tends to point to guilt but does not prove it. Also, evidence that does not come directly from an eyewitness or from demonstrable fact.

> *The defense attorney said that the fact that the accused was spotted in the general vicinity of the scene of the crime was merely* **circumstantial evidence** *and did not prove his involvement in the act.*

Citation, *noun*

(1) A notice to appear in court to answer to charges of a minor crime, such as a traffic violation. Failure to appear, or in certain jurisdictions failure to respond by mail, may result in a warrant for arrest by the police. (2) Also, a reference in a written or oral argument to a previously decided case that dealt with the same points of law.

*(1) Kean received a **citation** in the mail after an automated traffic camera took a photo of her vehicle (and its license plate) crossing an intersection without stopping at a red light. She was given the option of appearing in court or pleading guilty by mail and paying a fine. (2) In arguing for dismissal of the case, the defense attorney included **citations** of several cases where similar types of evidence were found to be not probative of guilt.*

Civil (SIH-vill), *adjective*
Anything relating to issues between individuals or organizations, as distinguished from criminal laws and actions. This includes most disputes regarding contracts, property, family relations, accidents, and estates.
*Mr. Jones engaged a lawyer to file a **civil** lawsuit against his neighbor to recover damages caused by the fall of the tree.*

Civil action, *noun*
A lawsuit for a civil matter and not involving criminal law.
*The plaintiff filed a **civil action** against the manufacturer of the machinery, alleging failure to honor the terms of the warranty.*

Claim, *noun*
A demand for money due, for damages, or for the enforcement of a right.
*In their **claim** for damages, the plaintiff alleged that the loss of use of the manufacturing equipment cost the company $10,000 per week for eight weeks.*

Class action, *noun*
A lawsuit brought on behalf of oneself as well as others who have been affected by an identical or similar damage. For example, an attorney who represents a person who claims to have been injured as the result of taking a particular medication may file a suit on behalf of all persons with the same condition.
*The **class action** suit sought $100 million in damages from the pharmaceutical maker for pain and suffering inflicted on an estimated 5,000 users of the medication.*

Clause, *noun*
A separate element or stipulation in a contract or law.

*The employment contract included a "non-compete" **clause** that limited Mr. Jones from seeking a new job in the same industry for five years after leaving the company.*

Clear and convincing evidence, *noun*

In some civil cases, the highest level of burden of proof is the determination that evidence that has been presented is clear and convincing.

*The judge instructed the jury that they must be convinced they have heard **clear and convincing evidence**, enough to believe that it is substantially more likely than not that the charges are true.*

See also: Burden of proof

Clear title, *noun*

A title that is determined by a professional examiner to be free of reasonable risk of successful challenge by someone else who claims to own the property.

*The real estate attorney's examiner reported a **clear title** on the property, indicating no apparent reasons why the sale should not proceed.*

See also: Title, Title insurance policy, Cloud on title

Clemency, *noun*

An action by the governor of a state or the President to reduce a sentence or grant a pardon or reprieve without forgiving the crime itself. Also, an action by a government agency to lessen the severity of a penalty.

*The governor granted **clemency** to six convicted felons who have already served longer terms in prison than they would have been sentenced to under the new law.*

See also: Amnesty, Pardon, Parole, Reprieve

Close corporation, Closely held corporation, *noun*

A corporation that is either by a single shareholder or by a small group. The shareholders may be involved in the operation of the company, family relations, or otherwise connected.

*As a **closely held corporation**, it is nearly impossible for outside investors to gain control of the business unless the shareholders choose to open up ownership.*

C

Closed shop, *noun*

A place of employment where a collective bargaining agreement stipulates that all workers must be members of a union in order to obtain a job.

*The assembly plant was a **closed shop**, under terms of the master contract negotiated by the union that represented the workers there.*

See also: Open shop

Closing, *noun*

The completion of a transaction, at which papers are signed or certified and funds exchanged. A real estate closing includes the delivery of a title. A financial closing involves the payment for securities.

*The buyer and seller met at the office of the escrow agent for the **closing** on the sale of the property and home.*

See also: Title, Escrow, Escrow agent

Closing statement, *noun*

An attorney's concluding argument to a judge or jury, summing up evidence presented in a case and asking for a particular verdict. The argument can include points of law.

*In his **closing statement**, the defense attorney argued that the prosecution had failed to directly link Chin to the crime and reminded the jury of testimony from several witnesses that indicated that others—and not the defendant—had been involved.*

See also: Summation, Opening statement

Cloud on title, *noun*

Any encumbrance, lien, outstanding claim, or fault in a title which may affect the validity of a real estate transfer.

*The title search turned up a **cloud on title** for the land and the buyer's attorney recommended that the purchase not go forth until the encumbrance was cleared and a title insurance policy was obtained by the seller.*

See also: Clear title, Encumbrance, Quiet title, Quitclaim, Title insurance policy

Co-conspirator, *noun*

A person deemed by a prosecutor, grand jury, or other legal authority to have agreed with another to commit an illegal act.

*Collins and Muldaur were named as **co-conspirators** in the attempt to defraud investors out of millions of dollars through the resale of phony mortgages.*

See also: Co-respondent

Co-op, *noun*

A form of real estate ownership in which ownership in a property is held by a corporation which sells shares to individuals; residents receive a proprietary lease.

*The Murrays were approved by the tenants board and allowed to purchase shares in the **co-op** and obtain a lease on an apartment.*

Co-respondent, *noun*

A joint defendant in a lawsuit. Also, in a suit for divorce, a person named as contributing to the breakup of the marriage, such as having committed adultery with the respondent.

*After the lawsuit was filed, the plaintiff's attorneys asked the court to add the name of Edgar Gary as a **co-respondent** under the same claim for damages.*

See also: Co-conspirator

Co-sign, co-signer, *verb, noun*

To add your name to a promissory note or contract and in doing so take on shared responsibility for the repayment of the loan or the performance of the agreement. A person who signs in this way is called a cosigner.

*William's parents had to **co-sign** his lease because he had just graduated from college and did not have a detailed credit history.*

See also: Comaker

Codicil (KAW-de-sill), *noun*

An amendment or addition to a will that modifies, revokes, or clarifies one or more elements.

*The court noted that Mr. Poster had signed and attached a **codicil** to his will that removed his former partner from the list of beneficiaries.*

See also: Will

Cognizable (KOG-nye-ze-bel), *adjective*

Recognized as being within the jurisdiction and purview of a court and therefore appropriate for consideration.

The judge ruled that the suit was **cognizable** *and ordered it scheduled for hearing.*

See also: Jurisdiction

Coinsurance, *noun*

A form of insurance in which the issuer of a policy covers only a portion of any loss, requiring someone else to pay the remainder. (1) For example, a health insurance policy may require clients to pay a portion of covered expenses. (2) Or, a property insurance policy might exclude certain hazards, such as flood damage, and the owner of the property may choose to purchase a separate policy just to handle that risk.

(1) As a subscriber to a health insurance policy, Mary Jones is required to pay $35 for any visit to a doctor as **coinsurance***; any remaining charges are covered under her policy. (2) The company was required to purchase* **coinsurance** *to cover flood damage, a risk that is specifically excluded from its general hazard insurance.*

Collateral (ke-LAT-er-al), *noun, adjective*

(1) Property or other assets pledged as security for a loan. (2) Also, a proceeding or other event that is occurring concurrent with another legal case.

(1) Mr. Webster included his collection of antique automobiles as **collateral** *to secure the loan to start his business. (2) The court deferred its ruling on the case, noting that a* **collateral** *case in another jurisdiction could have an impact on its decision.*

See also: Security

Collective bargaining, *noun*

Bargaining by a group of workers for salaries, benefits, and work rules. In most situations the collective bargaining unit is called a union, and a contract that results is called a collective bargaining agreement.

The factory workers engaged in **collective bargaining** *to obtain a master agreement covering salary schedules and working conditions.*

See also: Union, Grievance

Collusion, *noun*

A situation in which two or more persons or businesses enter into a secret or illegal arrangement to deceive or defraud a third party.

*The real estate agent and the appraiser were charged with **collusion** in artificially deflating the selling price of the property for their own benefit.*
See also: Conspiracy

Comaker (KO-maker), *noun*

When there are two or more signers on a check or a promissory note, each is a comaker of the obligation and is liable for the entire amount involved.

*As a **comaker** of your son's application for an automobile loan, you are liable to make the monthly payments or pay the full amount due if he fails to make payments himself.*
See also: Cosigner, Promissory note

Commission, *noun*

(1) A fee paid to a broker or salesperson usually based on a percentage of sales. Also, a fee paid to an agent, financial representative, or other professional and based on the value of the transaction or of the amount of money managed in some way. (2) Also, the appointed authority to perform certain duties, usually on behalf of a government.

*(1) The broker was paid a **commission** of 7 percent for her work in arranging for the sale of the company's excess inventory. (2) Mr. Clapton was given a **commission** to act as appraiser for the town.*

Commitment letter, *noun*

An official notification to a borrower of the intention of a lender to give a loan.

*The bank sent a **commitment letter** to the borrower, including the details of the loan and setting the time and date for the closing.*
See also: Binder, Closing

Common stock, *noun*

The lowest and most basic class of stock issued by a corporation. By contrast, preferred stock is a class of shares that have priority over common shares when it comes to the payment of dividends or in the distribution of assets if the company is dissolved.

*The corporation announced it would offer a new round of sales of **common stock** to help fund its expansion into the Australian market.*
See also: Preferred stock

Community property, *noun*

A legal term applied in most states to property and assets received by a husband and wife during the period of their marriage. Some states exclude specific assets including inheritances and certain property and profits that were owned or received before marriage.

*The couple's beach house was determined to be **community property** because it had been purchased during the period they were married.*

Community service, *noun*

A form of alternative sentence in which a convicted defender is required to perform certain services in the community instead of going to prison or paying a fine.

*The judge sentenced both defendants to three months of **community service** working for the parks department to remove graffiti and repair sidewalks.*

Community standards, *noun*

A benchmark used in certain jurisdictions or under certain laws to determine whether something is obscene or otherwise offensive to the general consensus of the community.

*In his ruling, the judge said that though the artwork was repugnant and insulting, it did not rise to the level of obscenity when compared to **community standards**.*

See also: Obscenity

Commute (ka-MUTE), *verb*

An action by a government official or by a judge or judicial board to reduce a criminal sentence.

*The governor decided to **commute** the sentence of all persons sentenced to incarceration for more than five years under the old law now that the legislature has decided to reduce the penalty for the offense.*

Compensatory damages (com-PEN-sah-tory), noun

Monetary payment awarded for actual losses to persons or organizations, including intangible losses such as pain and suffering or absence of services. Not included are punitive damages intended as punishment for willful or negligent actions.

*The court awarded $100,000 in **compensatory damages** for losses caused by the closing of the factory because of the water main break.*

See also: Pain and suffering, Punitive damages

Comparables, *noun*

Properties in an area that are similar to others for sale in the area and are used by appraisers or real estate agents to establish an estimated selling price.

> *The real estate agent said that based on **comparables** in the neighborhood, the house should sell for about $475,000 in an ordinary market.*

See also: Comparative market analysis

Comparative market analysis, *noun*

A report prepared by a real estate agent or an appraiser used to compare selling prices for similar properties in a particular area. Some lenders require preparation of such a report as part of their decisions on whether to issue a mortgage; most seek to avoid lending more money than the home or property is worth.

> *Based on the **comparative market analysis** of other recent sales in the neighborhood, the lender offered to issue a mortgage of no more than $325,000, meaning that the buyer would have to come up with a down payment of $175,000 from other sources.*

See also: Comparables

C

Competent, *adjective*

In contracts and wills, someone deemed to be mentally and physically able to perform the task or make necessary decisions. In court matters, someone who is recognized as having the legal authority to act in a particular matter.

> *The court ruled that Mr. Webster was **competent** to act as executor of his brother's estate.*

See also: Disability, Consent

Complaint, *noun*

(1) The initial filing in a civil case, asserting that one party intends to seek damages or action by the court against another party. (2) Also, in some jurisdictions, a prosecutor begins an action by filing a criminal complaint (also called information or a petition) that charges a defendant with a crime and provides basic details of the allegation.

> *(1) Consolidated Widget filed a **complaint** in Common Court seeking unspecified damages from Intergalactic Doodad for breach of contract. (2) The county prosecutor filed a criminal **complaint** with the court, charging Mr. Smythe with grand larceny.*

Complicity, *noun*
Participation with or assistance to another person in the commission of an unlawful act.

*The prosecutor charged Janus with **complicity** in the bank robbery, alleging that he provided information to the actual participants in the crime about the layout of the building and its electronic monitoring system.*

See also: Accomplice

Compos mentis (KOM-pes MEN-tiss), *noun*
A Latin phrase meaning "having mastery of mind" or "of sound mind."

*The court required the prosecution to determine that the defendant had **compos mentis** before the trial could proceed.*

See also: Non compos mentis

Composition, *noun*
A settlement between parties that allows a borrower to pay off a loan with an amount less than the full amount due.

*The **composition** pays off the obligation of the borrower, relieving it of a liability that was threatening to force the company into bankruptcy.*

Compromise, *noun*
A settlement of a dispute in which both parties agree to accept less than what they had first sought.

*The arbitrator proposed a **compromise** solution to the contract dispute, reducing the amount due to be paid and shortening the length of the term of the agreement.*

Concur, *verb*
A decision by a higher court to agree with another court's ruling. Also, an opinion expressed by an attorney or a party in a court case agreeing with a point or ruling.

*The appeals court justice filed a **concurring** opinion, agreeing with the conclusions of the decision by other members of the panel but citing other reasons and precedents.*

Concurrent sentences, *noun*
A situation under which two or more sentences on different charges are served simultaneously.

*The judge ordered **concurrent sentences** of ten years in prison on each of the three charges.*

See also: Consecutive sentences

Condemn, *verb*

(1) An action by a government agency to take a property for public use under the power of eminent domain. (2) Or, an action to declare a structure dangerous or uninhabitable.

*(1) The city council voted to **condemn** three properties on Rolling Meadow Drive to permit widening of the road. (2) The building inspector entered an administrative order to **condemn** the structure at 50 Main Street because of violations of health and safety regulations.*

See also: Eminent domain

Conditional sale, *noun*

A form of sale where the original owner retains title to the goods until full payment is made or some other condition is met.

*Consolidated Intergalactic delivered and installed factory equipment to Transoceanic Trucking under a **conditional sale** that states that ownership of the equipment does not transfer to the buyer until the machinery has been fully configured and tested and final payment made.*

Condominium, *noun*

A form of real estate ownership in which two or more owners have title to individual portions of a building; they typically have joint ownership of the common areas such as entryways, hallways, utility rooms, and land.

*The Blacks purchased a **condominium** title that gave them ownership of a three-bedroom apartment in the building. The sale requires them to pay a proportional share of the cost of the upkeep and maintenance of the exterior structure of the building, mechanical equipment including elevators and furnaces, and property taxes.*

See also: Co-op

Confession, *noun*

A written or oral acknowledgment of guilt, or of having done something improper.

*In general, courts are very demanding that police or other law enforcement agencies fully inform citizens of their rights before allowing a **confession** into evidence.*

Conflict of interest, *noun*

A situation in which someone may have a personal or business interest in a matter that would interfere with the ability to act fairly and dispassionately in any way.

*The judge said that although there was no actual **conflict of interest** because his wife was an employee of the plaintiff, he would recuse himself from the case to avoid the appearance of a conflict.*

Conformed copy, *noun*

A copy of a document to which modifications or additions have been made to make it conform to the original.

*Both parties initialed a **conformed copy** of the contract that included changes made to the original.*

Conjugal rights, *noun*

A right to companionship or sexual relations in a marriage.

*Denial of **conjugal rights** has been used as one cause for action in a divorce proceeding.*

See also: Conjugal visit

Conjugal visit, *noun*

In certain jurisdictions, a permitted visit by the spouse or sometimes an unmarried person with whom a prisoner has a relationship, for the purposes of sexual relations.

*The county sheriff said the facilities at the courthouse lockup did not have facilities to permit **conjugal visits** to prisoners by spouses or significant others.*

See also: Conjugal rights

Consecutive sentences, *noun*

A situation under which two or more sentences on different charges are served separately; one sentence must be fully served before the next begins.

*The judge ordered **consecutive sentences** of ten years in prison on each of the three charges.*

See also: Concurrent sentences

Consent, *noun*

A freely given permission for something to happen, or an agreement to do something.

*The issue of **consent** is at the heart of many criminal trials regarding rape.*

See also: Age of consent, Competent

Consenting adult, *noun*

An adult (that is, not a minor) who freely agrees to engage in an action or permit something to happen.

*Over the years, many formerly illegal sexual acts have been made permissible when performed by **consenting adults**.*

See also: Consent

Conservator (con-SER-ve-tor), *noun*

A guardian appointed by a court to protect and manage the financial affairs of another person who is unable to do so because of medical or mental impairment.

*The court appointed attorney Gene Bross as **conservator** for the financial affairs of Fred Carlin.*

See also: Guardian

Consideration, *noun*

Payment in some form. Consideration is an essential element of a contract or agreement.

*As **consideration** for services performed, the signer agrees to pay $50 per hour and will reimburse the cost of any out-of-pocket expenses as specified in this contract.*

See also: Quid pro quo, Agreement, Contract

Consign (kin-SINE), Consignment, *verb, noun*

(1) To give goods to someone else to sell to others. (2) Also, to give goods or documents to someone else for delivery to another person.

*(1) The company delivered a shipment of product to a dealer on **consignment**, with the agreement that the seller would pay the manufacturer for items actually sold. (2) The attorney **consigned** the documents to an overnight delivery service.*

Consolidate, *verb*

(1) To combine two or more similar or related legal actions into a single matter for consideration by the court. (2) Also, to bring together two or more loans or other financial instruments.

*(1) The court approved a motion by the defense to **consolidate** the two lawsuits from the unrelated trucking companies since both were asking relief for the same issue. (2) The borrower received approval from the lender to **consolidate** the two loans into a single obligation and refinance the amount based on current interest rates.*

Conspiracy, *noun*

An agreement, usually made in secret, between two or more persons to engage in an illegal act, or to achieve something by illegal means.

*Federal prosecutors accused the two men of engaging in a **conspiracy** to defraud investors.*

See also: Collusion

Constitutional, *adjective*

A law or action that is in harmony with the U.S. Constitution, or the constitution of a state. An action that is not in keeping with a constitution or expressly forbidden by the document is considered unconstitutional.

*The defendant argued that his **Constitutional** right to a speedy and public trial had been violated by his lengthy, secret incarceration.*

Construction, *noun*

When there is ambiguity or uncertainty as to the meaning of a law, an element of a constitution, or an agreement between two parties, a lawyer or judge may seek to determine its construction.

*Much of the pretrial arguments concerned the **construction** of the contract between the two parties, determining which laws applied to the case. The justice pledged he would apply strict **construction** to the law, not expanding its interpretation because of current events or social mores.*

See also: Liberal construction, Strict construction

Construction loan, *noun*

A short-term loan to finance the cost of construction, usually offered to contractors or homeowners before a longer-term mortgage is issued.

*Many **construction loans** are set up to disburse funds as they are needed for the completion of the building project and become due after completion; they may also be set up to automatically convert to a standard mortgage at closing.*

See also: Mortgage, Promissory note

Construe (con-STRU), *verb*

The process of discerning the meaning of words in a document, law, or legal decision based on accepted legal and more general definitions.

*The judge chose to **construe** the terms of the contract to mean that Consolidated Intergalactic could not demand payment without delivering the entire order specified in the agreement.*

Consumer, *noun*

Someone who purchases goods, services, or real property for personal (non-business) reasons.

*The lawsuit asked for damages to compensate any **consumer** of the product who suffered losses related to faulty electrical design.*

Contempt, *noun*

A judicial finding of disrespect to the judge or court officers or willful disobedience of an order.

*The judge found both defense attorneys in **contempt** for their repeated interruptions of the closing statement by the prosecution.*

Contest (kin-TEST), *verb*

To dispute or challenge the validity of a will or some of its elements.

*Schwartz's son directed his attorney to **contest** the will, saying that it had been altered in the final weeks of his father's life under duress.*

See also: Duress

Contiguous (kin-TIG-you-us), *adjective*

Connected to or next to something, usually applied to issues of real property.

*The title included transfer of two pieces of **contiguous** property.*

Contingency, Contingent, *noun*

A future event or situation that may or may not occur.

*The contract includes several provisions to deal with possible **contingencies** including significant changes in the marketplace or unforeseen accidents. The sale of the home was made **contingent** on the ability of the buyer to obtain a mortgage within fifteen days after the agreement was signed.*

See also: Contingency fee

Contingency fee, *noun*

An arrangement under which a plaintiff and an attorney agree that fees for the lawsuit would be paid as a percentage of the money obtained as the result of a successful court case or a settlement of the suit. In most such arrangements, the attorney is not paid if the plaintiff does not collect from the defendant.

*Many civil lawsuits are paid for on the basis of a **contingency fee** that is given to the attorney as a percentage of the proceeds received from the lawsuit.*

See also: Contingent liability

Contingent liability (con-TIN-jint), *noun*

An obligation to perform an action or pay an amount of money that only takes effect if a certain future event or condition occurs.

*Mary Brown has a **contingent liability** to supply the product on the same terms if Consolidated Intergalactic is unable to do so.*

See also: Contingency fee

Continuance, *noun*

A postponement or adjournment of a trial or other court proceeding until a specific later date, or until a specific action has been accomplished by one or the other party.

*The judge ordered a two-week **continuance** of the trial to permit the defense to obtain depositions from two witnesses who have moved out of state.*

See also: Adjournment

Contraband, *noun, adjective*

Goods that are illegal to possess, own, or sell.

*Customs officials confiscated several hundred boxes of **contraband** pharmaceuticals illegally imported from a foreign country and not approved for sale in the United States.*

Contract, *noun*

An agreement, defined with specific terms and obligations, which obligates performance of a service or delivery of a product in return for payment called a "consideration."

*Mr. Kohn signed a **contract** to deliver to Ms. Rembrandt, within ten days, twelve framed paintings of dogs playing poker, for a payment of $12.50 per artwork.*

See also: Agreement, Consideration

Contributory negligence, *noun*
An action, or failure to act, by the plaintiff that is deemed to have been negligent and helped cause the injury or loss that is the cause of a lawsuit.

*The defendant argued that the accident was primarily due to **contributory negligence** by the plaintiff and was not the fault of his client.*

See also: Negligence

Controlled substance, *noun*
A drug that has been classified by federal or state authorities as one that may only be dispensed by prescription and only under controlled circumstances. In general, controlled substances are those which are considered addictive or intoxicating, such as narcotics.

*The defendant faces charges of possessing **controlled substances** for the purposes of sale.*

Conversion, *noun*
Treating someone else's property as if it were yours, or intentionally depriving another person of the use of their own possessions.

*Webster was accused of **conversion** of Smith's property without permission by selling items temporarily left at his home.*

See also: Theft

Conveyance, *noun*
The formal transfer of the title to property, or an interest in property, from one person to another.

*The **conveyance** of the title for the land occurred following completion of the closing of the mortgage.*

Convict (CON-vict), *noun*, (con-VICT), *verb*
(1) Someone who has been found guilty of a crime. (2) Also, to find someone guilty of a crime.

*(1) As a **convict**, Elray is not eligible to apply for a job with the school district. (2) The jury voted to **convict** Elray on all four counts of felony armed robbery.*

See also: Verdict, Conviction, Acquit

Conviction, *noun*
The act of finding someone guilty of a crime, or a record of having been found guilty.

*As a result of Crisp's **conviction** on bank fraud charges, he is not eligible to serve as an executive of any regulated financial company.*
See also: Verdict, Convict, Acquit

Cooperative, *noun*
A jointly owned business enterprise for the purchase or management of goods, or for other activities, established for the benefit of its members.
*Residents established a **cooperative** to purchase food and other items in large quantities at discount for resale to members.*
See also: Cooperative housing, Co-op

Cooperative housing, *noun*
A building which is jointly owned by individual owners of apartments or other units.
*Members of the **cooperative housing** own shares in the managing corporation for the building as well as their individual apartments or office spaces.*
See also: Co-op, Cooperative

Copayment, *noun*
The amount of money paid by an insured member of a health insurance plan directly to a health care provider. Some plans also have a deductible, which requires the member to pay all costs up to a particular amount after which the insurance plan takes over payment.
*A typical health insurance plan may require the member to make a **copayment** of about $25 for basic medical services, and then the plan reimburses the provider for the remainder of the fee.*
See also: Out-of-pocket expense

Copyright, *noun*
The set of rights retained by an author, composer, or other creative person or an entity representing them.
*In general, under **copyright** law a piece of intellectual property cannot be used by another person or company for the period of time specified by law without permission from the owner of the copyright.*
See also: Intellectual property

Coroner, *noun*
A person officially designated to investigate deaths that appear to have been the result of something other than natural causes. In some

jurisdictions the coroner does not necessarily possess a medical degree or license.

> The **coroner** ruled that the cause of death was homicide, specifically as the result of knife wounds.

See also: Medical examiner, Autopsy, Inquest, Post mortem

Corporation, *noun*

A form of business organization in which a company acts as if it were a person. The principals or shareholders of a corporation have only liability for the actions or debts of the company. The corporation can also issue shares of stock to raise funds for operations or capital expenditure.

> By registering with the state as a **corporation** and following all necessary regulations in doing so, the company was given a legal standing of its own.

See also: Incorporate, Limited liability

Corpus delicti (KOR-pes di-LIK-tie), *noun*

Literally, the "body of the crime," it is the substantial fact of a crime. In common (but not necessarily legal) terms, it is often used to refer to the body of a murder victim.

> In his argument before the court, the prosecuting attorney claimed that the **corpus delicti** provided overwhelming evidence of the aggravating nature of the crime.

C

Cost basis, *noun*

In financial and tax calculations, the amount of money originally invested in purchase of a security, adjusting for stock splits and reinvested dividends or distributions.

> In calculating the capital gains tax on the sale of shares of stock, the accountant obtained the **cost basis** for the original purchase.

See also: Basis

Costs, *noun*

The expenses of mounting a legal case.

> The judge found for the defendant, and ordered the plaintiff to pay the **costs** of the failed lawsuit.

Counsel, *noun, verb*

(1) An attorney, counselor, or lawyer; someone licensed to practice law.
(2) Also, to give legal advice.

(1) The defendant engaged Smith, Smith, Smith, and Smythe as legal **counsel** *for his case. (2) He* **counseled** *his client to consider the prosecutor's offer to allow pleading guilty to a lesser misdemeanor instead of going to trial on the more serious felony charge.*

Counterclaim, *noun*

A lawsuit filed by a defendant in response to a claim by another party and included in the answer to the original lawsuit.

Consolidated Videogames filed a **counterclaim** *against Intergalactic Toys, denying it had used images from Intergalactic's products and instead accusing Intergalactic of violating a non-compete clause in an existing agreement between the two companies.*

See also: Cross claim, Offset, Recoupment, Setoff

Counteroffer, *noun*

A response to a proposed contract, or settlement of a dispute, that does not accept the offer but instead puts forth different terms.

The defendant made a **counteroffer** *to settle the dispute before going to trial.*

See also: Settlement

Court order, *noun*

A directive from a court or judge to perform an act, or not to act in a particular way.

The **court order** *required the immediate suspension of sale of the item and the appointment of a guardian to account for the inventory until the lawsuit was settled.*

See also: Writ, Habeas corpus

Courtesy, *noun*

Something done out of politeness or consideration for someone else. A so-called professional courtesy, in which a law enforcement officer or an attorney does a special favor for someone else, may be in violation of conflict of interest rules or laws.

The code of conduct in judicial proceedings requires professional **courtesy** *amongst lawyers, the judge, and all other officials at all times.*

Covenant (KUV-eh-nint), *noun*

A promise made as part of a contract or in a deed for transfer of real property.

The contract included a **covenant** *promising Consolidated Widget the exclusive right to market the product in the state of Ohio.*

See also: Restrictive covenant

Credit bureau, *noun*

An agency that collects information and stores records about personal borrowing including credit cards, automobile loans, and mortgages, and maintains records of reports from lenders about repayment history.

Consumers can request a copy of their current credit score from a **credit bureau** *and check for inaccuracies in reports.*

See also: Credit report, Credit score

Credit card, *noun*

A way to make payment without the use of cash. A credit card is a link to a short-term unsecured loan; when a customer charges purchase of a product or service, the amount is added to that person's outstanding balance. In most cases, if the full amount due is paid when billed, no interest rate is assessed; if a balance remains after the due date, interest is charged.

The best way to use a **credit card** *is to pay off your full balance each month when the bill is due, avoiding interest charges on the balance due.*

See also: Debit card

Credit report, *noun*

A report from a credit bureau or other source on an individual's or company's history of borrowing and repaying loans including credit cards, mortgages, and other obligations.

Most lenders consult an applicant's **credit report** *before deciding whether to issue a loan; they also record major obligations with the bureau so that a borrower's current record is available for review.*

See also: Credit score, Credit bureau

Credit score, *noun*

A numerical rating of a person's credit history based on their history of establishing and using loans, mortgages, and credit cards. The higher the score, the greater the creditworthiness of the borrower.

C

*The most common **credit score** system in the United States uses a scale that runs from a low rating of 300 to a top score of 850.*

See also: Credit bureau, Credit report

Creditor (CRED-it-or), *noun*

A person or company that is owed money or other consideration.

*As part of the bankruptcy ruling, the court suspended payment to all current **creditors**.*

Creditworthiness, *noun*

A determination of whether a person or a business is reliable enough to be given credit or lent money, based on either a credit history, credit score, or a survey of assets.

*The greater a person's **creditworthiness**, the more likely a lender will be willing to make a loan or increase the amount of the loan at a preferred rate of interest.*

See also: Credit report, Credit score

Cross claim, *noun*

A claim filed by one defendant against another defendant on the same side of a lawsuit. By contrast, a counterclaim is a filing against a party on the other side of a lawsuit.

*The plaintiff filed a **cross claim** against the distributor of the product seeking compensation for losses caused by the failure of the equipment; another suit accuses the manufacturer of negligence in the design and assembly of the devices.*

See also: Counterclaim, Offset, Recoupment, Setoff

Cross examine, cross-examination, *verb, noun*

Questioning of a witness called by the other party in a lawsuit or criminal trial.

*The adversarial nature of a legal proceeding means that both parties get to question witnesses called by either side; after direct examination, the other party is given the chance to **cross examine** a witness. In his **cross-examination** of the prosecution's eyewitness, the defense attorney brought out several significant inconsistencies in the testimony.*

See also: Examination, Direct examination, Redirect

Cruel and unusual punishment, *noun*
Punishment that is disproportionate to the crime, or barbaric.

*The Eighth Amendment to the U.S. Constitution bars **cruel and unusual punishment** as well as excessive bail or fines.*

Curtilage, *noun*
The land that surrounds or encompasses a house.

*The lease included the right to make use of the house as well as the **curtilage** within the fenced boundaries of the property.*

Custodial parent, *noun*
As the result of a separation or divorce proceeding, the parent given primary responsibility for the care of a minor.

*The judge ruled that the mother would be the **custodial parent** of the child, but ordered that the father be granted regular visitation rights.*

See also: Guardian, Guardian ad litem

Custody, *noun*
(1) Have control over property. (2) Also, in domestic situations having control and responsibility for a minor child. (3) Also, in police terms, the holding of an accused or convicted person.

*(1) Pending a final decision, the court allowed the original owner of the vehicle to maintain **custody**. (2) The court awarded **custody** of the child to her father. (3) George was taken into **custody** by the State Police at the scene of the accident and later charged with driving while under the influence of alcohol.*

See also: Arrest, Detain

Cy pres (sigh-PRAY), *adverb, adjective*
From an old French term, meaning "as near as possible." When a testator's intentions in a will or trust cannot be followed exactly, the court or an executor will attempt to follow the wishes as closely as possible.

*Because the intended recipient of the bequest was no longer in existence, the executor decided that a **cy pres** donation to a similar charitable organization would be appropriate and legal.*

C

71

Damages, *noun*

The amount of money a plaintiff is seeking, or is awarded, in a lawsuit.

*The suit asks for payment of $50 million in **damages** for loss of use of his eyesight as a result of the accident.*

See also: Injury

Days delinquent, *noun*

The number of calendar days since the due date that a borrower is delinquent in making a payment. Also known as contractual delinquency.

*According to the notice from the lender, Dylan was thirty-five **days delinquent** in making at least the minimum monthly payment on the loan and was now in default.*

See also: Default, Delinquent

De facto (di-FAK-toe), *adjective, adverb*

A Latin phrase meaning "in fact." A court or other legal authority may rule that a person or agency may act as if it had authority to do so even if not all requirements have been met.

*The judge ruled that the stepfather had properly acted as a **de facto** guardian for his wife's children.*

De jure (DEE JOOR-ee), *adverb, adjective*

Literally, "from the law." Something that is de jure is brought into existence and is maintained because of legal requirements or procedures. By contrast, something that is de facto is something that exists as a matter of fact or nature.

*A business corporation is an entity that exists **de jure**, following the legal description for the state in which it is registered.*

De novo (di-NO-voh), *adjective*

A Latin term meaning "anew," as in starting over as if no proceedings had ever occurred.

*The appeals court determined that the original trial had not been conducted properly and ordered a trial **de novo**.*

Dead hand, *noun*

An unwanted or undesirable effect of a past event, especially in regards to the disposal of property after the death of its former owner.

*The previous use of the land as a firing range and explosives disposal site had a **dead hand** influence on its marketability. The estate was burdened by a*

dead hand *restriction on the sale of the property which required that it not be disposed of for at least twenty-five years after the death of the last direct heir.*

Deadly force, *noun*
An exercise of force that is so severe that it could possibly result in the death of the person against whom it is used.
> *The law limits the situations under which law enforcement officers can use **deadly force** in dealing with violent persons.*

Death certificate, *noun*
An official document signed by an attending physician, coroner, or medical examiner stating a date, time, location, and cause of death for a person.
> *The medical examiner withheld issuance of a **death certificate** until the results of the autopsy and toxicology reports were completed and evaluated.*

See also: Coroner, Medical examiner

Death penalty, *noun*
The punishment of execution by the state or federal government.
> *Having been found guilty of a capital offense, the judge imposed the **death penalty** on the defendant.*

See also: Capital punishment

Death tax, *noun*
An informal name given to taxes imposed on an estate.
> *An estate attorney can assist in setting up trusts and other legal means to minimize or avoid **death taxes**.*

See also: Estate tax

Debenture (de-BEN-shur), *noun*
A bond issued by a corporation that is unsecured and based only on the general credit of the company.
> *The sale of **debentures** by the company is similar in effect to the obtaining of an unsecured loan from an individual or financial institution.*

See also: Debt, Obligation, Promissory note

Debit card, *noun*
A way to make payment without the use of cash. A debit card is a form of secured loan, linked to a checking account or an investment account.

When a customer uses a debit card to make a purchase, the funds are immediately deducted from the associated account.

In general, a **debit card** *that is linked to a checking account does not offer all of the protections against fraud or disputes with a merchant that a credit card issuer may provide.*

See also: Credit card

Debt (DETT), *noun*

(1) An obligation to pay a certain amount of money, to deliver certain goods, or perform a particular act. (2) Also, the total amount of money owed by a company or person.

(1) The board of directors voted to increase the company's maximum amount of **debt** *to $20 million. (2) The court-appointed agent determined that Ms. Baez had incurred $25,000 in* **debt**.

See also: Debenture, Obligation, Promissory note

Debt-to-income ratio, *noun*

A calculation used by some lenders to assess an applicant's ability to handle new debt. Assuming there is a reasonable level of income, the lower the ratio the more creditworthy a borrower.

The **debt-to-income ratio** *is calculated by dividing gross monthly debt obligations by gross monthly income.*

See also: Creditworthiness

Deceased, *noun*

A person who has died.

The executor of an estate is designated to manage the disposition of the assets of a **deceased** *person.*

See also: Decedent

Decedent (di-SEE-dent), *noun*

In civil cases, including issues involving wills, trusts, and estates, the person who has died.

The court ruled that the **decedent**, *Mr. Jefferson, had intended that none of his children receive proceeds from his estate.*

See also: Deceased, Executor, Estate, Testator

Decision, *noun*

A ruling, judgment, or finding of facts by a judge, arbitrator, or government agency.

*The arbitrator's **decision** found that the plaintiff was entitled to full payment under terms of the contract.*

See also: Judgment, Ruling

Decree (di-CREE), *noun*

A judgment by a court or an official order from an agency or authority.

*The court's **decree** ordered Mr. Applebom to repay all of the defendant's legal expenses.*

See also: Court order, Writ

Decriminalize, decriminalization, *verb, noun*

To repeal a law making an act a criminal violation or to change a statute so that an act becomes a misdemeanor or violation instead of a crime.

*The legislature voted to **decriminalize** the possession of small amounts of marijuana, changing the law so that persons found with two ounces or less face a small fine, confiscation of the material, or both.*

See also: Misdemeanor

Dedication, *noun*

The gift of land by a person or business to the government to be used for the public good such as for a park, school, recreational facility, or road. Sometimes the conveyance of the land is made as part of a deal to allow other commercial development or zoning changes.

*The **dedication** to the town of the land along the river will allow establishment of a park and picnic area.*

Deductible, *noun*

In an insurance policy, the amount that the holder of the policy must pay in a loss before the insurer will make payment.

*If an automobile policy has a $1,000 **deductible** and damages are $3,000, the insurance company will pay $2,000 to the repair shop and the owner of the car is responsible for the remainder.*

See also: Copayment, Out-of-pocket expense

Deduction, *noun*

An expense that a personal or business taxpayer may subtract from total income before the calculation of taxes is performed.

*For most individuals, the largest single tax **deduction** on their federal return is for the cost of mortgage interest.*

See also: Itemized deduction

Deed, *noun*

A written and signed document that transfers full ownership or an interest in ownership of real property. In most jurisdictions the conveyance of the deed must be certified by a notary public and registered with local government.

*The transfer of the **deed** for the property was made after completion of the closing of the mortgage.*

See also: Title

Deed of trust (Trust deed), *noun*

An alternative to a mortgage or a secured loan in some states, in which the borrower (the trustor) places the legal title to real property with a neutral, third party (the trustee) who holds it until the full amount of the debt is repaid or other obligations performed. Also known as a trust deed.

*The house and land were conveyed in a **deed of trust** to an attorney to secure the loan until it was repaid.*

See also: Mortgage

Defalcation (de-FAL-kay-shun), *verb*

An improper use or appropriation of funds, especially in a situation where someone has a fiduciary responsibility such as a person who is a trustee, a public official, or corporate officer.

*The councilman was charged with **defalcation** of funds in the town's emergency services account by assigning government crews to pave the driveway at his home.*

See also: Embezzlement, Fiduciary, Malfeasance

Defamation, *noun*

The act of making an intentional and willful false statement about someone that tends to damage that person's reputation. A spoken or oral statement is considered slander while a statement that is published, printed, or broadcast is considered libel.

*The suit alleges that the false statement that Mr. Brack had filed for bankruptcy multiple times was a **defamation** of his character.*

See also: Defame, Libel, Slander

Defame, *verb*

To damage the reputation of another person through spoken statements.

The plaintiff claimed that the defendant had set out to intentionally ***defame*** *him by making false and damaging statements.*
See also: **Defamation, Libel, Slander**

Default (di-FAULT), *noun, verb*

(1) The failure to make a scheduled payment on a loan. (2) Also, the failure to respond to a summons or other court order by a deadline.

(1) The loan went into ***default*** *on May 1 after Consolidated Intergalactic failed to make a payment on the due date. (1) Mr. Jones* ***defaulted*** *on his mortgage. (2) Ms. Jones was found by the court to be in* ***default*** *for not providing the information demanded in the court order.*
See also: **Days delinquent, Delinquent**

Default judgment, *noun*

A ruling by a court or agency that gives an award to a plaintiff if a defendant fails to respond to a complaint within the time period specified by law.

The court clerk entered into the records a ***default judgment*** *against the plaintiff after the party did not respond to the lawsuit within thirty days.*
See also: **Default**

D

Defendant, *noun*

In civil matters, the person or party of whom relief or damages are sought. In criminal cases, the person accused of committing a crime.

In a criminal case, the burden is on the prosecution to prove that a ***defendant*** *is guilty of an infraction.*
See also: **Accused, Plaintiff**

Deficit (DEH-fi-sit), *noun*

A shortcoming in an account or budget, or a payment that is less than the total amount due.

The accountant reported that the company's balance sheet showed a ***deficit*** *of $3 million for the quarter, mostly as the result of costs due to the unexpected sharp decline of the value of the dollar against European currencies.*

Defraud (di-FRAWD), *verb*

To obtain money, property, services, or anything else of value from a person or company on the basis of falsehoods or deceit.

*The employee was charged with **defrauding** the company of $500,000 over the course of three years through issuance of checks to accomplices for services that were never rendered.*

Deliberate (di-LIB-er-it) *adjective*, (di-lib-er-ATE), *verb*
(1) Done on the basis of premeditation or planning. (2) Also, the act of a jury or a panel of judges to consider the facts and the law to reach a decision.

*(1) The defendant was accused of causing a **deliberate** accident. (2) The jury **deliberated** the case for three days before reaching a verdict.*

Delinquent, *noun, adjective*
The failure to pay an amount due, or to perform a duty on time.

*The lender notified the borrower that he was **delinquent** in making the expected monthly payment and said that if the funds were not received within ten days the loan would go into default.*

See also: Default, Days delinquent

Delinquent taxes, *noun*
Taxes that are past due and unpaid.

*A state or local government can take real property where there are **delinquent taxes**.*

See also: Delinquent

Delivery, *noun*
A formal or symbolic handing over of money, property, documents, or other objects. A delivery may mark the fulfillment of a contract or compliance with a court order.

*The **delivery** of the transcripts was accepted by the clerk of the court.*

Demand, *noun, verb*
(1) A claim or formal request. A party could demand payment or action as part of a contract. (2) In a lawsuit, a plaintiff generally has to show that a demand was made before the suit was filed.

*Terms of the contract have not been followed; we **demand** immediate payment.*

Demise (di-MIZE), *noun*
(1) Death of a person. (2) Also, the failure of a business or agreement. (3) Also, a deed that conveys real property only for the lifetime of a person.

*(1) Upon the **demise** of the defendant, the criminal court case was dismissed. (2) As a result of the **demise** of the corporation, all current contracts and obligations were turned over to a court-appointed administrator for disposition. (3) The **demise** deed allowed full use of the property during Mr. Smith's lifetime, but upon his death the land and home were to be sold by an executor and the proceeds given to a designated charity.*

Demographics, *noun, adjective*
Necessary information collected by a lender, government agency, employers, or other appropriate entity about customers and applicants.

*Typical **demographic** information maintained about applicants includes name, address, date of birth, and driver's license information.*

See also: Right to privacy

Demurrer (dee-MURR-er), *noun*
A response by a defendant in a lawsuit that says that even if the facts alleged by the plaintiff are true the claim is invalid.

*In a written **demurrer**, the defendant acknowledged the principal facts claimed by the plaintiff but argued that there was no legal basis for a lawsuit.*

Deportation, *noun*
The involuntary expulsion of a non-citizen from the country.

*The federal court approved the **deportation** of the six illegal aliens arrested in a raid on a sex slave ring.*

Deposition (deh-pih-ZI-shen), *noun*
A recording of testimony from a witness, under oath, before trial.

*Mr. Shrub was questioned by attorneys for both sides in a **deposition** about the company's hiring practices.*

Depreciation, Depreciate (di-PRE-she-ay-shun), *noun, verb*
An actual or calculated loss of the value of an asset over time because of deterioration or obsolescence.

*For taxation purposes, the company determined that its manufacturing equipment would be fully **depreciated** at the end of a seven-year period.*

*The auditors challenged the **depreciation** schedule for capital assets, saying that the pace of technological change had already made much of the company's equipment of little actual value.*

See also: Recapture, Accelerated depreciation

Depression, *noun*

A sustained and severe recession that typically includes high levels of unemployment and deflation (falling prices) for products because of lack of demand and other factors.

*Historians say the United States has suffered several economic **depressions** in its history including the Great Depression from 1929 to 1939 which was precipitated by a collapse of banking and financial institutions.*

Derelict, *noun, adjective*

(1) Something or someone who has failed to perform an act. (2) Also something or someone who is abandoned or in poor condition because of neglect.

*(1) The plaintiff alleged that the caretaker was **derelict** in his duties to maintain the property. (2) The home was declared a **derelict**, in danger of collapse. The man, who had no known means of support, was considered a **derelict**.*

Descent (di-SENT), *noun*

The specified rules for passing the contents of an estate to heirs when there is a lack of a valid will, a condition called intestate.

*Under rules of **descent**, Mr. Jones' estate will pass to his wife if she is still living or be divided equally amongst his living children.*

See also: Estate, Heir, Intestate, Will

Desertion, *noun*

The act of abandoning someone, usually a spouse or children, without an intent to return.

*In divorce proceedings that depend upon a finding of fault, the **desertion** from the marriage by one spouse is a common reason for granting the petition.*

See also: Abandonment

Detain (de-TAIN), *verb*

To arrest, take into custody, or delay someone or something.

> *The police acted to **detain** all witnesses to the murder so that they could be identified and interviewed.*

See also: Arrest, Custody

Deter (dee-TERR), *verb*

To discourage or restrain someone from taking action, especially through the use of fear.

> *The basic purpose of a police foot patrol is to **deter** crime.*

Devise (de-VIZE), *verb*

The giving of real property under terms of a will.

> *Mr. Jones said he wanted to **devise** his home to his daughter as part of his will.*

See also: Bequeath, Bequest

Devolution (deh-vo-LU-shun), *noun*

(1) The transfer of real property under predetermined rules of the law.
(2) Also, the transfer of rights or powers from one person or one government official to another.

> *(1) The title to the property was transferred to heirs under rules of **devolution**. (2) The powers of the office of mayor passed to the newly elected officeholder by **devolution**.*

D

Dilution (dye-LU-shun), *noun*

A reduction in the value of existing shares of stock by the issuance of new shares.

> *The corporation's sale of 100,000 new shares of common stock caused the **dilution** of the value of existing shares by 50 percent.*

See also: Common stock

Direct deposit, *noun*

A means for the issuer of payroll, dividend, or other payments to have funds sent electronically to a bank account or other financial institution for immediate credit.

> *Many employers offer their employees the option for **direct deposit** of their paychecks into personal checking accounts.*

Direct examination, *noun*

The questioning of a witness by the party that called the person to testify. The opposing party can then conduct a cross-examination of the witness.

*In his **direct examination** of the witness, the prosecution sought to establish the basic facts of the crime and the involvement of the defendant in its commission.*

See also: Examination, Cross-examination, Redirect

Disability (DISS-ah-bil-ity), *noun*

(1) A condition, disease, or injury that prevents someone from performing ordinary physical functions including the assignments of his employment. (2) Also, in insurance and employment situations, something which makes it impossible for someone to perform his or her ordinary occupation or in extreme cases any equivalent employment. (3) Also, in legal terms, an impediment to making a contract such as being a minor or being judged mentally incompetent.

*(1), (2) Jones was unable to continue in his job because he developed a permanent **disability**. (3) The contract was ruled invalid because of the **disability** of the minor to enter into a binding agreement.*

See also: Competent

Disbar (diss-BAR), *verb*

To remove an attorney from the Bar, meaning the list of attorneys who have a license or other approval to practice law in a particular jurisdiction. The act of disbarment is generally related to improper conduct in the practice of law or in other matters.

*As a result of the attorney's conviction on charges of felony fraud, the judge moved to immediately **disbar** him.*

Disclaim (diss-CLAIM), *verb*

(1) To renounce or quit any claim to property; (2) to deny responsibility, such as a refusal by an insurance company to pay a claim; (3) to renounce any future responsibility; (4) to deny the validity of something or to deny a connection to it; (5) to renounce a valid or legal right.

*(1) Ms. Greene instructed her attorney to **disclaim** any interest in the land. (2) The insurance company said it would **disclaim** the request for payment because the insured had engaged in skydiving, an activity specifically excluded from coverage. (3) In dissolving the partnership, both sides agreed to **disclaim** any responsibility for actions by the other from that*

point forward. (4) Clifton **disclaimed** any involvement in the importation of counterfeit handbags, saying that the product had been represented to his company as authentic. (5) The defendant **disclaimed** his right to a speedy trial, preferring to allow his attorneys more time to prepare his defense.

See also: Disclaimer

Disclaimer, *noun*

(1) A statement that denies something, including a refusal to accept responsibility for certain acts; (2) a renunciation of ownership; (3) a repudiation of another party's claim.

(1) The offer included a **disclaimer** denying warranty or repair service for any listed activity considered not ordinary use of the equipment. (2) The conveyance of the property included a **disclaimer** of further interest in the land by the seller. (3) The defendant response included a **disclaimer** to all of the principal allegations by the plaintiff.

See also: Disclaim

Disclose (diss-CLOSE), *verb*

To reveal something previously kept secret or hidden.

In his pretrial deposition, the witness **disclosed** he had been involved in a series of loan arrangements similar to the one that is at issue in the lawsuit.

D

Discovery, *noun*

A process before a trial or hearing in a civil or criminal action where one party obtains access to all of the information, including documents and depositions, obtained by the other party. In many types of trial, discovery is a right afforded both parties.

During pretrial **discovery**, the defendant's attorney obtained a list of current salaries that was later introduced in the trial as evidence.

Discrimination, *noun*

Treating one person, or a class of persons, differently from others. Under federal and state laws, individuals or groups are guaranteed protection from discrimination based on specific protected attributes including race, sex, sexual orientation, ethnic origin, and religion. Other laws offer more narrowly defined protection against discrimination on the basis of age, or in certain occupations or situations where sex or sexual orientation might require a distinction.

*The lawsuit alleges Consolidated Intergalactic had a pattern of **discrimination** against Fiji Islanders in hiring, promotion, and salary rates.*

See also: Equal protection

Disinherit (diss-in-HERR-it), *verb*
An action to remove someone from a will, or to specifically exclude someone from inheriting anything from an estate.

*After a long period of estrangement from her children, Mrs. Jones instructed her attorney to **disinherit** them and instead distribute all of her estate to her brother and his family.*

See also: Will, Estate, Descent

Dismissal (dis-MISS-el), *noun*
(1) A ruling by a court that a lawsuit or criminal prosecution is ended without a judgment. (2) Also, the withdrawal of a criminal charge by a prosecutor or a civil lawsuit by either party.

*(1) In his **dismissal** of the case, the judge ruled that there was insufficient evidence to go to trial. (2) The district attorney asked for **dismissal** of the case because of newly found exculpatory evidence.*

Dispossess, *verb*
To eject or remove a person or business from real property or premises.

*The landlord received a court order to **dispossess** a tenant who had violated terms of a lease.*

See also: Eviction, Eject, Ejectment

Dispute (di-SPYOOT), *verb*
To question the truth or validity of something.

*The defendant's attorney called a series of witnesses to **dispute** the other side's allegations of involvement in the bank fraud.*

Dissolution, *noun*
The termination of a legal relationship, including a marriage or a business partnership.

*The court ordered the immediate **dissolution** of the marriage, approving the distribution of assets agreed to by both parties. As part of the **dissolution** of the business, the partners agreed to a distribution of assets.*

See also: Divorce, Separation

Distrain (di-STRAIN), *verb*

To seize someone's personal property to serve as security for payment owed.

> *The landlord received court permission to **distrain** the renter's possessions as security; if the rent is not paid within the time period specified by law, the landlord can sell the property.*

See also: Eviction

District attorney, *noun*

An elected or appointed official in a county, city, or other jurisdiction and assigned to oversee the prosecution of crimes. Also known as a prosecutor or in some jurisdictions as the state's attorney.

> *The **district attorney** convened a grand jury to consider an indictment against the mayor on charges of defalcation of city funds.*

See also: Prosecutor, State's attorney

Dividend, *noun*

A portion of a company's earnings or profits distributed to shareholders. Also, a distribution from the surplus earnings of an insurance policy or a bond.

> *The board of directors voted to issue a **dividend** of fifty cents per share to all shareholders of record on March 1.*

See also: Interest

Divorce, *noun*

The termination or dissolution of a marriage by court order.

> *The judge ordered the approval of the petition for **divorce** submitted by attorneys for both parties in the marriage.*

See also: Dissolution, Separation

Docket, *noun, verb*

(1) The collection of cases that are scheduled for a court's calendar. (2) Also, to add a case to a court's calendar.

> *(1) The civil court **docket** is filled for the next six months. (2) The judge instructed the clerk to **docket** the hearing for the next morning at 8:00 A.M.*

Domain, *noun*

(1) In business law, the rights of ownership. (2) Also, the scope of a subject or issue.

*(1) The owner of the land exercises **domain** over its use, within the restrictions of zoning, environmental, and criminal laws. (2) The judge ended the line of questioning, saying it was outside of the **domain** of the matter before the court.*

See also: Eminent domain

Domestic partnership, *noun*

A relationship between two people, other than marriage. In some jurisdictions this includes homosexuals in a committed relationship.

*Under some state laws, both parties in a **domestic partnership** gain some of the rights of a married couple.*

Domicile (DAW-mi-sile), *noun*

The place where a person makes a permanent home or intends to return, or the place where a business has its headquarters.

*The court ruled that it had no jurisdiction in the case because the corporation had its **domicile** in another state. The court found that although the defendant had residences in several states, his **domicile** was in Florida.*

Dominant estate, *noun*

A deed or easement that gives someone else rights over another person's property.

*The deed gives **dominant estate** to a neighbor for a portion of the parcel of the land, permitting construction and use of a road that cuts across a corner of the property.*

Donation, *noun*

A gift, especially money, given without receiving something of value in return.

*The food bank is entirely supported by **donations** received from local merchants and individuals and receives no government support.*

See also: Gift

Double jeopardy, *noun*

Being put on trial a second time for the same offense, if the previous trial resulted in an acquittal or conviction. This is a specific element of the Fifth Amendment to the U.S. Constitution.

*In certain circumstances, it is not considered to be **double jeopardy** if a person is prosecuted for the same crime under separate state and federal laws.*

Dower (DOW-er), *noun*

A widow's share of her deceased husband's estate as set forth in law in some states. In general, the surviving spouse is given the election to choose between dower rights or those spelled out in her husband's will.

*Under **dower** rights, Eleanor was entitled to one-third of her husband's estate after his death. Instead, she elected to accept the more generous bequest in his written will.*

See also: Bequest

Down payment, *noun*

An initial payment that is less than the full amount of a selling price or contract total.

*The Carlsons made a **down payment** of $5,000 to the contractor to cover the initial purchase of supplies for the renovation project; the remainder is due upon completion of the work.*

Draft, *noun, verb*

(1) A legally binding instrument such as a check by which a person or organization directs a bank or other financial institution to pay money to the bearer of the document. The person writing the draft is the drawer. The institution holding the funds is the drawee and the recipient of the funds is the payee. (2) Also, an uncompleted version of a document, prepared for editing or amendment, and not submitted to a court or other authority for approval or acceptance. (3) Also, to prepare and sign a check or other instrument.

*(1) Mr. Webster gave the vendor a **draft** to cover the expenses for the repair. (2) The proposed law was circulated, in **draft** form, to seek suggestions from other legislators. (3) The court ordered Ms. Claptop to **draft** a check for the full amount of the contract and deliver it to the plaintiff within 24 hours.*

See also: Check, Cashier's check, Certified check, Endorse, Negotiable instrument

Driving under the influence (DUI), *noun*

Operating a motor vehicle while impaired by the effects of alcohol or other intoxicants, including drugs.

*Jones was charged with **driving under the influence** of alcohol after he failed a field sobriety test; a blood test conducted at the county jail showed an alcohol level significantly higher than the legal minimum for the charge.*

See also: Driving while intoxicated (DWI), Under the influence

Driving while intoxicated (DWI), *noun*

Operating a motor vehicle while impaired by the effects of alcohol or other intoxicants, including drugs.

*In some jurisdictions, a second conviction for **driving while intoxicated** is grounds for immediate loss of a driver's license for a period of six months.*

See also: Driving under the influence (DUI), Under the influence

Drug possession, *noun*

The crime of having or controlling illegal drugs for any purpose, including personal use, distribution, or sale.

*The motorist was arrested for **drug possession** after the state trooper found a bale of marijuana in plain sight in the back seat of the car after the driver was stopped for a routine traffic violation.*

Due process, *noun*

The promise of fair treatment in criminal and civil cases through the availability of all of the available protections and remedies in the law.

*Defendants are guaranteed the **due process** of law regardless of their financial or other status.*

Dummy corporation, *noun*

A company created to serve as a front or cover for a legitimate company. It may be set up to conceal the activities of another corporation in negotiating for purchase of property, or could be employed for illegal purposes such as an attempt to evade taxes.

*The company set up a series of **dummy corporations** to purchase various parcels of land that were eventually brought together to serve as the site of the new factory; the board of directors feared that the price of the land might be driven up if sellers knew the true identity of the buyer.*

See also: Shell corporation

Duplicitous, *adjective*

In legal terms, a charge or a plea that contains more than one allegation or more than one defense.

*The judge dismissed one of the charges against the defendant, ruling that it was **duplicitous** of another.*

Duress (dew-RESS), *noun*

The use of threats, false imprisonment, force, or other improper means to force someone to act against their own wishes.

*The court ruled that the contract was invalid because it had been signed under **duress** after the plaintiff was threatened with physical harm.*

See also: Contest

Earnest money, *noun*

Money paid as evidence of good faith to proceed with a contract.

*The purchase agreement included a check in the amount of $1,000 as **earnest money** to secure the real estate contract; the funds will be applied toward the full amount due at the time of closing.*

See also: Closing

E

Easement, *noun*

A right to make use of or pass through property for a specific purpose, such as permission for a utility company to install pipes or towers.

*The deed includes an **easement** to permit the electricity company to install towers and wiring that cross a corner of the property.*

See also: Interest, Encumbrance

Effective tax rate, *noun*

Expressed as a percentage, an individual or company's actual income tax paid divided by net taxable income before taxes.

*The calculation of the **effective tax rate** shows the impact of tax credits, incentives, and other steps taken to lessen the amount of taxable income.*

See also: Tax bracket

Eject, *verb, noun*

(1) To dispossess or remove an occupant from a property through a legal process. (2) Also, a lawsuit to dispossess someone from a property.

The court order allows the landlord to **eject** *Mr. Anderson from the apartment.*

See also: Dispossess, Ejectment

Ejectment, *noun*

A legal action to eject a holdover tenant or a squatter from real property.
The landlord filed for **ejectment** *of the tenant who had remained in the premises after the end of the lease period.*

See also: Eject, Eviction, Holdover tenancy

Electronic Funds Transfer (EFT), *noun*

A transfer of funds by electronic means without the use of physical exchange of checks or other financial instruments. EFT can be used to pay bills or for direct deposit of paychecks and other payments.
Farmer arranged for **electronic funds transfer** *to pay his monthly mortgage bill on the due date.*

Emancipation, *noun*

The act of setting a minor child free of the control of parents in order to live on his or her own or under the supervision of others.
The court ordered the **emancipation** *of the seventeen-year-old, declaring that he would be better off living and working on his own rather than in the difficult circumstances presented at the home of his biological parents.*

Embezzle, embezzler, *verb, noun*

(1) To steal or misappropriate money or property from an employer or someone for whom you have a fiduciary trust. (2) Also, a person who commits the crime of embezzlement through the fraudulent taking of funds or property from an employer or someone for whom the person has a fiduciary trust.
(1) Jones was charged with attempting to **embezzle** *$10,000 from the trust fund by making purchases for his own use. (2) The clerk was accused of being an* **embezzler** *after it was found that the proceeds of company accounts had been diverted for personal use.*

See also: Embezzlement, Fiduciary, Defalcation

Embezzlement, *noun*

The theft or misappropriation of money or property that is owned by a company or government, or has been placed under someone's trust.

*The company's accountant was arrested and charged with **embezzlement** of funds from his employer.*

See also: Embezzle, Embezzler, Fiduciary, Defalcation

Eminent domain, *noun*

The right of a government or government agency to take private real estate for public use, with compensation.

*The school board asked the City Council to take the land and home adjacent to the high school under **eminent domain** to allow for the construction of new classroom buildings.*

See also: Condemn, Domain, Just compensation

Emotional distress, *noun*

One form of claim for damages in a lawsuit alleging intentional acts or negligence by another.

*The suit asked for $200,000 in damages for **emotional distress** caused by the collapse of the tent during the wedding reception.*

Encroachment, *noun*

(1) The act of trespassing or intrusion onto someone else's property. (2) Also, the act of infringing upon or acting to curtail a right.

*(1) The lawsuit claimed that the neighbor's fence and driveway was an **encroachment** upon their property. (2) In the filing to the court, the plaintiff alleged that the state's action was an **encroachment** on civil rights.*

See also: Infringe, Trespass

Encumbrance, *noun*

An interest, right, or obligation that limits the complete title to a piece of real property.

*The buyer's attorney noted that the title for the land has an **encumbrance** that gives the local utility company the right to enter upon the property and to install underground pipes when necessary to serve other customers.*

See also: Easement, Interest

E

Endorse, endorsement, *verb, noun*

To sign your name on the back of a check or elsewhere on a negotiable instrument or draft to make it cashable or (in some cases) transferable to another party. Also spelled indorsement in some legal papers.

*Charles **endorsed** the check and deposited it into his bank account.*

See also: Draft, Negotiable instrument, Indorsement

Endowment, *noun*

The donation of money or other items of value to establish a scholarship, professorship, or other benefit for a public or educational institution; the endowment can be made as part of a gift or bequest in an estate or during the lifetime of the donor.

*Elinor Jones made an **endowment** of $1 million to her alma mater to establish a new course in feng shui studies.*

See also: Bequest

Enjoin (en-JOIN), *verb*

An action by a court to order someone or some organization to perform a particular act, or to cease performing a particular act.

*The judge said he would **enjoin** the defendant from shipping any further product until the case was settled.*

See also: Injunction

Enticement (en-TICE-mint), *noun*

To tempt someone to do something illegal, or something they do not wish to do, by making something seem desirable or attractive.

*The defendant was accused of offering large cash bonuses as **enticement** to convince employees of a competitor to reveal trade secrets.*

Entrapment, *noun*

An act by law enforcement or government agencies that serves to entice or induce someone to commit a crime they would not otherwise have done.

*The defense alleged that the arrest was the result of an organized effort at **entrapment** by local police.*

Equal protection, *noun*

The right for all persons to have equal access to the court and be accorded equal treatment by the law and judges.

*The concept of **equal protection** under the law, added to the U.S. Constitution in the Fourteenth Amendment in 1868, eventually became the underpinning for civil rights and antidiscrimination statutes.*
See also: Discrimination

Equity, *noun*
(1) Fairness or equality in legal proceedings. (2) Also, the net value of an asset after any outstanding debts and other obligations have been subtracted.

*(1) In the divorce proceedings, the court ruled that all community property would be divided between the parties as a matter of **equity**. (2) The couple's **equity** in the house was only $10,000 after the amount of the outstanding mortgage was deducted.*
See also: Equal protection, Mortgage

ERISA, *noun*
The Employee Retirement Income Security Act of 1974 sets minimum standards for retirement and health benefit plans in the private sector.

*Most companies that offer benefits to their employees must follow the rules and regulations set by Congress in **ERISA**, the Employee Retirement Income Security Act of 1974.*

Erosion (ee-RO-jun), *noun*
The gradual breaking down or reduction of profits, rights, or other matters.

*The legislature decried the **erosion** of personal privacy rights that have occurred in recent years in the name of security.*

Erroneous, *adjective*
In legal terms, something that is not in accordance with established law.

*The appeals court overturned the lower court's ruling, saying that the judge had been **erroneous** in applying the law to the facts of the case.*

Error, *noun*
A mistake in a court's ruling or judgment, or in the application of proper judicial procedures. An error can cause a mistrial, a retrial, or an appeal. The error can occur during pretrial petitions or motions, scheduling, during a trial, in dealings with a jury, or in a verdict or judgment.

*The appeals court threw out the verdict because it said the judge committed an **error** in his instructions to the jury.*

Escape clause, *noun*

A clause or provision in a contract that allows one or the other party to end the agreement or be relieved of a specific obligation under certain circumstances.

> *The contract includes an **escape clause** that allows Transoceanic Trucking to end the agreement if average gasoline prices exceed $4 per gallon for a period of thirty days or more.*

See also: Obligation

Escheat (ess-SHEET), *noun*

The forfeit of all real and personal property to the state if a person dies without any heirs, or without any named beneficiaries in a will.

> *When Jones died, his property was taken by the state under the rules of **escheat** because he had no heirs and had not prepared a will that gave instructions of his wishes to make any bequests to others.*

See also: Bequeath, Bequest, Estate

Escrow (ess-KROW), *noun, verb*

(1) An account or other form of storage set up to hold funds and documents related to a deal or contract in progress. For example, an escrow agent or an attorney may hold a down payment or deposit for a real estate deal before it is finalized (usually called a closing). Or a landlord may be required to hold security deposits from tenants in an interest-bearing escrow account. (2) Also, to place funds or documents into a secured account.

> *(1) The contract for sale of the property required that the buyer's deposit be held in **escrow** by the title agent who will conduct the closing. (2) The lease required the landlord to **escrow** the security deposit and last month's rent in a bank account and to return funds, plus interest, to the tenant if all of the terms of the contract are fulfilled.*

See also: Impound

Escrow agent, *noun*

A person who acts on behalf of both parties in a real estate transaction, holding funds and documents (including deeds and title) until agreed-upon steps are completed.

> *In some states, the closing of a real estate transaction is accomplished through an **escrow agent** who makes the final transfer after both parties are satisfied in all of their conditions.*

See also: Escrow, Title

Estate, *noun*

(1) In matters related to probate, the estate is all of the personal and real property owned by the person who has died (the decedent) before its distribution according to the terms of a will. (In the absence of a will, property is distributed in keeping with state laws.) (2) Also, in general law, estate can also be used to refer to the degree and nature of interest a person has in current or future ownership in real property.

(1) At the time of his death, Mr. Collins' **estate** *was valued at approximately $1.2 million. (2) Under terms of the contract, Mrs. Borchert has a full* **estate** *in the land and buildings.*

See also: Will, Heir, Intestate, Probate, Escheat, Personal property

Estate tax, *noun*

A tax levied on the value of an estate before it is distributed to heirs. Also known as a Death tax.

Shrum had worked with an estate planner to transfer many of his assets before his death in order to avoid paying much of the ordinary **estate tax**.

See also: Death tax

E

Euthanasia (yu-then-ASIA), *noun*

The killing of a person suffering from an incurable and very serious disease for reasons of mercy. Active steps resulting in euthanasia are illegal in most states. Also called a mercy killing.

The judge authorized the hospital to disconnect artificial breathing and feeding apparatus in keeping with the family's wishes, resulting in **euthanasia** *of the patient.*

See also: Mercy killing

Evade, *verb*

To escape or avoid something, such as to evade prosecution or arrest or to evade taxes.

The judge issued an arrest warrant after the prosecutor reported that the accused had left the jurisdiction to **evade** *arrest.*

See also: Tax evasion

Eviction, *noun*

The act of dispossessing someone of ownership or use of land. Also, a removal of a tenant from rented or leased premises under terms of a court order or other legally permitted process.

*The landlord received permission for the **eviction** of the tenant who was four months in arrears on payment of rent.*

See also: Distrain

Evidence, *noun*

Information or other forms of proof used to attempt to establish facts in a legal proceeding.

*The prosecutor entered the crime scene photographs as **evidence** in the murder trial.*

See also: Exhibit, Material, Immaterial

Ex parte (eks-PAR-tee), *adjective*

From the Latin, "for one party." Motions, orders, or other actions for the benefit of only one party in a dispute.

*White's attorney received an **ex parte** hearing before the court to seek an immediate restraining order against the defendant; a full hearing was scheduled for a week later.*

Ex post facto, *adjective*

A Latin phrase for "after the fact," used to indicate a law or ruling that is intended to be retroactive, affecting an action already done.

*Under the United States Constitution, it is not permitted to criminalize conduct **ex post facto** if the action was legal at the time it occurred.*

Examination, *noun*

The formal process of questioning a witness in court.

*In his **examination** of the witness, the defense attorney sought to establish a pattern of false statements.*

See also: Cross-examination, Direct examination, Interrogation, Redirect

Excise tax, *noun*

A levy on the manufacture or sale of products, and sometimes services. It is distinguished from a tax on real property or income. The word excise means tax, and sometimes is used in that form.

*The state levies an **excise tax** on the sale of all goods, with the exclusion of groceries and clothing for personal use.*

See also: Ad valorem, Sales tax

Exclusion, Exclude, *noun, verb*

(1) A particular risk or item that is not covered under terms of an insurance policy or indemnification. (2) Also, in a legal proceeding, evidence or testimony that is not permitted to be used. (3) Also, an exception to a law or regulation.

*(1) The life insurance policy **excludes** coverage for deaths caused as the result of skydiving, scuba diving, and hang gliding. (2) The court order **excluded** testimony that was taken before the defendant was advised of his rights to be represented by an attorney.*

Exculpate (EKS-kul-pate), *verb*

Literally, to free from a charge. To show that someone, or a business, is not guilty. This refers to the process of disproving a charge, not to a court's ruling.

*The attorney argued that the forensic evidence completely **exculpates** his client of any involvement in the crime.*

Execute, *verb*

(1) To fulfill the obligations of a contract or court order. (2) Also, to sign and make valid a contract.

*(1) Consolidated Intergalactic **executed** its contract for delivery of widgets one week ahead of schedule. (2) Mr. Wilhoit **executed** the contract by signing it and giving the vendor a deposit.*

See also: Contract

Executor (eg-ZEK-ye-tor), *noun*

A person named in a will or appointed by a court to carry out the instructions made in the will.

*Jones was named by the probate court as **executor** of the estate.*

See also: Decedent, Estate, Testator

Exhibit, *noun*

(1) A document or object introduced as evidence in a court proceeding. (2) Also, a paper that is incorporated into the main document of a pleading or a contract or other legal document.

*(1) The plaintiff introduced the lease agreement as an **exhibit** in the lawsuit. (2) **Exhibit** A of the contract, attached to the main document, listed the sliding scale of prices for products covered under the agreement.*

See also: Evidence

Exonerate (ig-ZA-ne-rate), *verb*

To free someone from blame or guilt, or from obligation or responsibility.

The finding of not guilty served to **exonerate** *the defendants of blame for the crime they were charged of committing.*

Expectancy, *noun*

An interest in property or an estate that may become actual in the future.

Samantha has an **expectancy** *of receiving the land and house that is in the estate of her father.*

See also: Estate

Expert witness, *noun*

A person who has advanced education or experience in a particular matter and is presented to the court to offer an opinion about a particular matter even though they have no direct involvement as a witness in the specific lawsuit or criminal case.

The defense asked the court to accept the testimony of an **expert witness** *on computer fraud.*

See also: Testimony

E

Expunge (ek-SPONGE), *verb*

To delete or erase an obligation or a record.

In certain classes of crime, a court has the discretion to order that records of conviction be **expunged** *after a period of time. As an element of the bankruptcy proceeding, the judge agreed to* **expunge** *existing debts.*

Extended warranty, *noun*

A contract which provides additional protection against the cost of certain problems with products after the expiration of the original manufacturer's warranty.

Experts advise consumers to carefully read and understand the terms of an **extended warranty** *before purchasing a policy; some plans are extremely limited in the scope of coverage they provide for product failures.*

Extortion, *noun*

Obtaining money or something else of value through threat or intimidation.

*Manes was accused of felony **extortion** for demanding money under threat of disclosing embarrassing personal details of Clifton's past.*

Extradition, *noun*

The transfer of custody of someone accused of or convicted of a crime in one jurisdiction to another state or country for further prosecution.

*The Commonwealth of Massachusetts notified Wyoming authorities that it was seeking the **extradition** of Charles Winston to face charges in Boston.*

Eyewitness, *noun*

A person who has personally seen an event or transaction and can therefore give firsthand testimony in a legal proceeding.

*Maureen was an **eyewitness** to the crime and was subpoenaed to give testimony in the trial.*

See also: Testimony

Fact, *noun*

An actual event or item, as proven in a trial through the presentation of evidence. In a court case, the judge or the jury is the "finder of fact."

*The **facts** of the case were not disputed by either party; the dispute centered on the quality of the product delivered.*

Factor, *noun*

(1) A merchant who sells products on behalf of a manufacturer or supplier, earning a commission instead of making a profit based on a markup between wholesale and retail costs. (2) Also, a person who lends money to a business with a loan secured by accounts receivable. (3) Also, something that helps lead to a result.

*(1) The shop owns none of its inventory, instead acting as a **factor** to sell products for manufacturers, earning a commission based on sales revenue. (2) Short on cash, the company received a loan from a **factor**; the note was secured by a lien on accounts receivable. (3) The defense attorney denied that the company's product was a **factor** in the failure of the elevator.*

Family court, *noun*

In many states, a special court division that deals with domestic disputes and the care and custody of minors.

*The foster parents petitioned the **family court** seeking that they be granted permanent custody of the child they had been caring for over the past five years.*

See also: Juvenile court

Fault, *noun*

Responsibility for an act, failure to act, or accident.

*The court found Mr. Brenner at **fault** for the accident and allowed the lawsuit for damages to proceed.*

FDIC (Federal Deposit Insurance Corporation), *noun*

A federal agency that insures deposits by individuals in a bank.

*The **FDIC** offers coverage for personal deposits in checking and savings accounts and certificates of deposit up to a specified limit per account at a particular financial institution.*

See also: SIPC

Federal court, *noun*

The federal court system enforces federal statutes as set by the U.S. Congress.

*The **federal court** system exists independently of state court systems that deal with disputes that arise from laws of the individual states.*

Fee, *noun*

(1) A charge for services rendered. (2) Also, an absolute title, or legal ownership, for land transferred for payment.

*(1) The **fee** for recording a document with the County Clerk is $25. (2) The land was granted by Harry Jones to Fred Weiner in **fee**.*

See also: Fee simple, Title, Habendum

Fee simple, *noun*

The most absolute form of ownership of real property.

*A **fee simple** title conveys all available legal rights to the owner, without any qualification.*

See also: Title, Fee, Freehold, Habendum

Felony, *noun*

A crime considered serious, usually carrying a punishment of a term in prison and sometimes capital punishment. By contrast, a less serious misdemeanor is usually punishable by a fine or by a shorter sentence served in a local jail.

> *Breaking and entering into a home where the residents are present is usually considered a **felony**. In many states, any crime where the perpetrator used or threatened deadly injury is a **felony**.*

See also: Misdemeanor

FICA (Federal Insurance Contributions Act), *noun*

The federal law under which employers and employees are generally required to pay a portion of an employee's wages to the government for use in paying retirement benefits.

> *Money collected through **FICA** withholding and payments funds the federal Social Security system.*

See also: Social Security

Fiduciary (fe-DOO-she-err-ee), *noun, adjective*

(1) A person, business, or professional (such as an attorney, agent, or designated representative) who is given the ability or obligation to act for another in matters that require total trust and honesty. (2) Also, involving trust as exercised by a person or professional in acting on behalf of another.

> *(1) The agreement engaging the attorney appointed him as **fiduciary** for all matters involving the company's foreign exchange activities. (2) The title agent has a **fiduciary** responsibility not to release funds or execute transfers of property until all of the terms of the agreement have been satisfied.*

See also: Trustee

Finance charge, *noun*

An additional fee, usually in the form of interest on an outstanding balance, for a purchase paid for in installments.

> *On a typical credit card account, borrowers must pay a **finance charge** for any outstanding balance not paid by the due date.*

See also: Minimum finance charge, Installment loan, Revolving credit

Finder's fee, *noun*

A payment made to a person, agent, or other entity who brings together the parties of an agreement.

> *The real estate agent received a **finder's fee** for locating a tenant for the open office space.*

Finding of fact, *noun*

The finding of fact is the end result of a legal proceeding, the determination of the actual and true facts in a case.

> *A judge or jury weighs the testimony and evidence presented in a case in preparation for the **finding of fact** that leads to a verdict or judgment.*

See also: Verdict

Fine, *noun*

A financial penalty imposed by a court, government agency, or authority.

> *The company was ordered to pay a $100,000 **fine** for violating state regulations regarding use of wetlands.*

Fine print, *noun*

Details and conditions of an agreement presented in small type or otherwise hard to find. In colloquial use, fine print often refers to text that may be deliberately obscure and sometimes deceptive.

> *The **fine print** in the offer included some provisions that invalidated some of the major provisions of the deal.*

First degree, *adjective*

A crime categorized as most serious, and usually eligible for the most severe punishments.

> *Wright was convicted of **first degree** murder because the jury felt that the crime was premeditated and especially heinous.*

See also: Aggravated, Special circumstance

Fiscal year, *noun*

A twelve-month period used for computation of profit or loss, or for settling accounts for a business or other organization. The fiscal year does not need to correspond to a calendar year, which runs from January 1 to December 31.

> *For accounting and tax purposes, Consolidated Intergalactic's **fiscal year** runs from February 1 of one year until January 31 of the following.*

See also: Calendar year

Fixed-rate mortgage, *noun*

A mortgage with an unchanging interest rate for its entire term.

*When interest rates are very low, it generally makes sense to lock in the rate with a **fixed-rate mortgage**.*

See also: Adjustable rate mortgage

Fixture, *noun*

A piece of equipment or an alteration that is attached to a structure or to land in a permanent fashion.

*The lease states that all major alterations to the premises must be approved by the owner and any such **fixture** must be left in place at the end of the contract.*

See also: Improvement

Flat tax, *noun*

A tax set at a fixed percentage of income, profit, or expenditure. As such it is not progressive, meaning that those with low incomes pay the same rate as those with high income.

*The proposal calls for a **flat tax** of 10 percent on the cost of all purchases of goods and services as a replacement for the federal income tax.*

See also: Progressive tax, Regressive tax

Forbearance, *noun*

The act of refraining from the exercise of a legal right. A lender may choose to forbear collection of a debt to give a debtor more time to pay.

*Instead of foreclosing on the home because the borrower was in default, the lender agreed to a **forbearance** on payments for six months to allow the borrower to recover from illness; during that time interest will accrue and will be added to the total amount owed.*

Forcible entry, *noun*

The forced or violent taking of possession of land against the wishes or will of the person or entity entitled to possession.

*The suit alleges the defendants made **forcible entry** onto the land by breaking down a locked gate and taking possession of the property.*

See also: Breaking and entering, Break-in

Foreclosure, *noun*

A legally sanctioned taking of an owner's rights in property that was pledged as security for a loan to satisfy a debt that is in default.

*The bank sought the court's permission for **foreclosure** on the premises because the borrower had failed to make loan payments for four months.*

See also: Security

Forensic, *adjective*

Scientific or medical techniques applied to the investigation of a possible or actual crime.

*The prosecution called in a **forensic** scientist to explain how the blood splatter evidence proved the involvement of the defendant in the murder.*

Forfeiture (FOR-fit-chur), *noun*

The loss of property or rights or privileges as the result of a legal determination of a violation of law.

*The judge found for the plaintiff and ordered the **forfeiture** by the defendant of all profits related to the sale of the infringing products.*

See also: Fine

Forge, *verb*

To produce a false or altered version or imitation of a document, financial instrument, or other item of value for the purposes of deception or fraud.

*The prosecutor charged that the accused had **forged** the driver's license he used to prove his identity in applying for a job with the state.*

See also: Forgery, Utter

Forgery, *noun*

The crime of making or altering a document, financial instrument, or other item of value for the purposes of fraud.

*The plaintiff's expert witness testified that the painting was a modern **forgery** of a classic work of art, produced with the intent of defrauding collectors.*

See also: Forge, Utter

Formulary, *noun*

A list of preferred prescription drugs for a health plan; coverage may only be offered for drugs included in the formulary or there may be different price tiers for various medications.

*The HMO's **formulary** includes a list of drugs that are preferred for use under the health plan's prescription coverage as well as other medications*

*that require special approval before the insurance company will provide
full or partial payment for them.*

See also: HMO, PPO, Single-payer

Franchise, *noun*

(1) A right to engage in a particular form of business under government
permission or license. Examples include taxi companies, trash hauling,
and street vending. (2) Also, the right to vote. (3) Also, an arrangement
between a manufacturer or supplier and a seller granting the right to sell
goods or services under a brand name or as part of a chain.

*(1) The city council issued a **franchise** to Ace Orange Taxi Company to
offer on-call cab service within the city limits and to and from the airport.
(2) The **franchise** to vote was extended to women in all American states
in 1920. (3) Lumberton Pet Shop entered into a **franchise** agreement to
operate under the PetKing brand.*

Fraud, *noun*

Intentional deception, falsehood, or other dishonest words or conduct
used to improperly obtain money, goods, or services.

*Mary MacCarney was convicted of **fraud** in the obtaining of a bank loan
to finance a car purchase.*

F

Freehold, *noun*

A recognized form of permanent and absolute possession of land or
property, with the right to dispose of it in any manner or at any time.

*The property was held as a **freehold**, allowing Jones to sell it or pass it to
his heirs in his will.*

See also: Fee, Fee simple, Habendum

Frivolous suit, *noun*

A lawsuit that is determined to have no merit or legal basis.

*The judge dismissed the lawsuit at a preliminary hearing, calling it a
frivolous suit intended only to harass the defendant.*

See also: Abuse of process, Vexatious

Full disclosure, *noun*

A legal requirement in business transactions and certain government
or political positions requiring the revelation of any information that is
pertinent or related to the situation.

*The seller included a **full disclosure** statement of its various invest-ments in manufacturers and distributors of its products.*

Gag order, *noun*

An order by a court prohibiting the parties and attorneys in a lawsuit or criminal trial from discussing the case with the media or in public.

*The judge issued a **gag order** on all parties in the case, seeking to avoid difficulties in obtaining an impartial jury for the trial.*

Garnish, *verb*

To withhold funds from a paycheck or direct withdrawal from a bank account to pay a debt or a claim.

*The court order allowed the plaintiff to **garnish** the wages of the defen-dant to pay off the damages in equal amounts over a six-month period.*

See also: Garnishment, Attachment, Obligation

Garnishment (GAR-nish-ment), *noun*

A court-approved attachment of wages, funds, or other assets. The per-son whose assets are attached is called the garnishee.

*The judge granted the request from Sam's Florists for a **garnishment** of $50 per week from Ms. Clifton's wages until the full obligation had been repaid.*

See also: Garnish, Attachment, Obligation

GDP (Gross Domestic Product), *noun*

The total market value of all goods and services produced in a specific year.

*The calculation of **Gross Domestic Product** adds all consumer, gov-ernment, and investment spending plus the value of exports minus the value of imports.*

General counsel, *noun*

The lead attorney for a business or organization. A general counsel who works only for the business is called a house counsel or in-house counsel.

*The company's policies call for any questions regarding employment issues to be directed to the **general counsel** before any action is taken by a supervisor or the human resources department.*

See also: In-house counsel

Generation-skipping transfer, *noun*

A gift that bypasses one generation to go to younger generations, for example skipping over children to go to their grandchildren.

> *In some situations, a **generation-skipping transfer** may trigger a transfer tax collected from the recipient of the bequest.*

See also: Transfer tax

Gerrymander (JER-ee-man-der), *verb*

To arrange or map an electoral district in such a way as to give one political group a particular advantage. The term is derived from the name Elbridge Gerry, governor of Massachusetts in 1812, who approved a reshaping of the state's districts in 1812; one oddly shaped area looked like a salamander and the resulting district was called a "Gerry-mander."

> *In some instances, lawsuits have successfully challenged the **gerrymandering** of an electoral district when it was apparent that the purpose was to deprive a group of citizens of their civil rights.*

Gift, *noun*

The voluntary transfer of money or property without any expectation of payment in return, and while both the donor and the recipient are alive. A gift made to someone under terms of a will is called a bequest.

G

> *The Roses made a **gift** of $12,000 to each of their grandchildren in keeping with the limits of the federal gift tax exemption.*

See also: Bequest, Donation

Gift in contemplation of death, *noun*

A conditional gift of personal property (not real property) made during the lifetime of a donor, given with the expectation that the giver will die within a reasonable period of time. The actual ownership of the property does not pass until the donor dies, and by definition the giver may take back the gift in the event of recovery from illness or other life-threatening conditions. An occasionally used Latin term for this is gift causa mortis.

> *Packer gave to the museum a **gift in contemplation of death** of his collection of antique typewriters.*

See also: Inter vivos

Gift tax, *noun*

A tax imposed under federal law on gifts of a large value made during a donor's life. In 2008, gifts with a cumulative annual value of $12,000 or less were not taxable. (Be sure to consult a tax specialist for specific advice in filing tax returns.)

*The federal **gift tax** must be paid by recipients on cash or property in excess of a minimum value.*

Good faith, *noun*

An intent to act honestly and without intent to take unfair advantage.

*The judge ruled that Mr. Phister had acted in **good faith** in his efforts to fulfill the contract.*

Good faith purchaser, *noun*

A person or entity that makes a purchase in good faith, without reason to believe there was a problem with the sale or that someone else had a claim to the property.

*The **good faith purchaser** had no notice of any problems regarding ownership of the property.*

Good will, *noun*

An intangible asset of a company consisting of its reputation, its trade marks and brands, and its regular customers.

*Although it is an intangible asset, when a company is sold the price may include a value placed on its **good will**.*

See also: Intangible, Intellectual property, Tangible property

Governing law, *noun*

The particular law or body of laws in a jurisdiction which applies to the situation involved in a case. The issue of governing law may come into play in a civil matter when the two parties are domiciled in different jurisdictions.

*In certain types of civil suits, the plaintiff (or both parties) may choose to initiate an action in a particular jurisdiction and proceed under the **governing law** in effect there.*

Grace period, *noun*

In a contract, a period of time after a due date in which a payment may be made without penalty. In laws or regulations, a period of time after a due date when payment or action can be made without penalty.

*The contract allows for a thirty-day **grace period** after the due date before penalties and interest are applied to the outstanding contract.*

See also: Default, Delinquent

Grand jury, *noun*

A special jury empanelled in state or federal jurisdictions to hear evidence presented by a prosecutor and decide whether there is sufficient evidence to indict a person for a particular crime. In some court systems, grand juries have been replaced by preliminary hearings before a judge. An ordinary jury that hears testimony in a trial is sometimes called a petit jury (pronounced "petty").

*The prosecutor asked the **grand jury** to indict Mr. Black on charges of embezzlement from the trust fund.*

See also: Jury, Petit jury

Grand theft, *noun*

A felony crime of stealing items exceeding a monetary value set by state law or court ruling. In most states, theft of items below this same monetary value is considered petty theft.

*The prosecutor determined that the value of the items stolen was in excess of statutory minimums and thus charged the defendants with **grand theft**.*

See also: Petty theft

Grandfather, *verb*

A provision that exempts a person or organization from its provisions because of operations that were in effect before a law or regulation was put into effect.

*The legislature chose to **grandfather** businesses and land owners from the zoning restrictions if they had conducted (and continued to operate) business in a manner that had been permitted in previous years.*

See also: Grandfather clause

Grandfather clause, *noun*

A clause in a law or regulation that permits persons or businesses operating under a previous set of rules to continue to do so; they are "grandfathered" in the new law.

*The town's new zoning code includes a **grandfather clause** that allows existing nonconforming businesses to continue to operate even if a new business would not be permitted in their area.*

See also: Grandfather

Gratuitous (greh-TU-ih-tus), *adjective*

Voluntary, or done without receiving any compensation in return.

*Timms donated ten hours per week, on a **gratuitous** basis, to assist the members of the organization.*

See also: Pro bono

Green card, *noun*

A permanent resident document that allows certain foreigners to remain in the United States under certain conditions including providing a needed job skill.

*In most instances, it is necessary for an alien to obtain a **green card** in order to obtain long-term employment in the United States.*

See also: Alien, Resident alien

Grievance (GREE-vince), *noun*

A formal complaint, usually filed under terms of a collective bargaining agreement by either an employee, the union, or the employer.

*The shop steward filed a formal **grievance** against the supervisor on behalf of Edmund Jones, alleging that he had been improperly disciplined.*

See also: Collective bargaining, Union

Gross income, *noun*

In tax preparation, the total taxable income of a person or business from all sources, before allowable deductions are made.

*Mr. Grant's **gross income**, before deductions, was $75,000. His net taxable income was $43,000 after items such as mortgage interest and other deductions were made.*

See also: Taxable income

Guarantee, *verb, noun*

(1) A formal promise, usually in writing, that a debt will be paid or a contract fulfilled. If a guarantee is offered by a third party, it is a promise to pay a debt or fulfill a contract on their behalf if they fail to do so. (2) Also, an assurance of the quality and durability of a product, stating specific conditions under which the manufacturer or seller will repair or replace it if it fails.

*(1) Consolidated Intergalactic signed a letter of **guarantee** on behalf of Freyco, promising to deliver product if the subcontractor is unable to do so.*
*(2) The camera came with a two-year limited **guarantee** against failure caused by workmanship or defective parts; units will be repaired or replaced during that period of time.*

Guaranty, *noun*

A promise to pay another person's or another organization's obligations or perform contracted duties in case of default.

*The agreement included a **guaranty** that in the event of the inability of the contractor to complete the job a third party would assume the obligation and liability.*

See also: Obligation, Bond

Guardian, *noun*

A person recognized by the courts as having the power and responsibility to manage the financial, medical, or other legal affairs of another person determined to be incapable of handling these matters without assistance. The person under guardianship is called a ward.

*As **guardian** for Sam Graham, he is able to manage all business and personal affairs.*

See also: Guardian ad litem, Conservator, Custodial parent, Ward

Guardian ad litem (Guardian ad LIT-em), *noun*

A guardian appointed by a court to represent the interests of a minor or an incompetent adult in legal proceedings.

*The judge named Mary Smith **guardian ad litem** for George Walker who had previously been found incompetent to make legal decisions on his own.*

See also: Guardian, Custodial parent, Custodian, Incompetent

Guilty, *adjective*

A finding by a court that a person has committed a crime or offense, either as the result of a trial or because the defendant has admitted guilt or did not contest the charge.

*The jury found the defendant **guilty** of all charges brought against him.*

See also: Verdict

GVWR (Gross Vehicle Weight Rating), *noun*

In motor vehicle regulations, the maximum permitted weight for a car or truck when fully loaded with passengers and cargo.

*Most states have different classes of license and registrations for vehicles that are within specified ranges of **Gross Vehicle Weight Rating**.*

G

Habeas corpus (HAY-bee-as KOR-pes), *noun*

A court order directing law enforcement officials to bring before a judge or court a person held in custody in order to determine whether the prisoner is being lawfully detained. The Latin phrase means "you have the body."

*The defense attorney asked for an order of **habeas corpus**, seeking to have his client released because he had not been properly charged.*

See also: Writ, Court order

Habendum (ha-BEN-dum), *noun*

In a deed or conveyance, the specific description of the estate or the interest to be granted to another.

*The **habendum** states that the buyer shall have and hold the premises in fee simple.*

See also: Fee, Fee simple, Freehold

Habitable (HA-be-ti-bil), *adjective*

A structure that is deemed to be safe for human habitation, in accordance with health regulations and building codes. A structure that does not meet this requirement is considered uninhabitable.

*The lease requires the landlord to maintain the premises in **habitable** condition at all times.*

See also: Implied warranty of habitability

Harassment (he-RASS-mint), *noun*

A crime of repeated, unwanted actions that serve to threaten, upset, or annoy another person.

*Jones was charged with **harassment** after he was observed repeatedly taunting a patron at the hockey match.*

See also: Sexual harassment

Hate crime, *noun*

A specific class of crimes motivated by bias or hatred of an individual or group of individuals because of their race, religion, sexual orientation, or other such identity.

*Because the assault was deemed to have been directly specifically at a group of Asian students, the charges were classified as a more serious **hate crime**.*

H

Head of household, *noun*

The person who is considered the primary source of income or having principal responsibility for a family.

> *Mary signs all documents and manages the finances of the family and is considered the **head of household**.*

Health Savings Account (HSA), *noun*

A special form of savings account that offers tax advantages to individuals who have a health insurance plan with a high deductible.

> *Funds contributed to a qualified **Health Savings Account** are not subject to federal income tax at the time of deposit and can be used for most medical expenses without tax liability.*

Hearsay, *noun*

A report by a person of words uttered by another person, usually disallowed in a court proceeding as second-hand evidence.

> *The defense objected to the testimony, saying that it was a **hearsay** report and not direct evidence of words or actions by the defendant.*

See also: Eyewitness

H

Heat of passion, *noun*

An action said to have occurred as the result of extreme anger or provocation. In some criminal cases this may serve to reduce the charge or indictment to a lesser crime.

> *The defense strategy centered on establishing that the defendant's actions occurred in the **heat of passion** after he had been harassed by the plaintiff.*

Hedge, *verb*

A pair of investments made in a way to counterbalance each other so that if one loses value the other increases. A hedge may involve shares of stock, commodities, or any other financial instruments or agreements.

> *As a **hedge** against market fluctuations, Sam's portfolio includes a mix of mutual funds and bonds that tend to react in opposite directions when the market rises or falls.*

See also: Hedge fund

Hedge fund, *noun*

An investment vehicle or fund that seeks to grow in value through the use of aggressive financial transactions.

> *Most financial advisors recommend that only sophisticated investors make use of volatile strategies such as **hedge funds** that seek to take advantage of short-term swings in the value of stocks, bonds, and commodities.*

See also: Hedge

Heir (air), noun

A person who inherits or is due to inherit property under the rule of law when a person dies without a will (intestate).

> *Kennedy was an **heir** to the substantial estate of the Collins family.*

See also: Bequest, Estate, Issue, Descent, Will

Held, *verb*

Having decided, ruled, or made a conclusion in a case or an element of the case.

> *The judge **held** that the motion for dismissal of the case was valid and ordered the release of the defendant and the end of the proceedings.*

H

HIPAA (Health Insurance Portability and Accountability Act), *noun*

A federal law that required the establishment of national regulations to protect the privacy of persons receiving health care services.

> *Doctors, hospitals, and insurance companies face strict limits on the nature of information about medical records under regulations put into place by Congress with the passage of the **Health Insurance Portability and Accountability Act**.*

HMO (Health Maintenance Organization), *noun*

A plan under which participants receive ordinary medical care from a specified group of doctors, hospitals, and other health care providers.

> *For subscribers to an **HMO**, most medical services are less expensive when they are obtained from a provider that is a member of the organization.*

See also: PPO, Single-payer

Hold harmless, *verb*

A guarantee to compensate someone for financial losses or release from liability, sometimes included as part of an agreement for services or the purchase of products. Also known as save harmless or to indemnify.

> *The contract promises that the company will **hold harmless** Sam in the event a lawsuit is filed by a third party.*

See also: Indemnify, Save harmless

Holder, *noun*

Someone in possession of property or a financial instrument that is written to his order or endorsed over to him.

> *As **holder** of the bond endorsed to him, James is entitled to cash it or transfer it in any legitimate way.*

Holdover tenancy, *noun*

A situation in which a tenant continues to occupy property or premises after the end of a lease or rental agreement, without the permission of the owner.

> *Because the landlord did not demand the tenant to move out of the apartment at the end of the lease, the residents asked the court to recognize their **holdover tenancy** and permit them to continue to pay rent at the previously agreed rate until the owner moved for eviction or offered a new contract.*

See also: Eviction

H

Homestead, *noun*

(1) A dwelling and the land that surrounds it. (2) Also, in some states, a special set of laws intended to protect a person's primary residence from being taken by others for any reason other than for repayment of a mortgage loan.

> *(1) The principal asset of the estate is the family **homestead** in Lake Placid. (2) Under terms of the **homestead** exemption, the family's home cannot be taken to satisfy consumer debt or civil penalties.*

See also: Premises

Homicide, *noun*

The killing of one human being by another. The act of murder is homicide with premeditation.

*The law makes a distinction between voluntary or willing **homicide** and an involuntary or accidental act which results in the death of another person.*

See also: Murder, Involuntary manslaughter, Justifiable homicide

Hostile takeover (HOS-til takeover), *noun*

An unwelcome bid to take over a publicly traded company by purchasing shares on the open market or, more commonly, making an offer to a sufficient block of existing shareholders to give the bidder a controlling interest.

*The investment firm launched a **hostile takeover** bid against Consolidated Intergalactic, offering to buy 51 percent of common stock at a $20 premium over the current trading price for the shares.*

Hostile witness, *noun*

A witness called by one party in a lawsuit or criminal trial who is considered hostile or adverse to that party's position in the case. If the witness is deemed by the judge to be hostile, the attorney can later cross-examine the same witness.

*Lebron was found by the judge to be a **hostile witness** and the defense attempted to show that his deposition contained misstatements.*

See also: Witness

Hung jury, *noun*

A jury that is unable to reach a verdict.

*The foreman reported to the judge that the jury was hopelessly deadlocked in its deliberations and the court declared an end to the proceedings because of a **hung jury**.*

See also: Mistrial, Retrial

Hypothecated, *verb*

One of the underlying principals of a secured loan, where the borrower obtains or retains legal ownership of a property but grants to the lender a lien on the property that prevents its resale or transfer until the debt is paid off.

*The mortgage for the property **hypothecated** on a lien that is granted by the borrower to the lender and will remain in place until the loan is retired.*

See also: Lien, Mortgage

Illegal alien, *noun*

A foreigner who has entered the United States without permission or who has remained in the country past the legal time limit for a tourist, a student, or a temporary worker.

*Employers are required to check the citizenship status of all job applicants to try to find **illegal aliens**.*

Illegitimate, *adjective*

(1) Not authorized by law. (2) Also, a child born to parents not married to each other.

*(1) Mr. Harrison was charged with **illegitimate** business practices. (2) Sam is the **illegitimate** son of Mary Brown and Charles Shew.*

Illicit (il-LI-sit), *adjective*

Illegal. In common usage, it is applied to activities that are considered socially unacceptable including extramarital relations or drugs.

*The employment contract includes a morals clause that permits termination for involvement in any **illicit** activity including use of drugs or unlawful gambling.*

Immaterial, *adjective*

An objection to evidence offered in a trial on the basis that it is not material (relevant) to the issue in the case.

*The prosecutor objected to the proposed testimony of friends of the accused, saying their opinions were **immaterial** to the question of whether a crime had been committed.*

See also: Material, Evidence, Inadmissible

Immunity, *noun*

(1) Exemption from certain types of prosecution or penalties granted by law to specific types of persons such as government officials or law enforcement officers. (2) Also, exemption from prosecution or penalties given by prosecutors or the court system when it suits the needs of the public.

*(1) Mr. Miller was granted **immunity** from prosecution in return for his testimony against his former employer. (2) Lt. Anderson has statutory **immunity** against claims of unlawful imprisonment because he is a police officer.*

See also: State's evidence

Impeach, *verb*

(1) The act of discrediting a witness by showing that testimony is false or that the witness was not qualified to testify. (2) Also, the process of trying a public office holder on charges of misconduct committed in the performance of their duty. The purpose of impeachment is the removal from office; in certain circumstances further charges could be brought in civil or criminal court.

*(1) The defense attorney sought to **impeach** the testimony of the eyewitness by demonstrating that she could not possibly have seen the robbery from her apartment window. (2) The state assembly voted to **impeach** the representative because of allegations he sought bribes from contractors in his district; the state senate will meet as a court to decide whether to remove him from office.*

Implied warranty of habitability, *noun*

In landlord-tenant law, a renter has the right to expect that the home or apartment will be in habitable condition for the entire period of the lease.

*The tenant abandoned the apartment and ceased making rental payments, claiming that the landlord had failed to uphold the **implied warranty of habitability** by not making necessary repairs.*

See also: Habitability

Implied warranty of merchantability, *noun*

A promise, inherent in any sale, that the product is properly conveyed, in saleable condition, and legal.

*In most situations, any sales contract includes an **implied warranty of merchantability** unless both sides agree that the product is sold "as is" or is noted as damaged or in need of repair.*

See also: Merchantability

Impound, *verb*

(1) To take property, records, money, or other items into the custody of a law enforcement agency, court, or government agency pending the outcome of a lawsuit or criminal case. (2) Also, to collect funds from a mortgage borrower over and above payments of principal and interest and hold them in a protected account, often called an escrow, and used to pay such things as property taxes or insurance.

*(1) The court ordered the sheriff to **impound** all of the vehicles owned by the manufacturer until both the criminal and civil suits against the*

company were concluded. (2) The mortgage agreement allows the bank to **impound** *sufficient funds to pay each year's property taxes and a sufficient amount of insurance to protect the lender's interest in the premises.*

See also: Escrow

Impress (im-PRESS), *verb*

To impose a trust onto property.

The court decided to **impress** *a trust onto the property, giving the family's attorney a fiduciary responsibility to maintain its value until a decision on disposition is made.*

Improvement, *noun*

A permanent change to real property that increases its value.

The lease permits the landlord to raise monthly rents to cover the cost of **improvements** *requested by the tenant or mutually agreed to by both parties.*

See also: Fixture

In common, *noun*

A form of ownership of property in which two or more people or entities share interest and responsibilities.

The deed conveys ownership of the premises to Harry Smith and Mary Jones **in common***, with rights to profits divided in proportion to their investment in the home and land.*

In-house counsel, *noun*

A lawyer or group of lawyers who are employees of a company and work only on legal matters related to its interests.

The **in-house counsel** *is required to approve all contracts and financial dealings of the company.*

See also: General counsel

In kind, *adjective*

Payment in a form other than money, such as trading services or products in barter or a combination of money and other items as a form of payment.

The attorney accepted payment **in kind** *from the carpenter, receiving a week's work on a storage closet for his office.*

See also: Barter

In loco parentis (in-LO-co pe-REN-tis), *noun*

A Latin phrase meaning,"in place of a parent,"this is the underpinning of many rules and regulations adopted by institutions such as schools or custodial agencies in taking care of a minor.

*The university's code of conduct includes rules for minors that permit it to act **in loco parentis** while the student is on campus.*

In personam (in per-SO-num), *adjective*

From the Latin phrase"toward a particular person."A lawsuit or a decision that is directed at a specific person only.

*The court's ruling was characterized as an **in personam** judgment and therefore applied only to the named defendant.*

In re (in-RAY), *preposition*

In a legal filing, shorthand for"in regard to"a particular matter.

***In re** the case of Hatfield v. McCoy, the court agreed to a change of jurisdiction to a county in another part of the state.*

Inadmissible (in-ad-MISS-a-bil), *adjective*

Deemed by law or the court as something that cannot be introduced as evidence.

*Judge Colbert ruled that the confession was **inadmissible** because the defendant had not been advised of his rights beforehand.*

See also: Immaterial

Incapacity, *noun*

(1) Unable to fulfill a responsibility because of medical problems. (2) Also, officially unable to perform a duty.

*(1) The power of attorney automatically became effective because of the medical **incapacity** of Mr. Kyle. (2) Under terms of the state law, employees of the Registrar of Voters have an **incapacity** to seek or hold any elected position or serve as an official of a political party.*

Incarceration (in-CAR-cer-ay-shun), *noun*

Confinement to a prison or other institution.

*The court ordered the **incarceration** of the convicted defendant for a period of fifteen years.*

Incite (in-SITE), *verb*

To provoke action or stir up feelings or emotions.

> *The prosecutor said that Lowell's actions served to **incite** a riot.*

Incompetent, *adjective*

(1) A person determined to be unable to handle his or her own affairs because of mental or other conditions (2) Also, in legal matters, someone who is determined to be unable to understand charges brought in a trial or to understand the legal proceedings.

> *(1) A guardian was appointed to manage Mrs. Breen's affairs after the court found she was **incompetent** to do so for herself. (2) The judge found the defendant **incompetent** to assist in his own defense and asked for an evaluation by a court-appointed psychiatrist to determine if a trial should go forward.*

See also: Disability

Incorporate, *verb*

To organize a business as a corporation, under rules set by the various states.

> *The owners decided to **incorporate** the company in Delaware because of various tax and operational advantages available there.*

See also: Corporation

Incriminate, *verb*

To say something or do something that tends to make someone appear guilty of a crime.

> *The prosecutor argued that the testimony of the co-defendant in the case clearly **incriminated** the accused.*

Indecent exposure, *noun*

The offensive display of a person's body in public, especially the genitals or female breasts.

> *The defendant was charged with **indecent exposure** after he was found sunbathing in the nude in the city park.*

Indemnify (in-DEM-ni-feye), *verb*

A guarantee to compensate someone for financial losses, sometimes included as part of an agreement for services or the purchase of products. Also known as hold harmless or save harmless.

*The contract promises to **indemnify** Sam in the event a lawsuit is filed by a third party.*

See also: Hold harmless, Save harmless, Indemnity

Indemnity (in-DEM-nih-tee), *noun*

A form of protection from loss or damages, or exemption from legal responsibility for particular actions.

*The contract included a promise that the manufacturer would purchase **indemnity** insurance that would protect any of its franchisees and authorized resellers from liability for civil damages.*

See also: Indemnify, Insurance

Independent counsel, *noun*

An outside or special counsel hired to deal with a legal matter because the attorneys who would ordinarily handle the situation have a conflict of interest.

*The contract permits both parties to agree to engage an **independent counsel** to arbitrate any disagreement.*

See also: Special counsel

Independent sales organization, *noun*

A business that resells products or services on behalf of others. For example, some companies offer franchises to sell cell phone or cable television services. In financial operations, an independent sales organization might serve as sales agents of an acquiring bank in selling credit card services to a merchant.

*The cable television company concentrates on providing services to its customers; it relies on an **independent sales organization** to market to consumers.*

Indict (in-DITE), *verb*

To formally charge someone with a crime.

*The grand jury voted to **indict** Mayor Jones on charges of defalcation of city funds.*

See also: Charge, Accuse, Indictment

Indictment (in-DITE-mint), *noun*

A formal charge voted by a grand jury, or sometimes as entered by a court.

The **indictment** charges that Clift engaged in a systematic process of fraud against investors in the company.

See also: Indict

Indigent (IN-di-jint), *noun*

A person who lacks sufficient funds for his or her own support or a family, or someone who is unable to pay fees required by a court. Also, a person unable to pay legal costs for defense in a criminal case.

*The court declared Mr. Albert to be **indigent** and appointed a local attorney to handle his defense.*

Individual Retirement Account (IRA), *noun*

A special account established by individuals that allows accrual of funds for retirement; interest and dividends earned are exempt from taxation as they are earned, and only subjected to taxation when it is withdrawn.

*Financial experts recommend that individuals set up and continue to make deposits to one or another form of **Individual Retirement Account** throughout their working years as a supplement to Social Security and other investments.*

See also: Roth IRA

Indorsement, *noun*

An alternate spelling for endorsement.

See also: Endorsement

Inducement (in-DOOS-mint), *noun*

An offer or effort that persuades someone to enter into a contract, or to perform an act.

*Consolidated Intergalactic offered special discounts to certain customers as an **inducement** to enter into long-term contracts.*

Infraction, *noun*

The violation of a rule or law, usually considered a minor offense.

*Many motor vehicle **infractions** are punishable only by a fine.*

Infringe, *verb*

(1) To use without permission someone's legally protected copyright, trademark, patent, or other intellectual property. (2) Also, to trespass or illegally enter a place.

*(1) The lawsuit claims that Consolidated Intergalactic **infringed** on the patents and the trade names of its competitor. (2) Jones said that his neighbor's fence **infringed** on his property.*

See also: Copyright, Intellectual property, Patent, Trademark, Trade name, Trespass

Inhere (in-HERE), *verb*

To vest or attach a right to a person or organization.

*All of us are beneficiaries of the rights that **inhere** to citizens of our democracy.*

Inherent (in-HERR-int), *adjective*

Existing in a person or an organization as part of its very definition.

*Many of our criminal laws are based on a belief that humans have an **inherent** right of safety.*

Inherit, *verb*

To receive money, property, or other things of value from the estate of a relative under terms of a will or by the process of the law for someone who dies intestate.

*Georgia stands to **inherit** the largest portion of her father's estate under terms of the will.*

See also: Bequest, Heir, Estate, Will, Disinherit

Inheritance, *noun*

Money, personal property, or real property received by someone from a relative through a will or trust, or as a result of state laws or a court ruling that set distribution from an estate.

*Marjorie received the title to the family home as part of her **inheritance** from her uncle.*

See also: Bequeath, Bequest, Heir

Inheritance tax, *noun*

A tax imposed on the recipient of property, money, or anything else of value under terms of a will or as a result of the process of law for someone who dies intestate.

*The heirs to the Murphy fortune are liable for **inheritance tax** on their portion of the estate.*

See also: Death tax

Injunction (in-JUNK-shen), *noun*

A court order prohibiting someone or a business operation from doing something. The order is issued before or during a court case, and usually is replaced by the ruling at the end of a trial or proceeding.

*The judge issued an **injunction** against further sales of the product until the lawsuit alleging infringement was settled.*

See also: Enjoin

Injury, *noun*

Harm done to a person, including physical injury, damage to reputation, or the loss of a right.

*The suit seeks compensation for **injury** including medical treatment as well as financial loss caused by the inability to perform the ordinary duties of his job.*

See also: Damages

Innuendo (in-yu-EN-doh), *noun*

An indirect hint or implication.

*The libel suit claimed that the plaintiff's reputation was damaged by **innuendo** that he was involved in a extramarital relationship.*

See also: Libel, Slander

Inquest (IN-kwest), *noun*

An investigation by an official coroner or other designated qualified experts into any death where the cause is not clear. In some jurisdiction, an inquest is required any time a person dies away from a hospital or medical facility.

*The county prosecutors said he would await the results of the **inquest** before deciding if there would be any charges brought in the case.*

See also: Autopsy, Post mortem, Coroner, Medical examiner

Insanity, *noun*

The condition of being severely mentally ill such that a person cannot distinguish fantasy from illusion, is unable to control behavior, or cannot conduct personal affairs.

*The court accepted the argument of the defense counsel that the defendant was not fit to stand trial because of **insanity** and instead committed the accused to a mental institution until such time as authorities determined a trial was possible.*

See also: Incompetent

Insider trading, *noun*

The buying or selling of stock, or other activities that lead to financial gain, based on information that is known only to officers or employees of a publicly held corporation.

*The chief executive officer of the company and its counsel were indicted on charges of **insider trading** after allegations that they sold thousands of shares of stock in the weeks before the company announced significant losses for the current quarter.*

Inspection, *noun*

The examination of documents or property to determine compliance with laws, regulations, or codes.

*The contract included a provision that allowed the buyer to conduct an independent **inspection** of the premises before the closing of the sale.*

Installment loan, *noun*

A type of loan in which the borrower makes periodic payments of a portion of the principal plus interest that is added based on the current outstanding principal.

*Automobile financing is a form of **installment loan** in which the monthly payment incorporates both a portion of the principal and interest; at the start of the loan the payment is mostly interest but by the end of the loan the payment is mostly allocated to reducing the principal.*

Institute (IN-sti-toot), *verb*

To begin legal proceedings.

*The plaintiff decided to immediately **institute** a lawsuit to seek payment of damages for the losses related to the failure of the joint venture.*

Instrument, *noun*

A formal, written legal document such as a contract, deed, or lease, or a financial document such as a bond or loan.

*A legal **instrument** needs to be properly endorsed by both parties in order to put it into effect.*

Insurance, *noun*

A contract between an insurer and an individual or business that provides for the payment of a portion or all of the amount of a particular loss. For example, a hazards policy may pay for the replacement or reconstruction cost of a home or other structure damaged by fire; policies issued by an insurer seek to define very closely the particular protections they cover, typically excluding losses caused by negligence or acts of war. Insurance policies can also be purchased to offer compensation for certain types of legal actions, including lawsuits for liability or infringement.

*The company purchased key executive **insurance**, a form of life insurance that provides payment in the case of the death of specified top officers of the business.*

See also: Indemnity

Intangible (in-TAN-je-bel), *noun, adjective*

Property that is incorporeal and cannot be physically touched, such as intellectual property or good will. Other forms of intangible property include savings accounts, shares of stock, and other financial instruments.

*As an author, the vast majority of his assets are **intangible** things such as copyrights, and his reputation and good will with publishers and readers.*

See also: Tangible property, Good will, Intellectual property

Intellectual property, *noun*

An intangible work that is created by a person or company. Examples include books, plays, and designs. In general, pieces of intellectual property can be protected by copyright, patents, or trademarks.

*The author engaged legal counsel to file a lawsuit alleging infringement of **intellectual property** by another writer.*

See also: Intangible, Tangible property, Infringe

Intent, *noun*

A willfulness or purposeful decision to engage in a particular action, or to not take an action.

*Many criminal laws make a distinction between acts made with **intent** as opposed to those that were involuntary or accidental.*

See also: Mens rea

Interest, *noun*

(1) A partial ownership of a business or a financial instrument. (2) Also, a right to property, including the right to take and use real property or an easement to travel through or otherwise make use of a portion of property. (3) Also, funds paid by a bank, a business, or an individual

for the right to use someone else's money. For example, a bank may pay interest on a deposit, or charge interest to a borrower with a loan or mortgage.

*(1) Consolidated Intergalactic has an **interest** in Transoceanic Trucking through the stock it received as payment in kind for services. (2) Under terms of the title, Texas Tea Drilling Company has an **interest** in the title that permits it to drill for gas or oil on the property. (3) The Left Bank of the Scioto pays 5 percent **interest** on certificates of deposit, and charges 6 percent interest on mortgage loans to customers.*

See also: Easement, Encumbrance, Dividend

Internal Revenue Code, *noun*

The set of rules and regulations established by the Internal Revenue Service that define how taxes are applied and the procedures and forms to be used for verification of income and eligibility for credits and deductions.

*Tax accountants must keep current on the changes to the **Internal Revenue Code** that are published each year by the Internal Revenue Service.*

Internal Revenue Service (IRS), *noun*

An agency of the U.S. Department of the Treasury, responsible for the administration and enforcement of most federal taxes including personal and federal income taxes, Social Security, and estate taxes.

*The **Internal Revenue Service** sets tax codes within the outlines established by Congress.*

Interpleader, *noun*

A suit argued between two parties to determine which is entitled to collect a debt or receive property from a third party.

*The insurance company filed an **interpleader** action, depositing the proceeds of the policy with the court which will determine which claimant is the actual beneficiary.*

Interrogation, *noun*

Questioning of a suspect or witness by police or other law enforcement authorities.

*Ian was brought to the police station for **interrogation** by detectives; he declined to answer questions and asked for legal representation.*

See also: Examination

Intervene, *verb*

To enter as a third party into an existing lawsuit to add a claim.

*Consolidated Intergalactic received the court's permission to **intervene** in the case of Normal Freight v. Occidental Accident Recovery.*

Inter vivos, *noun*

A conditional gift of personal property (not real property) made during the lifetime of a donor, given with the expectation that the giver will die within a reasonable period of time. The actual ownership of the property does not pass until the donor dies.

*Skelley made an **inter vivos** gift of his residence and property to the local historical association, with title to pass on the occasion of his death.*

See also: Gift in contemplation of death

Intestate, *adjective, noun*

A person who has died without having prepared a valid will.

*Fern Williams died **intestate**, not having authored a will.*

See also: Estate, Heir, Descent, Will, Administrator

Intoxication, *noun*

The condition of being made incapable because of drinking alcohol or using drugs. Various jurisdictions have differing definitions of intoxication and use different medical or empirical tests to establish the condition.

*The sheriff's deputy testified to the court about the tests he administered to the defendant to determine his level of **intoxication**.*

See also: Driving while intoxicated, Driving under the influence

Inure (in-YURE), *verb*

To result in a particular effect.

*The contract states that all profits that might result from the later sale of the technology would **inure** to the benefit of Kathy Long.*

Invalidate, *verb*

To make something null through the action of a court or the application of a law.

*The ruling served to **invalidate** all of the town's contracts signed in March because the council had voted without a proper quorum.*

Investment Company Act of 1940, *noun*

The federal law that provides the framework for regulation of investment companies.

*The Securities and Exchange Commission, which sets regulations for brokerages, mutual funds, and the issuance of shares of stock by publicly traded companies, was enabled by the federal **Investment Company Act of 1940**.*

See also: Securities and Exchange Commission

Involuntary manslaughter, *noun*

An unintended or accidental killing caused by negligence or recklessness.

*Keene was charged with **involuntary manslaughter** as the result of the death of his passenger in the automobile accident that police said was caused by excessive speed.*

See also: Manslaughter, Homicide

Irreparable injury, *noun*

An injury or damage that cannot be remedied or cured by the payment of compensation. Also known as irreparable damage.

*The plaintiff asked the judge to issue an immediate injunction against the construction damage because the cutting down of trees and damming of the stream would cause **irreparable injury** to the property.*

Issue, *noun*

(1) The point of law or a particular fact that is the subject of a legal proceeding. (2) Also, a person's direct descendants, including children, grandchildren, and great-grandchildren.

*(1) The trial centered around the **issue** of whether the new product was sufficiently indistinguishable from the plaintiff's product as to constitute an infringement. (2) The rules of descent state that the estate be first given to the decedent's spouse if living, or then divided by a specified formula to any living **issue** that was the result of their marriage.*

See also: Heir

Itemized deduction, *noun*

A specific type of expense or loss that must be detailed on a tax return in order to be claimed as a deduction against income.

*On personal tax returns, medical expenses can be an **itemized deduc-tion** from income if they exceed a particular percentage of the taxpayer's adjusted gross income.*

See also: Deduction, Standard deduction

Jeopardy, *noun*
In danger of being charged or convicted of a crime.
> *The district attorney warned Mr. Jones that he was in legal **jeopardy** of being charged as an accomplice in the crime before he asked him to submit to interrogation about the incident.*

Joint, *adjective*
Property, rights, or obligations shared or otherwise held together by two or more persons or organizations.
> *The shipping company was a **joint** operation by Consolidated Intergalactic and Transoceanic Freight.*

See also: Severalty

Joint and several liability, *noun*
An element of certain contracts that allows a creditor to sue one or more of the members of a group of parties if other defendants do not have sufficient resources to pay a judgment.
> *The contract says that the borrowers give the lender **joint and several liability** in the event of a lawsuit, allowing actions against any or all of the parties to the agreement.*

Joint custody, *noun*
An arrangement, ordered by the court, in which both parents will share custody of a child.
> *The ruling by the court gave **joint custody** of the children to both parents, accepting a proposed schedule agreed to by both sides.*

Joint venture, *noun*
An agreement between two or more people or businesses to work together on a specific project under terms laid out in the deal.

*Consolidated Intergalactic and Indonesian Nut Oils entered into a **joint venture** to build and operate a processing plant in Jakarta; under the deal, investment and proceeds will be split evenly.*

Judgment, *noun*

A ruling or final decision by a court.

*The **judgment** of the court required Consolidated Intergalactic to retro-actively compensate all of its employees from the Fiji Islands at pay rates equal to those of all others in the same job description. The company said it would appeal the **judgment** to a higher court.*

See also: Order, Ruling

Judicial, *adjective*

Relating to a judge, court, or a judicial proceeding.

*The contract gives both parties the option of submitting disagreements to an arbitrator instead of entering into a lawsuit and a **judicial** proceeding.*

Jumbo loan, *noun*

Loans that exceed the level set by federal agencies for certain programs including underwriting or insurance.

*Some mortgage brokers specialize in writing **jumbo loans** for clients not eligible for certain federal programs.*

See also: Mortgage

Jurisdiction, *noun*

(1) The authority given to a particular court to rule on legal matters. (2) Also, a specific geographic area, such as a town, county, court district, or state that is assigned cases.

*(1) The small claims court has **jurisdiction** over civil disputes with claims of no more than $5,000. (2) The defense attorney asked that the trial be moved to a different **jurisdiction** in hopes of finding an unbiased jury pool.*

Jury, *noun*

A group of citizens empanelled to hear a criminal or civil case and decide guilt or liability based on evidence presented to them in court.

*In most jurisdictions, a person accused of a serious crime or facing a sig-nificant civil lawsuit is entitled to a trial by **jury** rather than a hearing conducted only in front of a judge.*

See also: Grand jury, Petit jury

Jury nullification, *noun*

An action by a jury to acquit a defendant despite apparent guilt because of a refusal to apply a law despite instructions from the judge. They might do so because they feel the law is wrong or because the situation represents something that offends their sense of justice or morality. A defense attorney is not permitted to ask for jury nullification and in some instances the decision can be rejected by the judge.

*The foreman admitted that the verdict amounted to **jury nullification** because the panel felt that it was unfair to charge the woman with homicide for the mercy killing of her elderly husband.*

Just compensation, *noun*

(1) The legal concept that a person is entitled to be paid a fair amount for work performed, or compensated fairly for a loss. (2) Also, an element of the Fifth Amendment of the U.S. Constitution that promises that private property cannot be taken for public use without just compensation.

*(1) The lawsuit asked for **just compensation** for the damages suffered by the homeowner as the result of the construction accident. (2) The issue in the lawsuit concerned the proper amount of **just compensation** for the taking of the plaintiff's property by the county under eminent domain.*

See also: Eminent domain

Justifiable homicide, *noun*

A homicide that, as defined by law, was committed in self-defense or to protect another, or otherwise in a situation where it is determined there was no criminal intent.

*The prosecutor announced that no charges would be brought against the homeowner who shot and killed an armed intruder, declaring the act a **justifiable homicide**.*

See also: Homicide, Involuntary manslaughter

Juvenile court, *noun*

A special court assigned to deal with cases involving minors. Some courts deal only with allegations or crimes or infractions while others also become involved in the supervision of children who are abandoned or neglected by their parents. The procedure in most juvenile court procedures often involves collaboration amongst representatives of the state, the defendant, and the court rather than as an adversarial contest.

Minors who are accused of particularly serious crimes may be charged as adults, and would then be put on trial in a criminal court and not the **juvenile court***.*

See also: Family court

Kickback, *noun*

An arrangement by a company or an individual awarded a contract who pays money to a government official or an employee of the party to the agreement as a reward or as a bribe. Depending on the circumstances and whether the payment was made in secret or was disclosed, such a payment could constitute the crime of bribery.

The commissioner was convicted of charges that he demanded and received a **kickback** *from bidders for paving and construction services performed for the county.*

Kidnap, *verb*

The crime of taking a person against their will, through the use of violence, threat, or intimidation.

Orsillo was charged with **kidnapping** *the insurance salesman when he forced him into his truck and drove him fifty miles into the woods before releasing him.*

See also: Abduction

K

Landlord, *noun*

A person who rents or leases real property to a tenant. The landlord may be the owner of the property or a representative.

A **landlord** *grants leasehold interest in real property to a tenant, usually under terms of a written agreement.*

Larceny (LAR-sin-ee), *noun*

One form of theft, the taking of the personal property of another without permission and with the intention of keeping the property or disposing of it.

Jones was charged with **larceny** *for removing the lawn jockey from his neighbor's lawn and attempting to sell it on eBay.*

See also: Asportation, Burglary, Theft

Late payment fee, *noun*

A fee assessed when a payment on a loan or line of credit is missed or paid late.

*The credit card company assesses a **late payment fee** of $25, in addition to finance charges, if a client fails to make at least the minimum payment by the due date.*

Lawsuit, *noun*

A claim by one person or organization against another person or organization and filed with a court for hearing.

*The homeowner filed a **lawsuit** against the carpenter claiming shoddy workmanship and breach of contract.*

Leading (LEE-ding), *verb*

An attempt to ask a question in a manner that suggests a particular answer or the use of particular words.

*The prosecutor asked the judge to admonish the defense attorney for **leading** the witness in her questions.*

Lease, *noun*

(1) A contract between a landlord and tenant that sets forth the rights and obligations of both parties during the period of the lease. (2) Also, a means to obtain the use of an automobile or other piece of equipment through periodic payments; at the end of the lease period the vehicle or equipment is usually returned to lessor or purchased by the lessee.

*(1) The twelve-month **lease** calls for monthly rent payments of $500; the tenant is responsible for utilities. (2) A **lease** is one way for an individual or company to obtain the use of a vehicle as a monthly cost rather than as a capital expenditure.*

Legacy, *noun*

A gift made to a beneficiary (legatee) of a will. In strict legal terms, a legacy does not include real property.

*Sam's **legacy** to his grandchildren was a trust fund intended to pay for their college expenses or first home.*

See also: Devise

Legal tender, *noun*

Any form of money, in banknotes or coins, that are issued by the government and must be accepted in commerce or in payment of a debt.

*The U.S. dollar is a form of **legal tender** that is accepted for payment anywhere in the country; checks, money orders, and credit cards are not legal tender although they are accepted as a form of bank draft that can be converted into cash.*

Legitimate, *adjective*

(1) Legal or proper. (2) Also, referring to a child born of parents who are or were married.

*(1) The ruling affirmed that the expenditure was a **legitimate** use of county funds. (2) Of her two children, Fred was born after she was married and is considered her only **legitimate** offspring.*

See also: Illegitimate

Lemon Law, *noun*

A statute enacted into law in many states that is intended to help a buyer sue for damages or for replacement of a major purchase such as an automobile or certain appliances if a store or manufacturer is unable to make it work properly after a certain number of attempts over a specified period of time. Also, more generally, a law that is aimed at helping a buyer receive a refund or replacement for an item that is substantially defective. The term comes from the secondary meaning of the word "lemon," meaning something that is unsatisfactory or defective.

*Under the Massachusetts **Lemon Law**, a consumer has the right for a refund or replacement of a new automobile if a repair is attempted three or more times for the same substantial defect without success, during the first year or 15,000 miles of ownership.*

Liability, *noun*

(1) Legal responsibility for your acts, or lack of action. (2) Also, a financial obligation such as a debt.

*(1) The contractor bears **liability** for damages caused by his work. (2) Although Caldwell had about $200,000 in assets, his **liabilities** (including a mortgage, two auto loans, and other obligations) were in excess of $450,000.*

See also: Liability insurance

Liability insurance, *noun*

Insurance that protects the holder of the policy for some or all of the risk faced because of liability claims from third parties.

> *The company's **liability insurance** policy provides payment for legal defense against most claims for damages or for payment to settle such claims in or out of court.*

See also: Liability

Liable (LIE-eh-bul), *adjective*

Responsible as a matter of law or because of the terms of an agreement.

> *Whalen was found to be **liable** for damages caused by the failure of the newly installed pipes. The law says that trespassers are **liable** to prosecution. In some jurisdictions, a barkeeper who serves alcohol to an intoxicated person is **liable** for prosecution or a civil lawsuit for damages.*

Libel (LYE-bel), *noun*

A written or published defamation that harms someone's reputation. A spoken defamation is called slander.

> *The newspaper faced a **libel** suit filed by the doctors named in its series of articles about medical fraud.*

See also: Defame, Defamation, Slander, Innuendo

Liberal construction, *noun*

An interpretation by a court that considers the legislative history of a law including its overall intended purpose.

> *Using **liberal construction**, the federal judge applied an 1820 interstate commerce law to Internet sales.*

See also: Construction, Strict construction

LIBOR (LYE-bore), *noun*

The London Interbank Offered Rate (LIBOR) is a rate of interest that is based on the current rates used by banks lending funds to each other in the London wholesale money market.

> *Some adjustable rate mortgages set their interest rates based on the **LIBOR**, which is one measure of the current wholesale cost of funds for banks.*

License, *noun, verb*

(1) A governmental permission to perform a particular act or operate a certain type of business; (2) a certificate that proves that an individual

or a business has been given permission. (3) Also, the act of granting permission by a government agency; (4) a permission given by a private entity for use of intellectual property or trade names.

*(1) The restaurant received a **license** to sell liquor and beer to its patrons. (2) Janice carried her driver's **license** in her purse as she drove to the town hall to obtain a marriage **license**. (3) The state **licenses** tow truck drivers to pick up vehicles only after they complete a special training session. (4) Consolidated Intergalactic **licensed** National Feather Distributors to use its patents and trademarks.*

Lien (LEEN), *noun*

(1) A claim against property for services rendered, filed, and registered through a court process. (2) Also, a security interest in property filed by a lender.

*(1) The contractor filed a workman's **lien** against the deed of the house, seeking payment before the home could be sold to another person until the bill was paid. (2) Because the purchase of the automobile was financed through a bank, there is a **lien** on the certificate of title to the vehicle.*

See also: Lis pendens, Mechanic's lien

Life interest, *noun*

A right to hold and use property that is granted for the lifetime of a person but expires with that person's death.

*Gary donated his home and property to the nature conservancy but retained a **life interest** for himself and his wife.*

Limited liability, *noun, adjective*

A cap on the maximum amount of financial exposure an individual or a business faces in the event of a lawsuit or bankruptcy; the cap might be set by statute or be part of an agreement between parties.

*The agreement included a clause that provided for **limited liability** by the manufacturer for damages that might be caused as the result of failure of the parts that were custom-manufactured for the vendor.*

Limited liability company (LLC), *noun*

A form of business that allows owners to protect their personal assets from corporate liability, except for instances of willful negligence or criminality, while maintaining some of the tax advantages of a partnership. Shareholders are similarly protected although the value of shares may decline.

Some professional groups, such as attorneys, organize their business as a **limited liability company** *for tax purposes.*

See also: Corporation

Limited warranty, *noun*

A written guarantee for a product that defines the limits of the maker or seller's responsibility.

Most products are sold with a **limited warranty** *that includes exclusions for ordinary wear and tear or from use of the item for purposes not intended or authorized by the manufacturer.*

See also: Guarantee

Line of credit, *noun*

The maximum amount of money a customer is permitted to borrow from a particular financial institution. Credit cards usually have a stated line of credit. A home equity loan has a line of credit that represents a certain percentage (less than 100 percent) of the amount of equity the borrower has in a residence or other significant property. A borrower does not have to borrow the full amount of the line of credit and generally can repay the debt at any time.

The bank offered Samantha a **line of credit** *in the amount of $100,000, based on her equity in the home she owned.*

Liquid asset, *noun*

An asset that can be easily converted into cash, such as certificates of deposit or shares of stock.

Inventory, raw materials, and accounts receivable are not considered **liquid assets** *because they each may require an indefinite period of time to be converted into cash.*

Liquidate, *verb*

(1) To sell off all or a portion of the assets of a business in order to pay bills, legal costs, or to close down the business. Any excess after payment of creditors would ordinarily be distributed to shareholders and other investors. (2) Also, to eliminate a debt or other claim against a company or individual; in the case of a bankruptcy, a debt might be set at a fraction of its full amount under agreement between the parties or as the result of a court order.

*(1) As the company shifted its focus from manufacturing to providing service and consulting, the board of directors decided to **liquidate** much of its assets at factories around the world. (2) As part of the bankruptcy proceeding, the company and its creditors agreed to **liquidate** outstanding debt with payment that was approximately 50 percent of the original amount of the promissory notes.*

Lis pendens (LEES pen-DENSE), *noun*

A pending lawsuit or legal action.

*The litigant filed a **lis pendens** notice with the county clerk to alert any potential purchaser of the property that there was a claim against the owner.*

See also: Lien, Mechanic's lien

Litigant (LI-ti-gent), *noun*

One or the other party in a lawsuit.

*As a **litigant**, we hope to recover damages for the loss of use of our home during the period it is unavailable to us because of necessary repairs.*

Litigate (LI-ti-gate), *verb*

To bring a dispute into a court as a lawsuit, or to argue an issue in a proceeding.

*Because we have been unable to come to an amicable agreement, we have no choice but to **litigate**.*

Living will, *noun*

A document that when properly drafted and executed appoints one or more persons as their representative to make decisions on medical care and other related issues in the event the person is unable to do so.

*Under the **living will**, the designated representative is empowered to decide whether extraordinary medical measures are taken in the case of a life-threatening condition.*

Loan servicing, *noun*

The process of collecting and processing payments made on a loan, such as a mortgage, over the life of the note.

*Some mortgage companies turn over the **loan servicing** of their notes to a third party or may sell the promissory note to another company which will service the loan.*

Loan shark, *noun*

An illegal or unethical lender who charges an excessive interest rate.

*Esposito operated as an unlicensed **loan shark**, making loans at usurious rates.*

See also: Usury

Lockout, *noun*

An action by an employer to block employees from coming to work, usually as part of a labor dispute.

*Workers arrived at the gates of the plant on Monday to find the company had instituted a **lockout** that prevented them from entering.*

Lodge, *verb*

To make a formal complaint or claim to a court or other legal authority.

*Transoceanic Trucking **lodged** an appeal to the judgment.*

Loitering, *verb*

Staying in a place without permission and with no apparent purpose.

*Jones was charged with **loitering** on the college campus after he was found asleep on a bench at midnight.*

Loophole, *noun*

A gap, mistake, or ambiguity in a law or regulation that allows someone to avoid the intent of the rule.

*The legislature passed a bill intended to close a **loophole** in liability law that allowed repair services to avoid paying negligence claims by filing for bankruptcy; companies must maintain a fully paid liability insurance policy in order to maintain their business license.*

Loss, *noun*

(1) The value of an injury or damages caused by another, or by breach of contract. The value may be decided by lawsuit, by law, or as specified in an agreement. (2) Also, when property sells for less than the cost of manufacture and marketing, or real property sells for less than the owner's basis in the land and buildings, the transaction is considered a loss.

*(1) The jury determined the plaintiff's **loss** as a result of the accident to be $1 million in compensatory damages. (2) The company was forced to sell*

*off much of its inventory at a **loss** because of changing market conditions and the need to prepare to manufacture a new line of products.*

See also: Basis

Maim, *verb*

To inflict serious bodily injury on someone, especially if it results in mutilation or the loss of an ability to function normally.

*Caron was charged with assault with intent to **maim**, a first class felony.*

Maintenance, *noun*

Financial support for another person's living expenses, including alimony or child support.

*The court ordered monthly payments of $1,200 in **maintenance**.*

See also: Alimony, Child support

Majority, *noun*

The age at which a person is considered to be an adult for legal proceedings and other purposes. Also known as the age of maturity.

*Most states set the age of **majority** at eighteen, after which a person can make decisions on legal and business matters without the involvement of guardians and is subject to laws applying to adults.*

See also: Maturity, Minor

Make, *verb*

To execute a financial instrument, including the signing of a check or promissory note.

*Jones agreed to **make** a check within forty-eight hours to cover the entire amount of the outstanding bill; in return the contractor agreed to hold off filing a lawsuit for the amount due.*

Make whole, *verb*

To fully compensate a person or party such that they are in the condition they would have been in before they suffered damages or a loss.

*The defendant agreed to **make whole** the plaintiff for the costs of repairing the kitchen which flooded as the result of the failure of the new plumbing system.*

Maker, *noun*

The person who signs a check or promissory note and is thus responsible for payment under its terms.

*The **maker** of a check returned by a bank for insufficient funds is liable for the amount due; if the check was drawn on an account not owned by the maker, civil or criminal charges can be brought.*

Malfeasance, *noun*

Intentional misconduct in the performance of duties. Often used to refer to improper actions by a public official.

*The plumbing inspector was dismissed from his job for **malfeasance** after evidence was presented that he had accepted bribes from contractors.*

See also: Misfeasance, Nonfeasance, Defalcation, Embezzlement

Malice, Malice aforethought, *noun*

(1) An intentional effort to commit a crime. Many penalties are increased if the prosecution or plaintiff can establish malice. (2) Another form of the phrase is malice aforethought meaning that the perpetrator was aware that an act was criminal.

*(1) Winning a libel suit often requires establishing that the act was committed with **malice**. (2) The indictment charged that the assault was premeditated and committed with **malice aforethought**.*

Malpractice (mal-PRAK-tiss), *noun*

Actions or omissions by a professional (such as a medical practitioner, attorney, engineer, or designer) which do not meet the standards of their job, are illegal, or negligent, causing provable damages.

*Jason Borow alleged **malpractice** by his attorney for failure to file required forms on time.*

Mandamus (man-DAY-mus), *noun*

An order issued from a higher court that commands a lower court to perform an act, or an order from a court to a government agency or officer to perform an act.

*The Superior Court issued a writ of **mandamus** ordering the state prison authority to reduce overcrowding at its facilities to no more than 100 percent of approved capacity.*

See also: Court order, Order, Writ

Mandatory, *adjective*
Required by laws or regulations.

*It is **mandatory** for drivers to return their license plates to the motor vehicle bureau if they sell or otherwise dispose of their vehicle.*

Manslaughter, *noun*
The crime of killing a human being without premeditation (malice aforethought).

*The prosecutor agreed to reduce the charges from first degree homicide to **manslaughter** after investigation showed the defendant was provoked.*

See also: Homicide, Involuntary manslaughter, Malice aforethought, Murder

Marital deduction, *noun*
A provision of estate tax code that allows a person to give assets to a surviving spouse with a reduction or exemption from taxation.

*Under the provisions of the **marital deduction**, the transfer of the decedent's assets to his former wife was made without any tax liability.*

Marital trust, *noun*
A financial planning tool that allows for the transfer of property between spouses under terms of the federal estate tax deduction.

*The attorney set up a qualified **marital trust** to preplan for the transfer of assets in the event of the death of one or the other spouse.*

Market value, *noun*
The expected selling price for property of any kind in an open and orderly market, as opposed to the price that might be received in a forced or distressed sale because of foreclosure.

*The **market value** for the house was $500,000 but, because the family was forced to sell the house quickly to raise funds, they sold it well below the price they could have expected to receive if it had been listed for a few months.*

Marketable title, *noun*
A title to real property that has no known encumbrances or other problems and is therefore considered able to be purchased with a reasonable expectation there will be no successful challenge to its validity.

*The buyer's attorney conducted a search of the history of the property and concluded that the seller had a **marketable title**.*

See also: Title, Cloud on Title

Marriage bonus, *noun*

A provision of the tax code that would result in certain married couples together paying less in taxes than would two unmarried individuals with the same income.

*Various pieces of legislation seek to encourage young families by providing a **marriage bonus** in the tax code.*

See also: Marriage penalty

Marriage penalty, *noun*

A situation that arises for some taxpayers where a married couple together owe more in taxes than they would if they were single and filing separately.

*In his campaign for office, the Senator promised to work to end the **marriage penalty** built into the federal income tax code by offering a special offset to married couples who each earn about the same in salary per year.*

See also: Marriage bonus

M

Material, *adjective*

Testimony or evidence that is relevant and significant to the issues in a lawsuit, criminal case, or other legal proceeding.

*The attorney argued that the testimony of the expert witness was **material** to the defense case and should be allowed.*

See also: Immaterial, Evidence

Material witness, *noun*

A witness deemed by one or the other party in a lawsuit or criminal case to have information that is relevant and significant.

*The court ordered both sides to exchange their list of **material witnesses** before the trial began.*

Matter of record, *noun*

Anything which has been recorded by an official court reporter or clerk, including testimony, rulings, and evidence.

*The defendant's testimony in the case is a **matter of record**.*

Maturity, *noun*

(1) The date upon which final payment is due under a promissory note or other financial instrument. (2) Also, the age at which a person is considered to be an adult for legal proceedings and other purposes. Also known as the age of majority.

> *(1) The bond has a **maturity** date of July 1, 2015, at which time the full amount of the principal will be paid to the holder. (2) In most legal matters, a person is subject to laws and regulations that applies to adults once they have reached **maturity** on their eighteenth birthday.*

See also: Majority, Minor

Mechanic's lien, *noun*

A lien or encumbrance placed on real property by a carpenter, laborer, architect, or supplier who has not been paid; it is intended to prevent the sale or transfer of the property until the debt is satisfied.

> *The roofing contractor placed a **mechanic's lien** on the home after the owner failed to pay him for work completed.*

See also: Lien, Lis pendens, Encumbrance, Marketable title

Mediation (MEE-dee-ay-shun), *noun*

A means to resolve disputes in which an impartial third party—often specifically trained for the job—assists both sides in reaching a mutually acceptable settlement.

> *The litigants agreed to **mediation** to resolve the contract dispute.*

See also: Arbitration, Binding arbitration

Mediator, *noun*

An impartial third party who conducts mediation of disputes.

> *The contract required that any dispute between the parties be submitted to a professional **mediator** instead of going through the expense and time of a lawsuit.*

See also: Mediation

Medicaid, *noun*

A government program that helps pay for medical services and nursing home care for low-income persons. The program is primarily funded by the federal government with additional funds from state governments which administer the provision of services.

Applicants for assistance in paying medical or nursing bills through the **Medicaid** *program must have assets and income below a certain threshold in order to qualify.*

See also: Medicare

Medical examiner, *noun*

A medical professional, usually a doctor, who is appointed by a state or local jurisdiction to establish the cause of death of persons who die in places other than a hospital or not under a doctor's care.

Because of the circumstances, the police called the **medical examiner** *to the scene to pick up the body and conduct an autopsy.*

See also: Coroner, Inquest, Autopsy, Post mortem

Medicare, *noun*

A federal insurance program that helps pay for medical care and hospitalization for persons over the age of sixty-five or who meet certain criteria for disability. Medicare Part A covers the cost of hospitalization; Medicare Part B is supplemental medical insurance for services by doctors and tests. Some seniors purchase additional coverage for prescriptions and other services.

M

Medicare *is a single-payer health insurance plan, with all bills submitted to an agency of the federal government or to a private company that contracts to provide the same services to eligible persons.*

See also: Medicaid

Meeting of the minds, *noun*

The point at which both parties reach an agreement on the terms of a contract.

The two companies reached a **meeting of the minds** *on the terms of the joint venture and instructed attorneys to draw up a contract for execution.*

Megan's Law, *noun*

The informal name for a set of laws passed by the various states and by the federal government requiring the disclosure to the public of the names, addresses, and other information about convicted sex offenders who have been released from incarceration. The name is derived from the original law, passed in New Jersey, after the death of a young girl named Megan at the hands of a sex offender.

A common provision of **Megan's Law** *statutes is the notification to the community any time a convicted sex offender registers with a local law enforcement agency.*

Memorandum, *noun*

A note or brief communication.

The two parties signed a **memorandum** *of understanding before asking their attorneys to draw up a more formal agreement.*

Mens rea (MENZ RAY-ah), *noun*

A Latin phrase meaning a "guilty mind," referring to someone who commits a crime with knowledge that it is wrong.

The prosecutor argued that the accused committed the act with **mens rea,** *fully aware that what he was doing was a crime.*

See also: Intent

Merchantable, merchantability, *adjective, noun*

A product of sufficient quality or value to make it fit for sale under ordinary circumstances or a regular market.

The contract requires that all products be of **merchantable** *quality, and that the seller accept back or issue credit for any faulty goods.*

See also: Implied warranty of merchantability

Mercy killing, *noun*

The killing of a person suffering from an incurable and very serious disease for reasons of mercy.

In some court cases, judges or juries have considered special circumstances for someone accused of a **mercy killing** *of a spouse or loved one who was terminally ill and in great pain.*

See also: Euthanasia

Merger, *noun*

The combination of two businesses or entities into one; one of the parties will no longer exist as an independent operation.

As a result of the **merger** *Consolidated Intergalactic will become the world's largest importer of betel nuts; all of the employees and most of the facilities of International Consolidators will become part of the new company.*

M

Merits, *noun*

The substance of a case, notwithstanding any technical or procedural issues.

*The plaintiff asked the court to make a decision on the **merits** of the case and to reject a motion by the defendant to dismiss the lawsuit because of a flaw in the paperwork.*

Mesne profits (MEEN profits), *noun*

Any profits which accrue or are earned by a tenant who does not have legal ownership of real property.

*After winning a lawsuit establishing ownership of the land, the plaintiff asked the court to award the full amount of **mesne profits** received by the illegal tenant.*

Minimum finance charge, *noun*

A fixed or minimum fee charged by a credit card company on the outstanding balance for an account.

*When a credit card user does not pay the full outstanding balance on an account, the issuer of the card may have a provision in its agreement that allows it to assess a **minimum finance charge** for the billing cycle.*

See also: Finance charge

M

Minor, *noun*

A person who is younger than the age of majority; in most jurisdictions a minor is someone under the age of eighteen.

*As a **minor**, Fred is not permitted to be the sole signatory on legal papers.*

See also: Majority, Maturity

Miranda Rule, Miranda Rights, *noun*

The right of a criminal suspect to be informed of constitutional rights before being questioned. Included is the right to remain silent and not answer questions, the right to have legal counsel, and notification that anything said to a representative of law enforcement or court officer can be used against the person in court. The rule was set by the U.S. Supreme Court in 1966 and is named after a defendant who argued his constitutional rights had not been observed.

*In general, statements to a police officer or prosecutor given by a person who has not been advised of **Miranda Rights** may not be admissible in a court proceeding.*

Misappropriation, *noun*
The illegal or unauthorized use of another person's property (including real property, personal property, and intellectual property) or funds.
*The attorney was disbarred after a court found him guilty of **misappropriation** of his clients' funds for his own use.*

Misdemeanor (miss-de-MEE-ner), *noun*
A crime, less serious than a felony. In many jurisdictions a misdemeanor carries a possible jail sentence of one year or less.
*Petty theft and disorderly conduct are usually classified as **misdemeanors**, while grand theft and aggravated assault are felonies and can result in significantly greater penalties.*
See also: Felony

Misfeasance (miss-FEEZ-ance), *noun*
Performing poorly in doing an act that is required or expected.
*Jones was removed from his position for **misfeasance** in handling the filing of legal papers.*
See also: Malfeasance, Nonfeasance

Misnomer (miss-NO-mer), *noun*
A wrong name used in a legal document.
*The court ruled that although the contract contained a **misnomer**, it was possible to determine the proper and intended person and declared the agreement valid and enforceable.*

Misrepresentation (miss-rep-ree-zen-TAY-shun), *noun*
A false or misleading statement. In circumstances where someone has obtained money, goods, or services based on false information, a crime may have been committed.
*Walter Ballou was accused of **misrepresentation** on his loan application.*

Mistrial (MIS-try-el), *noun*

The termination of a trial before a final ruling or settlement is made because of an improper act by a witness, attorney, jury, or judge. Other reasons for a mistrial include a procedural error or a hung jury.

*The judge declared a **mistrial** after it was learned that several members of the jury had undertaken to perform research on their own.*

See also: Hung jury, Retrial

Mitigating circumstances, *noun*

Circumstances, conditions, or happenings which may be taken into account by a judge or jury in determining the severity of punishment after conviction. They do not excuse conduct, but can be considered in an exercise of mercy or fairness.

*The defense attorney asked the judge to consider the **mitigating circumstances** of the crime, including a documented history of ten years of harassment by his neighbor.*

See also: Aggravated, Special circumstance

Mitigation, *noun*

An act to ameliorate or reduce the severity of something.

*The state board ordered the builder to create new wetlands and forest as **mitigation** for his violation of environmental regulations.*

See also: Mitigating circumstances, Aggravated, Special circumstance

M

Modification, *noun*

A change made to a court order or judgment already on the record. A modification might be made because of a change in circumstances or to cure or rectify an error.

*The judge made a **modification** in the custody order to increase the visitation rights of the father because of improvements in his personal life brought to the court's attention by a social worker.*

Moiety (MOY-eh-tee), *noun*

A half interest in real property.

*The partners held the land in **moiety**, sharing the investment and rights of tenancy.*

Molestation (mo-les-TAY-shun), *noun*
The crime of committing a sexual act with or upon a child under the age of majority.
The defendant was accused of multiple counts of ***molestation*** *of a child.*
See also: Rape, Minor

Money laundering, *noun*
The act of moving illegally obtained funds through other channels in an attempt to obscure or hide its origins.
Banks are required to report many types of transactions to federal regulators in order to help prevent or bring to light attempts at ***money laundering****.*

Money market fund, *noun*
A mutual fund that invests in short-term securities such as Treasury bills and commercial paper. The goal of most such funds is to maintain the principal, with the interest rate increasing or decreasing based on market conditions.
Most ***money market funds*** *maintain a constant share price, with the interest rate varying based on the performance of securities held by the fund.*

M

Monopoly, *noun*
A single business or a group of related or interlocked entities that control such a significant portion of the procurement, production, or sale of a product or commodity that they are able to set prices or conditions.
Many federal laws regulate industries in a way meant to discourage the creation or maintenance of a ***monopoly*** *that restricts free trade.*

Month to month tenancy, *noun*
Tenancy of property that sustains on a month to month basis when there is not a written or oral rental agreement in place.
The lease states that at the end of the term the agreement will continue as a ***month to month tenancy*** *until and unless a new lease is offered and executed by both parties.*

Moot, *adjective*
An unsettled point of law, or something that was not of significance to a current dispute or case.

Both parties agreed that the issue of whether the contract had been signed on January 14 or January 15 was a **moot** *point.*

Moral turpitude, *noun*

A serious or major violation of ordinary standards of moral conduct.

The employment contract included a clause allowing the employer to immediately dismiss the employee for **moral turpitude**.

Moratorium (mor-i-TOR-ee-um), *noun*

(1) A suspension of activity on a particular matter. For example, a court might order a moratorium against hearing certain cases while a particular law or ruling is under challenge in a higher court. (2) Also, in a bankruptcy proceeding, a court ruling that suspends or delays repayment of a debt.

(1) The court imposed a **moratorium** *on new proceedings in cases related to the ordinance banning political signs, pending a ruling from a higher court on the constitutionality of the law. (2) The judge ordered a* **moratorium** *on demands by debtors while the company reorganized its finances.*

M

Mortgage, *noun*

A loan or promissory note in which the borrower gives the lender an interest in real property as security. In most situations, a mortgage is used to fund the purchase of land and a home or other building; a borrower can also use the equity that exists in one piece of real property as security for a mortgage with the funds to be used for other purposes.

The Beechers obtained a **mortgage** *from a local bank to allow them to purchase a home; the lender was given an interest in the property that will not be released until the full amount of the principal of the loan plus any accrued interest has been paid.*

See also: Assumption

Mortgage insurance, *noun*

An insurance policy that insures mortgage lenders against a borrower defaulting on a loan.

Some lenders may require a borrower, especially one with a less-than-optimal credit score or credit history, to purchase **mortgage insurance** *to protect the lender against a possible default on the loan.*

Motion, *noun*

A request or application to the court for a ruling or judgment.

> *The defense attorney entered a **motion** calling for the dismissal of all charges against his client because of the failure of the prosecution to establish the facts of the indictment.*

See also: Move

Move, *verb*

(1) To formally request a court to take an action. (2) Also, in parliamentary procedure, to ask a legislature or other group to act on a matter. The act of moving for action is called a motion.

> *(1) The attorney **moved** for dismissal because the prosecution failed to prove its case; the motion was denied. (2) The county commissioner **moved** for an immediate vote on the bill.*

See also: Motion

Multiple listing service, *noun*

In real estate sales, a multiple listing service (MLS) brings together the offerings of agents who are members of an association.

> *The agreement with the real estate agent required that the house be offered by a **multiple listing service** so that buyers who visited any member agency could find out details about the property.*

Municipal, *adjective*

Referring to a town or city that has its own local government. In some states, these are called incorporated or chartered governments.

> *Since the land is within the area of the **municipal** government, local zoning codes apply to the use of the property.*

Murder, *noun*

The premeditated killing of one human being by another.

> *Romney was charged with first degree **murder** for the killing of his neighbor with malice aforethought.*

See also: Homicide, Manslaughter, Malice aforethought

Mutual fund, *noun*

An investment vehicle in which a buyer pays for a share in a collection of various securities such as stocks or bonds.

*Buying shares in a **mutual fund** rather than purchasing shares in individual companies is one way to spread and reduce the risk of an investment.*

Narcotic, *noun*

Technically, an addictive drug including those derived from opium (opiates). In common usage, the term narcotic is also used to apply to any illegal drug.

*Laws regulating **narcotics** generally distinguish between those found with small amounts intended for personal use and those who are deemed to possess drugs with the intent to sell them to others.*

Naturalization, *verb*

The process of granting citizenship to a foreigner, or the process of becoming a citizen.

*The **naturalization** process in the United States includes the swearing of an oath of allegiance to the country.*

Necessity, *noun*

A situation in which a person has no reasonable option other than to violate a law or enter into civil jeopardy.

*The defendant argued that because the snowstorm blocked all roads, it was a matter of **necessity** to trespass across neighboring land in order to obtain food and medical supplies.*

Negate, *verb*

To overrule an order or judgment by a court. Other words to the same effect are annul or set aside.

*The appeals court **negated** the lower court's ruling and re-assigned the case to a new judge.*

See also: Annul, Quash, Set aside

Negligence, *noun*

A failure to take reasonable steps to protect others, or to take action that is unreasonable and results in injury or loss to others.

*The landlord was accused of **negligence** for not repairing the faulty staircase before it collapsed and injured the tenant.*

See also: Contributory negligence

Negotiable, *adjective*

(1) Something that can be the subject of discussion, bargaining, or modification. (2) Also, something that can be transferred or assigned so that it becomes legally owned by another person.

(1) The parties agreed on a franchising agreement with a stipulation that actual prices and terms for products to be sold would be **negotiable** *at the time any shipment was requested. (2) The parties agreed that the financial instrument was* **negotiable** *and could be sold or transferred at any time without changing the obligations it contained.*

Negotiable instrument, *noun*

A check, bond, promissory note, or other financial document that can be transferred to another by giving it to another person or entity. In some instances the instrument must be endorsed to the order of another person or entity while other such instruments are transferred to another by the act of delivery.

A bearer bond is a **negotiable instrument** *whose value belongs to whoever possesses it.*

See also: Check, draft, bond

Net income, *noun*

The money that remains after expenses have been paid, also called the profit.

The company reported gross revenues of $124 million for the quarter, with expenses of $101 million, making for a **net income** *before taxes of $23 million.*

See also: Profit

No contest, *noun*

In a criminal case, a plea in which a defendant neither admits nor denies guilt but submits to punishment as if guilty. Also known as nolo contendere.

Brooks pleaded **no contest** *to the charges and was sentenced by the judge to the statutory minimum penalty.*

See also: Nolo contendere

No-fault divorce, *noun*

A divorce decree issued without laying blame on one or the other parties in a marriage. The ending of the marriage is treated separately from the division of any assets or decisions about custody of children.

*The judge ordered a **no-fault divorce**, recognizing the request of both parties to end the marriage.*

See also: Fault

No-fault insurance, *noun*

A form of automobile insurance, available in a number of states, that directs that payment for minor personal injuries be made by the company that insures the vehicle in which they were riding or by which they were hit regardless of whether the driver was at fault. Some such policies apply the same principle to payment for cost of repairs: the driver's policy covers the expense regardless of which driver was at fault.

*The concept of **no-fault insurance** is intended to reduce the number of disputes that go to court to determine which driver or which insurance company is liable for payment of damages.*

See also: Fault

N

Nolle prosequi (NAH-lee PROSS-e-kwee), *noun*

From the Latin, meaning "to be unwilling to pursue." A decision by a plaintiff or prosecutor not to proceed further with a legal action.

*The prosecutor filed a notice of **nolle prosequi** with the court, notifying the accused that there was no intention to bring the case to trial.*

See also: Prosecution

Nolo contendere (NO-lo ken-TEN-de-ree), *noun*

A Latin phrase meaning, "no contest." A plea accepted in criminal proceedings in some jurisdictions that allows a defendant to accept conviction on a charge while neither admitting nor denying commission of a crime. In certain circumstances, this would allow a defendant to deny the same charges in a civil action.

*The defendant pleaded **nolo contendere** to the misdemeanor charges, neither denying nor admitting to the accusation.*

See also: No contest

Nominal damages (NA-men-el), *noun*

A small monetary award made to a plaintiff as an indication that the litigant prevailed in a lawsuit. A nominal award, perhaps $1, is a way of saying that the defendant was wrong but that there were no significant damages suffered by the plaintiff.

> *The jury found in favor of Bruce Wein, but awarded only $10 in **nominal damages** because it found that Mr. Wein did not suffer real damages.*

Non compos mentis (NAHN KOM-pes MEN-tiss), *noun*

A Latin phrase meaning "not having mastery of mind" or "not of sound mind."

> *A psychiatrist testified to the court about the mental state of the defendant before the judge ruled that the accused was **non compos mentis**.*

See also: Compos mentis

Nonfeasance (non-FEEZ-ance), *noun*

A failure to perform an act that is required or expected. This is distinguished from malfeasance and misfeasance.

> *Greene was accused of **nonfeasance** for failing to file required quarterly and annual reports.*

See also: Malfeasance, Misfeasance

Nonprofit, *noun*

An organization that is set up to provide charitable, educational, or other services and not for the purpose of making a profit. Various state and federal laws regulate how funds are spent and the types and amounts of taxes that are collected.

> *The soup kitchen was set up as a **nonprofit** organization; any funds left over after expenses and salaries are paid are set aside as an emergency fund to cover unexpected contingencies.*

Nonresident alien, *noun*

A tourist or temporary worker whose permanent residence is in another country and has not received permission to stay for an extended period as a resident alien.

> ***Nonresident aliens** are foreigners who have been allowed entrance to a country for a visit, and are usually barred from seeking or obtaining employment.*

Not guilty, *noun*

(1) At a criminal court hearing, a plea by the defendant denying the charges. (2) Also, in a verdict by a judge or jury, a decision to acquit.

> *(1) The defendant pleaded **not guilty**. (2) We the jury find the defendant **not guilty** of the charge against him.*

See also: Verdict, Acquit, Convict

Notarize, *verb*

The act of authenticating a document or witnessing a signature or other act by a notary.

> *The bank required the mortgage applicants to have the loan documents **notarized** at the time they sign them.*

See also: Notary

Notary (NO-te-ree), *noun*

A person authorized by a jurisdiction to perform certain specific legal tasks including witnessing the signing of documents and certifying contracts and real property agreements or deeds. The notary usually applies a special seal or embossed marking on paperwork, along with his or her own signature. Also called a notary public.

> *The personal services contract required that a **notary** public witness its signing.*

See also: Notarize

Nuisance, *noun*

(1) Unlawful interference with someone's reasonable use and enjoyment of their property. (2) Also, the unreasonable or illegal use of property in such a way as to cause a threat or inconvenience to others.

> *(1) The lawsuit alleged that the installation of 100,000 Christmas lights and a 500-watt sound system on the front lawn of the house was a **nuisance** and interfered with the plaintiff's right to enjoy their own property. (2) The building inspector declared the nightclub a public **nuisance** and ordered its owners to clean up the property and soundproof its walls to prevent disturbance to residents of neighboring structures.*

Null, *adjective*

Something that has no legal effect, is unenforceable, or has no value.

> *The court ruled that the applicable statute had been repealed and the charges were therefore **null**.*

See also: Void, Abrogate

Nuncupative (NUN-kyu-pay-tive), *adjective*
An unwritten will that is spoken or declared orally.
> *Some states allow putting into effect a* **nuncupative** *will given by a person who is mortally wounded or about to die from natural causes.*

See also: Will

Oath, *noun*
A sworn declaration to tell the truth. Someone under oath in a court or in giving a deposition is subject to prosecution for perjury for knowingly stating a falsehood.
> *When a witness swears an* **oath,** *he or she promises to tell the whole truth and nothing but the truth under penalty of prosecution for lying.*

See also: Affirm, Affirmation, Perjury

Objection, *noun*
An argument or motion made by an attorney that a statement or action by the opposing counsel, or by the judgment, is not in keeping with procedure or is not allowed.
> *The defense attorney entered an* **objection** *to the line of questioning by the prosecution; although the judge overruled the motion, the* **objection** *is on the record of the trial and may be reviewed by a higher court if an appeal is lodged.*

Obligation (ob-li-GAY-shun), *noun*
(1) The legal duty to perform an act or pay an amount due. (2) Also, any binding agreement that requires someone to perform an act or pay an amount due.
> *(1) A police officer has a legal* **obligation** *to arrest someone who commits a crime that he witnesses. (2) Under terms of the* **obligation,** *Mr. Ojeda was required to pay for services rendered within fifteen days of being billed.*

See also: Contract, Debenture, Debt, Promissory note

Obligee (ob-li-JEE), *noun*
A person who is owed money, items, or services under terms of a contract or financial instrument.

*As the **obligee**, Odetts is entitled to receive the monthly payment of principal and interest under the promissory note.*
See also: Obligation, Promissory note

Obscenity (ub-SEN-i-tee), *noun*
(1) Something that is considered to be extremely offensive. (2) In legal terms, obscenity is an offensive form of expression that is judged to exceed the constitutional guarantee of free speech.

*(1) As Justice Potter Stewart once wrote in a Supreme Court decision, **obscenity** is very difficult to define, but "I know it when I see it." (2) The student was suspended from school for ten days for uttering an **obscenity** at his teacher in response to a reprimand.*
See also: Community standards

Obstruct (ob-STRUKT), *verb*
The criminal offense of intentionally impeding a legal process or investigation.

*The district attorney brought charges against Mr. Schilling, alleging he attempted to **obstruct** justice by destroying evidence.*

Obstruction of justice, *noun*
The crime of interfering, or attempting to interfere, with the legal process. Acts included in this offense include threatening or bribing witnesses or members of a jury, concealing or destroying evidence, falsifying evidence, and interfering with an investigation or arrest.

*O'Reilly was charged with **obstruction of justice** after it was determined he had erased and destroyed computer and paper records related to the operation of his business.*

Occupancy, *noun*
The act of possessing real property. In some states, an owner must actually use or occupy land at least once in a specified number of years or make efforts to prevent others from entering or using real property in order to maintain ownership.

*The court ruled that the actual owner of the premises had not visited or used it for more than a decade and that therefore the squatters had gained possession by **occupancy**.*

Offset, *noun*

A deduction from the amount of money due under a debt made to offset a counterclaim. Also called a setoff.

> *In the settlement of the lawsuit, the defendant was ordered to pay the amount demanded by the plaintiff minus $10,000 as an* **offset** *for unpaid invoices for material already shipped.*

See also: Recoupment, Setoff, Counterclaim, Cross claim

Omission (oh-MISH-un), *noun*

A failure to perform something that was required by law or had been an element of an agreement.

> *The court's ruling stated that the* **omission** *of necessary legal documents had made it impossible for the case to be decided.*

On demand, *adjective*

A negotiable instrument that can be redeemed at any time rather than on a specified date or under certain circumstances. Certain types of promissory notes allow the lender to demand payment from the borrower at any time, while some instruments such as checks and some types of bonds can be cashed by the holder on demand.

> *A check is a form of* **on demand** *instrument since it can be deposited or cashed at any time once issued.*

On point, *noun*

Regarding a precedent or argument that is considered directly relevant to the matter at hand.

> *The judge said that the attorney's argument was* **on point** *and would be considered in the final decision.*

Open, *verb*

(1) To reconsider a case that had been closed or decided. (2) Also, a hearing or proceeding where the public is permitted to attend and observe.

> *(1) The judge ruled that he would* **open** *his prior ruling on the matter for reconsideration. (2) The legislator met in* **open** *session to consider amendments to the bill.*

Open shop, *noun*

A workplace that includes both unionized and non-union employees with equal pay and benefits for equivalent jobs.

*About half the states have right to work laws that require **open shops** that essentially prohibit unions from requiring workers to be members.*

See also: Closed shop

Opening, Opening statement, *noun*

An attorney's initial statement to a judge or jury, outlining a case or laying out a defense, before the trial begins. In most courts, the opening is limited to the facts of a case and its expected course and cannot include legal arguments.

*In his **opening statement**, Mr. Laver told the jury that the prosecution would present evidence that would show that the defendant had consistently misrepresented his credentials and training in selling his services as a consultant.*

See also: Closing statement, Summation

Opinion, *noun*

(1) In a court of law, an opinion is the explanation of a judgment. It may include reference to precedents, the facts of the case, and other related information. (2) Also, beliefs, inferences, and conclusions based on observation of an event or scientific or other professional analysis.

*(1) The court's **opinion** made reference to several similar cases that required similar assessment of the competence of expert witnesses. (2) The engineer expressed an **opinion**, based on his analysis of the evidence, that the bridge had failed because of corrosion that could have been repaired.*

Option, *noun*

A contractural right to purchase property, securities, or other items, or a right to obtain a particular service.

*The agreement included the granting of an **option** to the buyer to purchase an additional ten acres of surrounding land at a specified price; the option was in effect for a period of two years after the contract was executed and then automatically expired. As part of his employment contract, Raitt was granted an **option** to purchase shares in the company at the set price of $12 per share; the option must be executed within a 90-day period after the end of his second full year of employment.*

See also: Stock option

Order, *noun, verb*

Any directive issued by a court or judge, other than a judgment or legal opinion on a case. However, a judgment might include an order within the ruling.

*The judge issued an **order** that both parties in the case refrain from making public comments while the matter is still before the court.*

See also: Court order, Writ

Ordinance (OR-di-nans), *noun*

A law or statute passed by a local authority, such as a city or town.

*The town **ordinance** prohibits leaving dangerous chemicals at the waste collection site without prior approval by the department of public works.*

Origination fee, *noun*

A charge levied by some lenders to cover the cost of processing a loan.

*In most situations, an **origination fee** is an effort by a lender to obtain additional profit and the borrower can attempt to negotiate for its removal or reduction.*

Ordinary course of business, *noun*

The normal and routine activities of a business, excluding special and unusual circumstances.

*In the **ordinary course of business**, Consolidated Intergalactic has a policy that does not require its employees to work more than six hours of overtime in any week.*

OSHA, *noun*

The Occupational Safety and Health Administration (OSHA) is a federal agency that oversees enforcement of the Occupational Safety and Health Act.

*Nearly every business is affected by one or another regulation set forth by **OSHA** to protect workers from the risk of illness or injury in the workplace.*

Ouster, *noun*

The wrongful eviction or dispossession of the rightful owner or a person with a legal interest in a property.

*The lawsuit says that after the business partners argued, the defendant conducted a wrongful **ouster** of the plaintiff and his possessions from the premises they jointly controlled.*

Out-of-court, *noun*

Actions, including negotiations or a settlement, reached between parties without the direct involvement of the court.

> *The parties to the lawsuit reached an **out-of-court** settlement of the dispute and petitioned the court to dismiss the case.*

See also: Settlement

Out-of-pocket expense, *noun*

In a health insurance plan, the portion of medical services and procedures that must be paid by the member.

> *Included in **out-of-pocket expenses** under most health insurance plans are copayments and deductibles.*

See also: Copayment, Deductible

Over the credit limit fee, *noun*

A fee from a credit card issuer or an institution issuing a line of credit that penalizes a borrower for spending or withdrawing more than is allowed under their credit limit.

> *The bank assessed an **over the credit limit fee** of $50 when Jones ran up a balance higher than his credit limit; they also demanded that he pay down the balance to below its maximum level within fifteen days.*

Overrule, *verb*

(1) A decision by a judge to reject a motion or objection made in a trial.
(2) Also, an action by a higher court that a previous appeals court decision on a legal issue was incorrect.

> *The trial judge **overruled** the objection by the defense attorney, allowing the prosecution to continue with its examination of the expert witness.*

Overtime, *noun, adjective*

(1) Additional hours worked beyond the normal hours of employment.
(2) Also, payment made to workers eligible to receive additional money for working overtime.

> *(1) In most places of employment, workers paid an hourly wage have a regular work week of thirty-five to forty hours, with **overtime** rates and rules applying when daily or weekly time on the job exceeds ordinary schedules. (2) The **overtime** rate for hourly workers at Consolidated Intergalactic is time-and-a-half or 150 percent of the regular rate.*

Own recognizance, *noun*

A promise to return to court for a hearing or trial to answer criminal charges without having to pay or pledge bail.

*The defense attorney asked the judge to release the accused on his **own recognizance** because he had family and employment in the area and was not likely to attempt to flee the jurisdiction.*

Owner, *noun*

A person or entity with the right to control, use, sell, or dispose an interest in real or personal property.

*In most transactions, a buyer has a reasonable expectation that the seller of the property is the rightful **owner**, although that generally does not protect against claims by others that contest the sale.*

O

Pain and suffering, *noun*

Physical or mental distress or torment caused by someone else's wrongful act.

*The jury awarded $1 million in damages for **pain and suffering**, in addition to $250,000 in compensatory damages for repairs to the family home.*

See also: Compensatory damages, Punitive damages

Palimony, *noun*

A court-ordered payment made from one party to another as a substitute for alimony where the couple was not married but had lived together. The word was coined about 1979 as a combination of "pal" and "alimony."

*The court ordered Jones to pay monthly **palimony** to his former partner, with whom he had lived for five years.*

See also: Alimony

Par, *noun, adjective*

The face value of a share of stock, bond, or other similar financial instrument. Subsequent trading of the instrument may result in its value increasing or decreasing.

*The shares were issued with a **par** value of $10 but were selling for $75 to $80 per share on the open market.*

Paralegal, *noun*

A trained specialist who performs certain tasks under the supervision of a lawyer. For example, a paralegal may handle the preparation of deeds or titles.

*The law office dispatched a **paralegal** as its representative at the closing of the sale of the property; an attorney had already reviewed all of the papers.*

Paramount title, *noun*

In competing claims to the rightful possession of property, the superior or prevailing claim.

*The lawsuit established the Keene claim as the **paramount title** and rejected the claims of the other two parties to the beachfront property.*

See also: Title

Parcel, *noun*

A defined piece of real property, usually as a subdivision of what was originally a larger tract of land.

*The **parcel** offered for sale amounted to a two-acre section of the hundred-acre ranch.*

Pardon, *verb, noun*

The executive power of a state governor or the President, or in some jurisdictions a delegated board, to forgive someone convicted of a crime and eliminate any remaining penalties or incarceration.

*In issuing the **pardon**, the President said the prosecution had been a political matter and should never have been pursued.*

See also: Commute, Clemency

Parole, *noun, verb*

Release from incarceration before the completion of a sentence, as allowed by a judge or a board of parole.

*The **parole** board said that Harris demonstrated remorse for his crime and had not committed any infractions while in prison; he was **paroled** on the condition of good behavior and directed to be in weekly contact with an officer of the court for the next three years.*

Participate, *verb*

To invest in a business undertaking, such as to purchase a share, make a loan, or otherwise contribute to the startup or operation of an entity.

*Roberts chose to **participate** in the establishment of the bank, investing $2 million in capital funds.*

Partnership, *noun*
A for-profit business jointly owned or operated by two or more persons.
*Murphy and Olbermann operated their butcher shop for forty years as a **partnership**, dividing work responsibilities and profits based on their private agreement between themselves.*

Pass, *verb*
(1) To transfer property from one person to another, usually as an inheritance. (2) Also, to pronounce a sentence or judgment.
*(1) Under terms of the will, ownership of the family home will **pass** to Roman's daughter. (2) The judge said he would **pass** sentence on the defendant at a session in ten days.*

Patent, *noun, verb, adjective*
(1) A government-issued acknowledgment of the exclusive right to own, sell, or license an invention or improvement. (2) Also, to seek acknowledgment by the government of the ownership of an invention or improvement. (3) Also, something that is obvious and readily apparent.
*(1) Herlihy was granted a **patent** for his invention of a self-suspending windshifter. (2) Leary filed papers with the federal agency to **patent** his improved method for buckling shoes. (3) The lawsuit said that the wood-burning stove had a **patent** defect that caused embers to enter the room where it was used.*
See also: Intellectual property, Infringe

Paternity (pa-TER-nity), *noun*
Being someone's father.
*The DNA test was undertaken to determine the **paternity** of the child.*
See also: Paternity suit

Paternity suit (pa-TER-nity), *noun*
A lawsuit to establish paternity.
*The **paternity suit** sought to establish that O'Reilly was in fact the father of the girl and responsible for her support.*
See also: Paternity

Pawn, *verb*

To pledge personal property as security for a loan with a pawnbroker.

*When someone **pawns** an item they receive a cash loan in return; if they do not pay off the loan within the specified term, ownership of the item transfers to the person holding the item.*

Payor (pay-YOR), *noun*

The person or entity responsible for making payment to a payee as required.

*Under terms of the promissory note, Farrell is the primary **payor** each month to the lender.*

Pending sale, *noun*

A real estate transaction that is under contract, but has not closed.

*The real estate listing indicated that the home was **pending sale**, which means that the seller has agreed to a contract with a buyer but the actual transfer of title has not yet taken place.*

See also: Sale

Pension, *noun*

A regular payment to a retired employee from a fund maintained by a former employer, sometimes augmented by contributions made by the employee while still working.

*In retirement, Keefe received a monthly **pension** funded by the company that employed him for thirty-five years.*

See also: Annuity

Peremptory challenge, *noun*

Rejection of a potential juror by an attorney for either side without the need to state a reason. In most jurisdictions, attorneys are granted only a certain number of such challenges and a judge (or an appeals court) may throw out a verdict if it is determined that peremptory challenges were used in an improper way so as to discriminate in some way against a defendant.

*The defense attorney issued a **peremptory challenge** to five prospective jurors and they were excused from the panel.*

Perfect (per-FECT), *verb*

To complete or correct a document or case so that it is fully satisfactory to a court or for a business transaction.

*The attorney filed papers with the town clerk and the assessor's office to **perfect** the title on the property and allow it to be sold. The judge allowed both sides in the lawsuit a seven-day period in which to **perfect** their filings before he would take the matter under consideration for a ruling.*

Perjury (PER-jur-ee), *noun*

The crime of intentionally giving false or misleading testimony in a court proceeding or before an officer of the court including a notary public or clerk while under oath or after affirmation.

*Aquilino was convicted of **perjury** for giving a false alibi for Mr. Ronstadt in his testimony.*

See also: Affirmation, Affirm, Oath

Perpetuity (per-pe-TOO-i-tee), *noun*

A thing or a provision that lasts forever, or for an indefinite period. For example, the transfer of real property from one person to another can be stated as being made in perpetuity.

*The sales contract transfers interest in the property to the buyer in **perpetuity**.*

Personal property, *noun*

Any property owned or controlled by a person other than real property (land and structures on the land).

*Laws and regulations regarding the sale or transfer of **personal property** are generally much less complex than those that apply to real property.*

See also: Real property, Chattel

Petit jury (petty jury), *noun*

A designation used in some states and jurisdictions to indicate a jury that is hearing a criminal case or a lawsuit. It is called "petit" as in small, as opposed to a "grand" jury which makes indictments.

*After the defendant requested a trial by jury, the judge ordered the convening of a **petit jury** to hear the case.*

See also: Jury, Grand jury

Petition, *noun, verb*

A written request to the court asking for an order or other action.

*The attorney submitted a **petition** seeking a change of venue for the trial. The plaintiff **petitioned** the court for an injunction ordering the plaintiff to discontinue sale of the product until the contract dispute was settled.*

See also: Writ

Petty theft, Petty larceny, *noun*

The crime of theft of money or personal property valued below a particular amount.

*George was charged with **petty larceny** for theft of objects valued at less than $500.*

See also: Grand theft

Plaintiff, *noun*

A person or entity that brings a case against another in a civil action.

*The party that initiates a civil lawsuit is called the **plaintiff** and the other party is named as a defendant.*

See also: Accused, Defendant

Plea, *noun*

In a criminal proceeding, the response by accused persons to each charge made against them. Typical pleas include not guilty, guilty, and no contest.

*If a defendant does not respond to a judge's question as to how he or she pleads to the charges, the court ordinarily will enter a not guilty **plea** on the accused's behalf.*

See also: Guilty, Not guilty, No contest, Nolo contendere

Plea bargain, *noun*

The result of a negotiation between a criminal defendant and the prosecutor in which the accused agrees to plead guilty or no contest to a lesser charge instead of going to trial on more serious charges.

*The defendant entered into a **plea bargain** with the prosecutor, agreeing to plead guilty to involuntary manslaughter instead of the more serious first degree homicide charge.*

See also: Plea

Plead, *verb*

(1) In a criminal case, to enter a plea in response to a charge. Pronounced PLED. (2) Also, in a civil case, to file a document (sometimes called a

pleading) related to motions, complaints, or declaration. Pronounced PLEED.

> (1) *The defendant* **plead** *not guilty to all charges and, through his attorney, asked for a jury trial.* (2) *The defendant's attorney told the court he intended to* **plead** *for relief from the terms of the injunction, which he called unreasonable and damaging to his client.*

See also: Plea

Pledge, *verb*

To give or promise something as security for the repayment of a debt or the fulfillment of a contract. In most situations, failure to make good on the debt or the contract would result in the forfeiture of the money or property pledged.

> *Webster* **pledged** *the federal treasury bonds he owned as collateral for the temporary loan he received.*

See also: Security

Points, *noun*

Prepaid interest, collected at closing, that serves to reduce the annual percentage rate assessed on a mortgage loan.

> *In mortgage financing, each* **point** *is equal to one percent of the amount of principal in a loan.*

See also: Prepaid finance charge

Polygraph (POLLY-graf), *noun*

One name for a so-called "lie detector" that measures a number of physiological responses including pulse and breathing rates as a supposed indicator of whether someone is telling the truth.

> *Not all jurisdictions accept the use of* **polygraph** *reports as evidence of the truth or falsity of a defendant or witness.*

Possession, *noun*

The right that an owner or someone who holds an interest in something, such as a tenant, to control and use property. Possession is not the same thing as ownership.

> *The contract gives the tenant the* **possession** *of the apartment for the term of the lease.*

Post mortem (post MOR-tem), *noun*

A Latin phrase meaning "after death." One use of the term is as a synonym for an autopsy, a medical examination of a body to determine the cause of death.

> *The county coroner conducted a **post mortem** of the body, determining that Mr. Tyson died of natural causes.*

See also: Autopsy, Inquest, Coroner, Medical examiner

Pourover provision, *noun*

An element of a will that declares that transfer of property will occur after a particular event occurs.

> *The will included a **pourover provision** that said that transfer of the bulk of the estate's value would occur only after all of the surviving children had reached the age of majority.*

See also: Estate, Will

Power of appointment, *noun*

As part of a will or trust, the act of the owner of property to designate or appoint someone else to make decisions on the distribution of assets after the death of the donor.

> *In many wills, the donor gives some level of **power of appointment** to the executor in order to allow for the possibility that listed beneficiaries predecease the donor.*

Power of attorney, *noun*

A document signed by one person (the principal) giving another person or persons (the attorney-in-fact) the power to act on the principal's behalf. Depending on the specific rights granted in the document, the attorney-in-fact may be allowed to sell real property, manage bank accounts and investments, and sign papers on behalf of the principal. The power of attorney may be for a limited period of time or a specific purpose such as for the sale of a home and is thus nondurable. Or it may be durable, meaning that it stays in effect until and unless it is canceled by the principal. A third type is sometimes called a springing power of attorney, meaning that it springs into effect if a certain event occurs; for example, the power of attorney might only take effect upon the disability of the principal.

*Her father granted Judy a durable **power of attorney** to act on his behalf in all financial and legal matters.*

See also: Attorney-in-fact

PPO (Preferred Provider Organization), *noun*

A medical plan that brings together a group of doctors, hospitals, and other health care providers under contract. Participating members of a PPO agree to provide services at a specified fee to subscribers.

*In general, subscribers to a **PPO** pay a reduced rate for services when they use member providers and a higher rate if they choose (or are forced) to go outside of the network.*

See also: HMO, Single-payer

Pre-approved, *noun*

(1) In mortgage lending or automobile financing, a bank or other institution might inform an applicant that they will be able to obtain a loan up to a particular amount; with this information, the applicant can shop for or arrange to make a purchase knowing that the loan will be available when required for the transfer. (2) Also, a credit card issuer or other lender may choose to contact individuals with an offer for a pre-approved line of credit based on information obtained by the financial institution from a credit bureau or other source.

*(1) A car shopper who is **pre-approved** for an automobile loan can compare or even attempt to negotiate the dealer's offer for financing. A pre-approved home buyer may be more attractive to a seller than someone who has not yet applied for a mortgage. (2) People with a good credit history may receive regular offers of **pre-approved** credit cards.*

Preamble (PREE-am-bul), *noun*

The introductory section of a law, statute, or other legal document that states its purpose.

*The **preamble** to the contract outlines the meeting of the minds of the parties involved in the deal.*

Precatory (PREK-ah-tory), *adjective*

The wishes or advice of someone expressed in a will; the remarks do not have the power of a demand.

*In his will, Adams added **precatory** words expressing his hope that his son will keep the family compound and not sell, transfer, or subdivide it.*

174

Precious metals, *noun*

Commodities that have unusually high values and are in certain economic conditions considered as an investment that is a good hedge against inflation.

*Most investors consider gold, silver, and platinum as the best **precious metals** for commodity trading; some other metals such as iridium, osmium, and rhodium have special value in high-tech industries.*

Precedent (PREH-si-dent), *noun*

A previous legal decision or case (usually at an appeals court or superior court level) which establishes authority that must be followed in any future cases that are on the same point of law or otherwise similar.

*The defense attorney cited several recent **precedents** to support his motion to challenge the use of polygraph evidence in the trial.*

Predecease (pree-de-SEES), *verb*

For someone to die before someone else.

*The will states that if Crutchfield's son should **predecease** his father, his share of the estate would pass to a charity named in the document.*

P

Preference, *noun*

In a bankruptcy repayment plan, a creditor who receives a larger proportional share of available assets than others with a claim against a debtor.

*The court decided that because of its decades of partnership with the debtor, including a loan made to the company as it neared bankruptcy, Consolidated Intergalactic would be given **preference** in the distribution of the proceeds from the sale of the debtor's assets.*

Preferred stock, *noun*

A class of shares that have priority over common shares when it comes to the payment of dividends or in the distribution of assets if the company is dissolved. Unlike common stock, however, shares of preferred stock generally do not bring voting rights in the selection of the board of directors and other major decisions.

*The corporation announced it would sell **preferred stock** to allow a new round of expansion, choosing not to dilute the voting rights of present shareholders by issuing new common stock.*

See also: Common stock

Prejudice (PREJ-u-diss), *noun, verb*
(1) Bias or prejudgment in a case, amongst members of a jury, or in personal or business actions in violation of the law. (2) Also, to cause harm.

*(1) Mr. Lyman's attorneys filed a motion asking the chief judge to assign a new trial judge to the case because of a demonstrated **prejudice** by Justice Bregger. (2) The defendant's attorney charged that actions by the prosecutor served to **prejudice** his rights to a fair trial.*

See also: Bias

Preliminary hearing, *noun*
A hearing at which a judge determines whether there is enough apparent evidence to put a person on trial for a crime. It is not a determination of guilt.

*At a **preliminary hearing**, the prosecutor presented testimony from a forensic scientist that tied the accused to the crime; the judge found probable cause for a trial.*

See also: Probable cause, Bound over

P

Premature distribution, *noun*
A withdrawal from a financial instrument or plan, such as a qualified retirement plan, before the minimum age set by agreement or statute.

*Taking a **premature distribution** from an IRA plan usually subjects the investor to a tax penalty or fee.*

Premises, *noun*
In legal and real estate descriptions, land and any buildings and outbuildings located on it.

*Detectives obtained a warrant to search the **premises**.*

See also: Homestead, Situs

Premium, *noun, adjective*
(1) The annual or installment charge for an insurance policy. (2) Also, an extra charge for special services or priority.

*(1) The automobile insurance **premium** totals $1,150 per year, or $100 per month if paid in installments. (2) The dealer offers a **premium** level of service, including repairs by appointment and the use of a loaner car while your vehicle is in the shop.*

Prenuptial agreement (PREE-nup-shul agreement), *noun*

A written contract agreed to by two people before they marry identifying the possession of assets they will bring to the marriage, the way future income and possessions will be treated, and a plan for the division of assets if the marriage is later dissolved. Colloquially called a "pre-nup."

*Astor and Rothschild met with an attorney to draw up and execute a **prenuptial agreement** to enumerate their assets and provide for their division if their upcoming marriage were to fail.*

Prepaid credit card, *noun*

A way to pay for goods and services without the use of cash, a prepaid credit card is actually not based on credit but is instead closer to a debit card. The prepaid credit card is secured by an amount of money that has been deposited with a financial institution; when the card is used, expenditures are deducted from the balance.

*When you use a **prepaid credit card**, charges are immediately deducted from funds on deposit with the issuer.*

See also: Credit card, Debit card

Prepaid finance charge, *noun*

Charges collected at a real estate closing.

***Prepaid finance charges** at a real estate closing often include points, loan application fees, title search, and other costs.*

See also: Points

Prepayment, *noun*

Paying off all or a portion of a loan before its due date, including the right to terminate a secured loan if the associated loan or vehicle is sold. Loans are usually structured so that at the start, more of the payment is allocated to interest than principal.

*Most loans allow the borrower the right of **prepayment** before the full amount or a portion of the loan amount is due.*

Preponderance of evidence (pri-PON-de-rince), *noun*

The standard of proof required to win a civil action; preponderance means the weight, power, or strength of evidence is sufficient to convince; it is thus possible for a single bit of evidence to outweigh a larger body of testimony.

*A civil court judge or jury is asked to decide if the **preponderance of evidence** weighs in favor of the plaintiff or the defendant.*

See also: Standard of proof

Prerogative (pri-RA-ga-tive), *noun*

(1) A right or privilege that is available only to a particular individual or group of individuals. (2) Also, an archaic term for any writ or court order to government agencies, public officials, or to another court.

*(1) Among the **prerogatives** of a state governor or U.S. President is the issuance of pardons. (2) The Superior Court issued a **prerogative** to the state Division of Licensing ordering it to issue an operating permit to the bus company without waiting for a resolution of the ongoing lawsuit regarding the distribution of assets from the bankruptcy proceeding of a company with which it had a joint venture.*

Prescription, *noun*

A means of establishing a claim to real property on the basis of a continued and uninterrupted use over a long period of time. Many states establish a statute of limitations that established the period that would be required before such a claim would be valid.

*The attorney for the neighbor demonstrated for the court the fact that his client had been using a portion of the property as an access road for more than twenty years without challenge by the landowner, and that therefore the neighbor had acquired an interest in the land by **prescription**.*

Presentment, *noun*

(1) A report by a Grand Jury to the court, made without request by a prosecutor, that a public crime (an illegal act by a public official, or a crime against the general public) has been committed. (2) Also, a demand to a borrower for payment of a promissory note on its due date.

*(1) The Grand Jury made a **presentment** to the court that recommended additional charges beyond those asked for by the prosecutor. (2) The lender issued a **presentment** to the holders of its promissory note, notifying them of the upcoming due date on the instruments.*

See also: Grand jury

Pretrial (PREE-trial), *adjective*

A conference convened by a judge or other court official that brings together attorneys for both sides in a lawsuit or criminal trial to discuss discovery, scheduling, and other issues before the trial began.

*At the **pretrial** conference before the high-profile trial, the judge advised both the prosecutor and the defense attorney of his expectations regarding behavior inside and outside of the courtroom.*

See also: Discovery

Prevail (pri-VAIL), *verb*
To win by persuasion in a court proceeding.

*The plaintiff's argument **prevailed** over the defendant's motion for dismissal.*

Prima facie (PRY-ma FAY-sha), *adjective*
A Latin phrase meaning "at first look," it is used in legal arguments to state that something is obvious and true "on its face."

*As an element of its burden of proof the prosecution was required to present **prima facie** evidence that the crime of murder had taken place.*

Prime rate, *noun*
The interest rate banks charge when making loans to their most-favored or most creditworthy customers. The prime rate is indirectly related to the interbank or Fed Funds rate set by the Federal Reserve Board.

*Some credit cards and other consumer loans have their interest costs tied to the published **prime rate**.*

Principal, *noun, adjective*
(1) In criminal law, the main actor in a crime; secondary participants are called accessories. (2) Also, the owner or managing director of a business. (3) Also, the main location for a business.

*(1) The prosecutor identified Terry Crisp as the **principal** in the crime, saying that he led the others in their scheme. (2) Sam White is owner and **principal** of the business. (3) The company has operations around the country, but its **principal** place of operation is in Boston.*

Principle, *noun*
An underlying legal, moral, or ethical standard.

*The rules of procedure in a court are based on the basic **principle** of equal protection before the law.*

Priority, *noun*

A right to payment or satisfaction of a person or entity's claim ahead of someone else.

> *The owners of preferred bonds have **priority** ahead of ordinary share-holders in repayment in the event of bankruptcy.*

Pro bono, *adjective, adverb*

For the public good, something done without payment.

> *In some jurisdictions, lawyers are expected to perform a certain amount of **pro bono** legal representation to clients who cannot afford to pay for services.*

See also: Gratuitous

Probable cause, *noun*

A court hearing in a criminal case to determine if there is sufficient reason to believe that a crime has been committed and that there is sufficient evidence to pursue the prosecution of a particular person. This is not a judgment as to the guilt or innocence of the accused, but it does require the prosecution to convince a judge that a trial is warranted.

> *At a **probable cause** hearing the prosecution presented the testimony of a police officer who described the facts of the murder and outlined a strong connection between the accused and the crime. The judge ordered the matter bound over to a trial.*

See also: Habeas corpus, Bound over

Probate, *noun*

A judicial proceeding to determine if a will is genuine and proper, and to monitor the distribution of the estate.

> *After the death of Mr. Wilson, his will went to **probate** where it was found to be genuine; per the decedent's wishes, his family attorney was appointed as executor.*

See also: Executor, Probate court

Probate court, *noun*

A special court that deals in the process of probating a will.

> *The **probate court** certifies wills and in some states oversees the distribution of assets of persons who die intestate.*

See also: Probate, Will, Intestate

Probative, *noun, adjective*

(1) Furnishing proof or evidence. (2) Also, describing an examination aimed at proving something.

> *(1) The defense counsel told the judge his line of questioning would be **probative** of his client's alibi for the time period of the crime. (2) The court approved special testing of the evidence that the prosecution said would be **probative** of the alleged link to the defendant.*

See also: Material, Immaterial

Probity, *noun*

Absolute moral uprightness.

> *The code of conduct for judges expects **probity** in all actions inside and outside of the courtroom.*

Procedure, *noun*

(1) The steps of the legal process. (2) Also, the allowed methods used by a law enforcement agency or a prosecutor in investigating a case, questioning witnesses or suspects, and the handling of evidence.

> *(1) The highest court or the administrative court for each state sets **procedure** for local jurisdictions in the handling of civil and criminal cases. (2) In certain circumstances, a violation of ordinary **procedure** by prosecutors or law enforcement agencies can result in a court dismissing a case.*

P

Process, *noun*

The means by which a person is given official notice of a legal action, or is formally notified to appear in court.

> *In a lawsuit, the **process** generally includes a deadline by which the defendant must file a response or pleading.*

See also: Process server

Process server, *noun*

A person, either a certified individual or an officer of the court (including a law enforcement official, clerk, or attorney), who delivers a summons or other legal paper and can testify that the act was accomplished.

> *The attorney for the plaintiff asked the sheriff's department to be the **process server** for the lawsuit, contacting the defendant and officially delivering notice of the initiation of the case.*

See also: Process

Proffer (PRAW-fer), *verb*
To offer evidence, or to present something in hopes it will be made part of an agreement.
*The defense **proffered** the testimony of an expert witness.*

Profit, *noun*
The financial gain from a business or investment after the cost and expenses have been deducted.
*The company showed a **profit** of $32 million on sales of $250 million for the year.*
See also: Net income

Progressive tax, *noun*
A method of taxation in which the effective tax rate goes up as the amount that is subject to the tax increases.
*The income tax structure in the United States levies a higher percentage against higher incomes and thus is a **progressive tax**.*
See also: Flat tax, Regressive tax, Effective tax rate

Prohibition (PRO-e-bi-shun), *noun*
A legal order forbidding a particular action. A prohibition may be aimed at a participant in a legal case, or at a lower court or public agency.
*The court ordered a **prohibition** against destruction of ballots by the elections office until a ruling had been made on the request for a recount.*
See also: Proscription

Promissory note, *noun*
A written promise (by a maker or obligor) to pay a sum of money usually consisting of the principal and interest of a loan to another person or entity (the payee, obligee, or promisee). It is the legal language of a loan.
*The lender produced a detailed **promissory note** with the details of the loan, and the conditions for its repayment, to be signed by the borrower.*
See also: Debenture, Debt, Maker, Obligation, Obligee, Principal

Proof, *noun*
The establishment or confirmation of a fact through the presentation of evidence.
*The prosecutor said that the results of the DNA testing was **proof** of the involvement of the defendant in the rape.*

Property tax, *noun*
A tax paid to state or local governments based on the value of real property.

Property tax is calculated by applying a percentage to the assessed value of land or property and buildings.

See also: Assessed value

Proprietary, *noun, adjective*
Something that is owned by someone or by an entity. This includes property of all types, including intellectual property.

*The company claimed that its product is based on **proprietary** software and any re-use of its code represents an unauthorized infringement.*

See also: Infringe

Proscription, *noun*
The act of banning or prohibiting something.

*The Congress enacted a series of laws aimed at the **proscription** of torture against detainees suspected of involvement in plans for terrorism.*

See also: Prohibition

Prosecution, *noun*
(1) The action of trying someone in a court for a criminal offense. (2) Also, the government's side in a criminal case. (3) Also, the performance of a duty or occupation.

*(1) The district attorney announced his office would seek the **prosecution** of anyone involved in the importation of the dangerous drug into the school. (2) The **prosecution** presented four days of testimony by expert witnesses and then rested its case. (3) The charge alleges widespread corruption in the sheriff's office in the **prosecution** of its duties.*

Prosecutor, *noun*
An elected or appointed official in a county, city, or other jurisdiction and assigned to oversee the prosecution of crimes. Also known as a district attorney or in some jurisdictions as the state's attorney.

*The **prosecutor** has some degree of discretion, as defined under the law, in deciding whether to prosecute an individual, the severity of the charge to be leveled, and the ability to enter into a plea bargain with a defendant.*

See also: District attorney, State's attorney

Prospectus (pro-SPEK-tis), *noun*
A document put forth by the proposed issuer of a security giving detailed information about the financial instrument and the issuer.
> *As required, the **prospectus** for the new offering of shares included information about the possible risks of making an investment in the company.*

Proxy, *noun*
(1) Someone who has been given authorization to act in another's place at a meeting, negotiation, or other such session. (2) Also, a written authorization to someone to act on behalf of another.
> *(1) Todd was named as a **proxy** for the CEO of the company with rights to vote on the matter under consideration at the meeting. (2) The signed **proxy** named Richardson as representative of the corporate officers in negotiations with the zoning board.*

Pseudonym, *noun*
Literally, a false name. A way to indicate a trade name or an alias.
> *In general, it is not illegal to operate a business or sell a product under a **pseudonym**, or to call yourself by another name, as long as it is not infringing on someone else's intellectual property or done for the purposes of fraud.*
See also: Alias, Also known as

Public defender, *noun*
A court-appointed or government funded attorney or group of attorneys who are available to defend someone accused of a crime who cannot afford the cost of a private attorney. In some jurisdictions, private attorneys can be assigned by the court to represent defendants on a pro bono basis or who are paid by the local government for their services.
> *The defendant told the judge he could not afford to pay for an attorney; the court assigned the **public defender** to represent him in the trial.*
See also: Right to counsel, Pro bono

Public domain, *noun*
(1) In copyright law, a work that is no longer protected by a copyright and is thus available to anyone to use without permission. (2) Also, land and water owned by the federal, state, or local government and thus belonging to the public.
> *(1) The works of great authors like Charles Dickens and Mark Twain are no longer protected by copyright and are thus in the **public domain**. (2)*

In many parts of New England, towns have a Commons area that is in the ***public domain***.

See also: Copyright

Public record, *noun*

Information, reports, transcripts, or documents which a public or government agency is required to maintain and make available to the public.

In general, all of the activities of a federal government agency, except for certain actions involving personal privacy and matters of national security, are on the ***public record***.

Publicly held corporation, *noun*

A company, organized as a corporation, with some or all of its ownership held by stockholders who can sell or transfer their shares to others.

As a ***publicly held corporation***, *Consolidated Intergalactic must follow many federal and state laws intended to prevent insiders from benefiting from knowledge not known to shareholders and the general public.*

Punitive damages (PYU-ni-tive damages), *noun*

Damages awarded in a lawsuit that are intended as a punishment or an example to others. Also known as exemplary damages. A litigant might also receive compensatory damages for actual losses.

The jury awarded $3 million in ***punitive damages*** *to the defendant, accepting the plaintiff's argument that the chemical company had been willfully negligent in not protecting residents of neighboring homes from injury caused by spills at the factory.*

See also: Compensatory damages, Pain and suffering

Purchase, *verb, noun*

(1) To acquire something through the payment of money or the exchange of something of value. (2) Also, a piece of property acquired in a way other than inheritance.

(1) The company decided to ***purchase*** *new vehicles in a cash deal. (2) The* ***purchase*** *was valued at $10 million.*

Purview (PER-vyu), *noun*

The range of a court's jurisdiction.

The court rejected the lawsuit saying it was outside of its ***purview***.

Qualified indorsement, Qualified endorsement, *noun*

A transfer of a financial instrument to an indorsee (endorsee), without any liability to the indorser (endorser). The document is usually noted as being "without recourse."

> *The promissory note was transferred to the holder who was given the right of a **qualified indorsement**, without recourse from the original issuer.*

See also: Endorse, endorsement

Quash (KWASH), *verb*

To annul or set aside an order because it is invalid.

> *The motion asked the judge to **quash** the summons because of errors in the description of the alleged crime.*

See also: Annul, Negate, Set aside

Query (KWEERY), *noun, verb*

(1) A question to be answered; (2) the act of posing a question.

> *(1) In his **query** to the judge, the foreperson of the jury asked for a clarification of the meaning of "beyond a reasonable doubt." (2) In his opening statement, the prosecutor said he planned to **query** witnesses about any and all connections they had with the importation of the counterfeit brand name watches.*

See also: Examination

Quid pro quo (kwid proh kwoh), *noun*

(1) A Latin phrase meaning "something for something." In a contract, this is the consideration exchanged between parties, such as money for services or money for property. (2) In a negative sense, quid pro quo can be used to refer to something given illegally or improperly in exchange for a favor.

> *(1) Consolidated Intergalactic agreed to set up a manufacturing facility in New Guinea as **quid pro quo** for a long-term contract to supply specialty oils. (2) The prosecutor charged that the gift to the legislator was intended as a **quid pro quo** for a favorable vote on the bill.*

See also: Consideration

Quiet enjoyment, *noun*

The right of an owner or tenant to use premises without disturbance or interference.

> *The tenant sued the landlord, claiming he had been denied the **quiet enjoyment** of his apartment because of the installation of a bowling alley on the ground floor of the building.*

Quiet title, *verb, adverb*
An action to free a title from the claims of others by bringing a lawsuit to establish a superior claim.

> *The plaintiff filed a **quiet title** action against Keillor, asking the court to declare the defendant's claim against the property invalid.*

Quit, *verb*
To vacate a premises or give up a claim to real property.

> *The owner **quit** the property and moved out of the court's jurisdiction.*

See also: Abandonment

Quitclaim, *noun*
A formal renunciation of a claim to a piece of property.

> *In some states, an owner may provide a **quitclaim** deed that relinquishes any future claim to the property; this does not necessarily protect any others who may have unresolved claims.*

R

Rape, *noun*
The crime of forcing another person to have sexual intercourse against her or his will or without giving consent. In general, the act requires actual penetration. A person can also be accused of attempted rape. A wife or husband cannot allege rape against their partner, although charges of assault can be brought.

> *The use of drugs or coercion to force someone to have sex without giving consent can also be the basis of a charge of **rape**.*

See also: Molestation, Sodomy

Ratify, *verb*
To indicate and confirm approval of a previous action that did not have prior approval.

> *The city council voted to **ratify** the contract for the purchase of parking meters; the city manager had signed the deal without receiving approval.*

Real estate agent, *noun*
A person who acts as a representative for a buyer or seller in a real estate transaction. In some states, an agent may hold a real estate license, or

may work under the supervision of a real estate broker who directly holds fiduciary and legal responsibilities.

*In most parts of the country, the majority of buyers and sellers are each represented by a **real estate agent** who helps would-be homeowners find a home and helps sellers market their property.*

See also: Real estate broker, Realtor

Real estate broker, *noun*

A broker is a real estate agent who is licensed by the state. In some situations, the broker is the owner or principal executive of a real estate agency.

*A **real estate broker** may supervise the efforts of associates or agents working at an agency.*

See also: Real estate agent, Realtor

Realtor, *noun*

A real estate broker or agent who is a member of a local real estate board that is affiliated with the National Association of Realtors.

__Realtors__ must pass a certification examination and follow a code of practices established by the national association in addition to meeting state licensing or supervision requirements.

See also: Real estate agent, Real estate broker

Real property, *noun*

Land, buildings, and anything permanently or firmly attached to the ground (such as light poles, wells, and outbuildings). Also included: anything growing on the land as well as any outside interests in the land such as easements or rights for oil or mineral development.

*By definition, **real property** is immovable or not practical to be moved to another location.*

See also: Personal property, Chattel, Intellectual property

Realize, *verb*

To receive something of value as the result of a transaction or deal.

*The foundation expects to **realize** about $12 million from the sale of the land it had been given by a donor.*

Reasonable doubt, *noun*

When a jury considered evidence in a trial, in most jurisdictions the highest standard of proof requires them to not have any reasonable doubt about a defendant's guilt before voting to convict.

*The judge instructed the jury they must be sure of guilt to a moral certainty and not have any **reasonable doubt** if they choose to find the defendant guilty.*

See also: Standard of proof, Preponderance of evidence, Clear and convincing evidence

Rebate, *noun, verb*

(1) A discount or return of a portion of the amount paid. (2) Also, to give a discount or return of a portion of the amount paid.

*(1) The contractor received a **rebate** of a portion of the cost of goods as an incentive by the merchant. (2) After announcing a major price cut, the manufacturer decided to **rebate** a portion of the price paid by early purchasers of the product.*

Rebuttal, *noun*

A line of examination, evidence, or testimony intended to disprove the legal position, argument, or evidence of the other side in a case.

*In his **rebuttal**, the prosecutor called an expert witness who testified that the defense's eyewitnesses could not possibly have seen the crime from their location.*

Recall, *noun, verb*

(1) To call back to the stand a witness who had previously testified. (2) Also, the act of nullifying or vacating an earlier order or judgment of the same court because of an error on the facts or because of changing circumstances. (3) Also, a move to remove an elected official before the ordinary end of term in office.

*(1) The prosecutor told the judge he intended to **recall** several of his primary witnesses in order to clarify several questions raised by the defense attorney in the case. (2) The judge said he would **recall** his earlier order barring the introduction of carpet fiber evidence and allow the prosecution to explore that line of questioning. (3) As the result of the **recall** election, the mayor was removed from office.*

See also: Redirect

Recapture, *noun*

In taxation, a regulation that requires the seller of property to pay to the government any unearned accelerated depreciation or deferred capital gains.

*The seller was required to pay back the prorated value of certain tax breaks on the investment because of a provision for **recapture** of such incentives when they are not fully earned.*

See also: Depreciation

Receiver, *noun*

(1) An independent person, sometimes a professional trustee or a neutral attorney, appointed by a court to take control of the property and business affairs of one of the parties in a lawsuit and to receive income while the right to those funds is being decided in a trial. In general, the other party in a lawsuit will ask the court to appoint a receiver when it is concerned that the money will not otherwise be available after the trial if they prevail in their case. (2) Also, a person appointed by the court to receive income, pay bills, and sequester profits while a bankruptcy proceeding was being heard. (3) Also, someone who accepts or purchases stolen goods with knowledge that they were illegally obtained.

*(1) The judge appointed Harry Jones, a retired accountant, as **receiver** for the business affairs of Transatlantic Bridgeworks for the duration of the lawsuit brought against the company. (2) Ballou was named as **receiver** for Transatlantic Bridgeworks while the court heard proposals for the reorganization of the company under bankruptcy rules. (3) Bruckett was named in the indictment as **receiver** of the stolen artworks.*

See also: Receivership

Receivership, *noun*

A condition of business operation in which the financial operations are under the control of a court-appointed receiver while a bankruptcy proceeding is under way to determine a reorganization or dissolution of the company.

*The appliance store continues to operate in **receivership** pending the final outcome of its petition to the bankruptcy court for a financial reorganization of its debts.*

See also: Receiver

Recession, *noun*

In economic terms, a period of business and investment downturn.

*Most economists define **recession** as two consecutive quarters in which the Gross Domestic Product has declined.*

See also: Depression

Recognize, *verb*

In financial terms, to include a gain or loss in tax calculations.

*The company said it would **recognize** a loss of $3.2 million on the sale of its betel nut processing facilities.*

Record (REK-erd), *noun*, (re-KORD), *verb*

(1) The transcript of testimony, rulings, and other spoken words as well as documents and evidence from a court session or a meeting of a public agency. (2) Also, to enter a document into an official registry. (3) Also, to make a tape or a transcript of events at a meeting.

*(1) The ordinance requires that the public **record** of the zoning board must be available for examination within three business days after any meeting. (2) The bank's representative visited the county clerk to **record** the mortgage lien. (3) The commission was directed by the county government to **record** all of its open meetings and make them available to the public.*

Recording fee, *noun*

A charge levied by government agencies to enter a real estate sale or purchase and the associated transfer of title into the public record.

*Depending on local real estate practices, either the buyer or seller is responsible for paying the **recording fee** associated with the sale or transfer of real estate.*

R

Recoupment, *noun*

The right of a defendant in a lawsuit to ask the court to withhold from any award made to a plaintiff in a lawsuit any money which is in turn owed by the plaintiff to the defendant.

*Although the defendant lost the lawsuit, its attorneys asked for the **recoupment** of the unpaid original amount of the sale from the damages awarded to the plaintiff.*

See also: Setoff, Offset, Counterclaim, Cross claim

Recourse, *noun*

The right to demand payment from the issuer of a financial instrument if there is a problem with cashing the check, promissory note, or other promise to pay.

*In general, the recipient of a check or other negotiable instrument has the right of **recourse** to demand payment in another form if the instrument is not accepted by others.*

See also: Endorsement, Indorsement

Recross, *noun, adjective*

Asking additional follow-up or clarifying questions of witnesses previously called by one side under cross-examination.

> *In his **recross** examination of witnesses, the defense attorney attempted to re-establish the chain of custody of evidence subjected to DNA testing.*

See also: **Direct examination, Recall, Redirect**

Recuse (ri-KYUZ), *verb*

When a judge steps aside for a case, or agrees to a request by one or the other party in a case to step aside. A recusal is usually made because of a conflict of interest or because of an actual or apparent bias.

> *The trial judge said he would **recuse** himself from the case because of a conflict of interest and ask the supervising judge to appoint a new trial judge. The supervising judge ordered the trial judge to **recuse** himself because of a conflict of interest.*

Red herring, *noun*

(1) Irrelevant or misleading information introduced into a legal proceeding or a financial dealing. (The term comes from an old English practice of using a smoked kipper—a red herring—as a device to train a hunting dog to follow a scent wherever it led.) (2) Also, in financial dealings, a registration statement filed with the Securities and Exchange Commission about an initial public offering that outlines some of the prospects and risks involved in investing in new shares of the company. Because the price of the shares and the number of shares is not usually known until just before the offering, a section printed in red—called a red herring—warns investors that the offering has not yet been approved by the SEC.

> *(1) The prosecution argued that the defense's attempt to introduce an international conspiracy theory into the case was a **red herring** intended to mislead the jurors. (2) In its prospectus for its initial public offering, the company included a standard **red herring** warning that advised would-be investors that statements in the document had not yet been approved by government regulators.*

Redaction (re-DAK-shun) Redact, *noun, verb*

An editing of a document to remove secret or confidential information before it is released to the public or revealed to someone who does not have a need to see the information.

Before the evidence was put on the record, the home addresses and telephone numbers of witnesses underwent **redaction***. The prosecution asked the court to* **redact** *the document so that the personal information of sexual assault victims was not revealed to the public.*

Redeem, *verb*
To buy back or reacquire property or a financial instrument.
The board of directors voted to **redeem** *outstanding callable bonds to reduce the company's outstanding debt.*

Redirect, *noun, adjective*
Asking additional follow-up or clarifying questions of witnesses previously called by one side under direct examination.
In his **redirect** *examination of witnesses, the prosecutor sought to address some of the questions raised about the accuracy of their initial testimony.*
See also: Direct examination

Redlining, *noun*
An illegal practice by mortgage and other financial institutions under which loans are only offered to buyers or homeowners in particular neighborhoods.
The objection to denying mortgages through **redlining** *is a belief that the decision is based on racial, ethnic, or other bias.*

Redress (REE-dress), *noun*
(1) A remedy or compensation meant to repair a wrong. (2) Also, the act of remedying a grievance.
(1) The arbitrator proposed payment of 10 percent of the proceeds from the contract as **redress** *for the dispute over franchise rights. (2) The underpinning of many of the rights of citizens is embodied in the First Amendment to the U.S. Constitution which prohibits the Congress from doing anything that would limit the right of the people to petition the Government for a* **redress** *of grievances.*

Reentry, *noun*
The act of taking back possession of real property by the owner.
The court ordered that the landlord had the right of **reentry** *to the premises because of the failure of the tenant to pay rent.*

Regressive tax, *noun*

A design for taxation that has the effective tax rate decrease as the amount subject to taxation increases.

*The effect of a **regressive tax** is to take a larger proportion of income from persons with lower income than from the rich.*

See also: Progressive tax, Flat tax

Rehabilitation, *noun*

(1) Questioning of a witness or introduction of new evidence with the intent of restoring the credibility of a witness. (2) Also, the repair or resolution of a debtor's financial status in a bankruptcy proceeding.

*(1) After the witness had undergone cross-examination by the defense attorney, the prosecutor asked the court to be permitted to introduce new evidence that was aimed at the **rehabilitation** of the witness' credibility. (2) The goal of the reorganization of debt was the **rehabilitation** of the debtor, with the hopes that the company would eventually be able to repay all outstanding debt and produce a profit.*

See also: Redirect, Recross, Bankruptcy

Release, *noun, verb*

(1) The act of giving up a claim to property, money, or other items. (2) Also, the act of relinquishing a right.

*(1) The document served to **release** the claim to the property that had been in dispute between the two parties. (2) Participants were asked to sign a **release** that removed liability by the league for injuries that might be suffered in the ordinary activities of the game.*

Relevant, *adjective*

Connected to or appropriate to the matter at hand. In a court, something that is related to the proving or disproving of the case.

*The prosecutor asked the judge to disallow the line of questioning by the defense, saying it was not **relevant** to the case and served only to confuse or mislead the jury.*

See also: Material, Immaterial, Red herring

Reliance (ri-LIE-ens), *noun*

Making an action, or failing to take an action, based on confidence in another person or on information provided.

*Our agreement to the contract was based on **reliance** in the representations made by the vendor.*

See also: Rely

Relief, *noun*

The remedy or compensation asked for or received in a court proceeding. The relief can include a financial award, the return of property, an injunction or other actions.

*The plaintiff asked for $100,000 as **relief** for the losses incurred by the inability of the vendor to deliver raw materials as promised.*

See also: Injunction, Remedy

Rely (ri-LIE), *verb*

To make a decision based on confidence in another person or information provided.

*In making our decision to enter into a contract, we chose to **rely** on the truthfulness of statements made by the salesman.*

See also: Reliance

Remainder, *noun*

An interest in real property that only becomes effective after a prior interest expires or is no longer effective.

*The foundation will receive title to the property in **remainder**, after the owner of the property dies.*

Remedy, *noun*

The redress sought from a court, or the relief granted by the court.

*The lawsuit sought a **remedy** for the damages caused as the result of the failure of the contractor to deliver goods as promised.*

Remise (ri-MIZE), *verb*

To give something up.

*The quitclaim deed stated that the owner agreed to **remise** all claim to the real property.*

See also: Quitclaim

Renounce (ri-NOUNCE), *verb*

To formally abandon a claim or right.

*After settling in Iceland, the Gustaffson family advised the U.S. Embassy they had decided to **renounce** their American citizenship.*

Rent, *noun, verb*

(1) The amount of money charged by a landlord for the use of real property. (2) Also, the act of hiring the use of equipment, a vehicle, or other item for a period of time, or the act of obtaining the use of real property through a lease or other agreement.

*(1) Under terms of the lease, the monthly **rent** for the apartment is $750.*
*(2) Jones signed a contract to **rent** the use of a truck for a week.*

Rent control, *noun*

Laws that seek to regulate the amount charged for rental of apartments, and sometimes to encourage the availability of housing for low-income tenants.

*New York City maintains **rent control** for a certain group of older apartments; the original intent was to prevent excessive rates.*

Renunciation, *noun*

(1) The act of renouncing a right or claim. (2) Also, the act of abandoning participation in a crime before it occurs.

*(1) The formal **renunciation** of the claim to ownership of the real property removed the cloud from the title and allowed the sale to go forward.*
*(2) The defense attorney presented witnesses who testified that the defendant had made a **renunciation** of the crime and did not participate in it or assist in it.*

See also: Renounce, Accomplice

Reorganization, *noun*

A restructuring of a corporation's debt, obligations, or financial structure as part of an effort to a bankruptcy proceeding or in preparation for the sale or merger of the company.

*The court approved the **reorganization** of the company and directed that its attorneys meet with all creditors to implement the plan for repayment of debt.*

See also: Bankruptcy, Chapter 11 bankruptcy

Repeal, *verb*

The annulment or removal of a law by a legislature.

*The state senate voted to **repeal** the ban on the sale of alcohol on Sundays; in order for the law to be enacted it must also be approved by the state legislature and be signed by the governor.*

Replevin (ri-PLEH-vin), *noun*
(1) The right to sue for the recovery of property improperly taken by another. (2) Also, an order by a court to temporarily or provisionally restore goods to their original owner pending the outcome of a lawsuit alleging improper taking.

*(1) The plaintiff filed a writ of **replevin** to institute a lawsuit for recovery of the property it says was improperly obtained by the defendant. (2) The court ordered the **replevin** of the goods to the original owner with instructions that the plaintiff not sell or transfer the property until the lawsuit had been settled.*

Repossess, *noun*
The act of taking back property that has been pledged as collateral for a loan when the borrower fails to make payments as scheduled.

*The finance company decided to **repossess** the automobile after the borrower fell three months behind in payments of principal and interest.*

Reprieve, *verb*
The postponement of the imposition of a criminal sentence by executive order such as by a governor or the President.

*The governor granted a last-minute **reprieve** of the execution sentence of the convicted murderer to allow further appeals to the courts.*

Repudiation (ri-pyu-DEE-ay-shun), *noun*
The refusal to fulfill an obligation or otherwise meet the demands of an agreement. Also, the denial of the existence of a contract or the existence of a valid agreement.

*In their **repudiation** of the contract, the company said it was not a valid agreement because of misrepresentations by the vendor.*

See also: Misrepresentation

Rescind (ri-SIND), *verb*
To cancel a contract by mutual agreement, or by the exercise of a rescission clause in the agreement. The act itself is referred to as rescission.

*The buyer chose to **rescind** the contract after determining that market conditions had changed abruptly.*

See also: Rescission

Rescission (ri-SI-zhen), *noun*

The act of canceling a contract by mutual agreement or by the exercise of a rescission clause in the agreement. By choosing to rescind, both parties are restored to the situation they were in before the contract was approved.

*The contract includes a **rescission** clause that allows the agreement to be cancelled within thirty days after signing without obligation or penalty to either party.*

See also: Rescind

Reservation, *noun*

A provision in a deed or other transfer that reserves to the grantor a particular right or portion of the property.

*The deed included a **reservation** that allows the seller to use the existing road through the property to access other property not included in the deal.*

See also: Reserve

Reserve, *verb*

To retain a specific right or claim to a portion of real property.

*In the deed of sale, the original owner **reserved** the right to exploit certain mineral or oil rights beneath the land.*

See also: Reservation

Residence, *noun*

A place someone uses as a home for an extended period of time.

*The defendant maintained and used a **residence** in Wyoming as a second home.*

Resident alien, *noun*

A foreigner who has received official permission to establish a permanent residence in the United States.

*As a **resident alien**, Jorge was given permission to seek and obtain employment and is protected by most of the rights given to citizens.*

See also: Green card

Residuary bequest, *noun*

In a will, a final bequest that indicates the donor's wishes for the disposition of any assets (the residue) that remain after all debts have been paid and specific bequests have been honored.

> Black's ***residuary bequest*** *asked that after distribution of bequests any remaining assets be donated to the county animal shelter.*

See also: Residue

Residue, *noun*

Any assets that remain in an estate after all expenses and debts have been paid and bequests honored.

> *As directed in the will, the* ***residue*** *of the estate was donated to the homeless shelter.*

See also: Residuary bequest

Respondent, *noun*

In a lawsuit, the person who is required to respond to any order of the court.

> *The subpoena ordered the* ***respondent*** *to file a response to the lawsuit by 5:00 P.M. on March 15.*

See also: Defendant, Subpoena

Rest, *verb*

To end the presentation of one side of a case, either the plaintiff or defendant in a civil matter or the prosecution or the defense in a criminal case.

> *The prosecution* ***rests*** *its case, giving the defense an opportunity to respond.*

Restitution (res-ti-TU-shen), *noun*

(1) A judgment or agreement between parties that returns property or money to a party to compensate for a loss. (2) Also, the restoration of both parties to their original condition after rescission of a contract.

> *The judge ordered the defendant to make* ***restitution*** *for the value of the stolen and damaged goods.*

See also: Rescission

Restraining order, *noun*

A temporary order or injunction to prohibit someone (or an entity) from taking an action.

*The court issued a **restraining order** demanding that the defendant not attempt to visit, call, or otherwise contact the plaintiff until a final order was made.*

See also: Injunction

Restrictive covenant, *noun*

An element of a deed that limits the future use of the land. A generally acceptable covenant would be one that prevents the buyer from making commercial use of the land and requiring it continue to be used for residential or agricultural purposes. In the past some covenants sought to prevent resale or transfer of land to particular classes of people.

*Modern courts have thrown out or allowed the removal of **restrictive covenants** from deeds when it was determined that the purpose of the limitation was to discriminate against persons because of their race, religion, or ethnic background.*

See also: Covenant

Restrictive indorsement, Restrictive endorsement, *noun*

A form of indorsement (or endorsement) of a financial instrument that limits the manner in which it can be cashed, deposited, or transferred.

*The recipient of the check added a **restrictive indorsement** stating that the check was "for deposit only."*

See also: Endorsement, Indorsement

Retainer, *noun*

A fee paid in advance to engage an attorney; the cost of services and expenses are deducted from the balance as they are incurred.

*The counsel asked for a $10,000 **retainer** to take on the case; an hourly rate of $100 for services rendered will be deducted from the balance.*

Retire, *verb*

(1) To pay off the outstanding balance of a promissory note. (2) Also, the movement of a jury panel into a closed room for deliberations on a verdict after the completion of the presentation of evidence and arguments.

*(1) The borrower made the final scheduled payment and **retired** the loan.*
*(2) The judge issued his instructions to the jury and then asked them to **retire** to the jury room to consider their verdict.*

See also: Satisfaction

Retirement plan, *noun*

A plan in which an individual or an entity sets aside money or makes other financial arrangements to provide for funds to be disbursed after retirement.

*In general, a **retirement plan** is primarily funded by the retiree through contributions during the years of employment and sometimes augmented by the employer, while a pension plan is mostly paid for by the employer.*

Retraction, *noun*

(1) The withdrawal of a legal document in any legal proceeding. (2) Also, the withdrawal of an offer for a contract. (2) Also, a formal correction in a publication or on a broadcast outlet, withdrawing an incorrect or false statement.

*(1) The **retraction** of the will changed the trial's outcome. (2) The company notified the job applicant that because of changing market conditions it was forced to make a **retraction** of its offer of employment. (3) As part of the settlement of the defamation suit, the newspaper agreed to publish a full **retraction** of the statements that were contested by the plaintiff.*

Retrial, *noun*

A second trial on the same issue. In civil matters, a retrial can be granted after a mistrial or hung jury or on the basis of a decision by an appeals court for error, bias, or the discovery of new evidence. In a criminal matter, a retrial can be instituted as the result of the same set of causes with the exception that under provisions of the Constitution, someone found not guilty cannot be tried again for the same offense.

*After the judge declared a mistrial, the prosecution immediately announced it would seek a **retrial** of the defendant and asked that the provisions of bail be continued.*

See also: Trial de novo, Mistrial, Hung jury

Retrocession, *noun*

The act of ceding back of interest in property to a person or entity that previously had the interest.

*The agreement included **retrocession** of the property to the original owner in exchange for a different parcel of land.*

Reverse mortgage, *noun*

A form of lending aimed at older homeowners that allows them to draw on the equity built up in their home without having to pay off the loan; under most such plans at the time of death or abandonment of the property the issuer of the reverse mortgage takes title and if there is any value beyond the amount due for principal and interest it is paid to the original owners or their estate.

*In certain circumstances, a **reverse mortgage** is a good way for older persons to drawn an income from the value of their home without having to sell it.*

Reversible error, *noun*

A mistake made in interpretation of the law or in legal procedure in a trial that is significant enough to cause a higher court to throw out the verdict.

*The defense attorney asked the appeals court to throw out the trial court's verdict because of a **reversible error** by the judge in the instructions to the jury.*

Revolving credit, *noun*

A form of credit that requires the borrower to make regular payments against the outstanding balance.

*Most credit card accounts are a form of **revolving credit** plan.*

See also: Finance charge, Installment loan

Rider, *noun*

An addition or amendment to a contract.

*The standard contract for services from the company also includes a **rider** that adds specific limitations or additional coverage. The insurance company added a **rider** to its basic homeowner's policy to add coverage for the insured's collection of antique butter dishes but excluded payment for damage caused by earthquakes.*

See also: Addendum

Right, *noun*

A moral or legal entitlement, such as the right to freedom or the right of free speech.

*You have the **right** to remain silent.*

Right of first refusal, *noun*

An element of a contract that gives one party the right to make a future purchase, or an additional purchase by matching the best offer made by another party.

*In signing the lease for the rental of the premises, the company was given **right of first refusal** to purchase the land and building should the owner decide to sell them at any time during the term of the lease.*

Right of survivorship, *noun*

A provision of joint tenancy or joint ownership of property that allows the surviving co-owner or co-owners to take over the interest of a deceased party to the contract.

*The lease states that in the event of death of any of the three signers of the contract, the interest in the property will pass by **right of survivorship** to the other tenant or tenants.*

Right of way, *noun*

The legal right, by law or by deed, given an individual, group of individuals, or the general public to travel along a specific route through the property of another.

*The town bylaw requires all residents with beachfront property to provide a marked and passable **right of way** from the road to the beach.*

R

Right to counsel, *noun*

The right of someone accused of a crime to have legal representation, as guaranteed by the Sixth Amendment of the U.S. Constitution.

*The judge advised the defendant of his **right to counsel** and inquired whether he could afford to hire a private attorney or wanted the court to appoint a public defender.*

See also: Public defender, Pro bono

Right to privacy, *noun*

The right, as defined by law, to have certain personal details kept confidential and not used by others without permission.

*In recent years, the **right to privacy** has been expanded by federal law to include a broad range of information about medical matters.*

Rights, *noun*

In general, a person's civil liberties.

*The basic outline of **rights** granted to American citizens were established in the first ten amendments to the U.S. Constitution, also known as the Bill of Rights.*

Robbery, *noun*

The crime of taking property or money directly from a person by force or under threat. The act of entering an unoccupied premises and stealing something is called a burglary.

*The defendant was charged with aggravated **robbery** for the theft of the woman's purse at knifepoint.*

See also: Burglary

Rollover, *noun, verb*

The act of moving assets from one tax-deferred or tax-free investment to another without losing the tax advantage.

*Field asked his financial advisor to transfer the funds in the pension account established by his former employer into a **rollover** IRA under his own control.*

R

Roth IRA, *noun*

A form of IRA (individual retirement account) that is funded with after-tax income.

*Since the owner of a **Roth IRA** is using money that has already been taxed, the plan exempts the investment from taxes throughout its existence and during its distribution in retirement.*

See also: Individual Retirement Account

Routing transit number, *noun*

A nine-digit code used in the United States on negotiable instruments including checks that identifies the financial institution from which it is drawn.

*The **routing transit number** is an essential detail needed to establish the pathway for electronic transfer of funds to and from financial institutions.*

See also: ABA number

Royalty, *noun*

A percentage of gross or net receipts or profits (as defined by agreement) paid to the creator of intellectual property by a publisher, manufacturer, or other user.

*The author receives a **royalty** of a percentage of the net receipts for the sale by the publisher of each of his books.*

Ruling, *noun*

A decision or order made by a judge or an administrator.

*The judge's **ruling** excluded all testimony from the expert witness because his credentials had been shown to be falsified.*

See also: Judgment, Order

Sale, *noun*

Transfer of title for property in exchange for money or something of value.

*Garrels agreed to the **sale** of her automobile for $12,500.*

Sales tax, *noun*

A tax levied on purchases of goods, and sometimes services. It is collected by the seller and paid to the government.

*There are many variations of **sales tax**, including some states that exempt clothing or food.*

Salvage, *verb, noun*

(1) The act of saving goods that have been lost, abandoned, or otherwise unavailable to the owner. (2) Also, payment made to a person or company that retrieves lost goods.

*(1) The company specialized in the **salvage** of cargo lost in shipwrecks and other accidents. (2) Consolidated Intergalactic made a payment of $575,000 in **salvage** to the company that retrieved its shipment of betel nuts after its jungle warehouse was destroyed by a flood.*

Sanction (SANK-shun), *noun*

(1) A financial penalty imposed by a court on a party in a court case, or to attorneys representing a party or defendant for violation of court rules. (2) Also, to allow something to occur, or to express approval of an activity. (3) Also, in international law, to put into place economic and other penalties against a country that is in violation of international agreements or laws.

*(1) The judge ordered a $500 **sanction** against the defendant's attorney for contempt of court. (2) The seizure of the automobile was given official*

sanction by the judge. (3) The trade organization put into effect a set of *sanctions* against the country for violations of human rights laws.

Satisfaction, *noun*
The full payment of a debt or the fulfillment of an obligation.
> *The borrower made payment of $2,000 in* **satisfaction** *of the debt.*

See also: Retire

Save harmless, *verb*
A guarantee to compensate someone for financial losses or release from liability, sometimes included as part of an agreement for services or the purchase of products. Also known as hold harmless or to indemnify.
> *The contract promises to* **save harmless** *Sam in the event a lawsuit is filed by a third party.*

See also: Hold harmless, Indemnify

Search, *verb, noun*
An examination of premises or a vehicle to find evidence of a crime. The U.S. Constitution requires law enforcement officers to obtain a warrant from a court in order to enter private property; there are exceptions that allow search of a home or vehicle if evidence is in clear sight.
> *Detectives, granted a warrant by the county court, executed a* **search** *of the suspect's home looking for stolen items.*

See also: Search warrant

Search and seizure, *noun*
The result of a search for criminal evidence that results in the removal of actual or potential evidence. The Fourth Amendment of the U.S. Constitution protects against unreasonable search and seizure and is the basis of the requirement for a court-issued search warrant in most situations.
> *The deputies conducted a* **search and seizure** *of the vehicle, removing it to a laboratory where it will be further examined for evidence of the murder.*

Search warrant, *noun*
A court order that permits a law enforcement agency to search a specific place for a specific purpose, based on a presentation that establishes the likelihood that evidence of a crime will be found.

*The sheriff asked the county court to authorize a **search warrant** to enter the premises of the suspects to look for stolen property related to the crime.*

See also: Warrant

Second mortgage, *noun*

An additional or secondary mortgage, sometimes called an equity loan, that taps into the value of a home. The holder of the first or primary mortgage has the right to collect money owed to it by the buyer before the holder of the secondary mortgage can seek to attach assets.

*The Solas family took out a **second mortgage** to fund a renovation of their home and now must make two monthly loan payments.*

See also: Mortgage, Equity

Secure, *verb*

To provide a backup to assure a lender that a debt will be paid or an obligation performed by giving the lender or other party a lien, mortgage, or other form of security interest in property or real property.

*The lender required that the borrower **secure** the loan by granting a lien on the title to the automobile.*

See also: Security

Secured credit card, *noun*

A form of credit card secured by a deposit account. Unlike a debit card, amounts charged using the card are not deducted from the account but instead must be paid as billed by the credit card company.

*A **secured credit card** is one way for persons with poor credit to improve their credit score.*

Secured transaction, *noun*

A loan or any other transaction in which property or real property is pledged as security in case full repayment is not made. Examples include home mortgages and automobile loans.

*The lender offered a lower interest rate on loans that were a **secured transaction** with collateral pledged.*

Securities and Exchange Commission (SEC), *noun*

The federal agency which sets regulations for brokerages, mutual funds, and the issuance of shares of stock by publicly traded companies.

*The **Securities and Exchange Commission** oversees most institutions and companies involved in the buying and selling of financial instruments that are publicly traded.*

See also: Investment Company Act of 1940

Security, *noun*
(1) An interest in property or a bond given to a lender to assure payment of a debt or fulfillment of an obligation. (2) Also, a form of ownership or the right to share in profits of a business obtained through investment.

*(1) The plumber signed over a **security** interest in his yacht to secure a loan to expand his mansion. (2) Shares are a form of **security** that allow investors to participate in the profits and the growth of a publicly traded company.*

See also: Secure

Security deposit, *noun*
A payment required by a landlord, or an agent for the rental or loan of a vehicle or other item, to be used if necessary to pay for repairs or damages that are not otherwise covered.

*The lease required payment of a $500 **security deposit** to pay for any damages that are more than ordinary wear and tear on the apartment.*

Security interest, *noun*
An interest given a lender or a party to a contract that allows them to take and sell property or real property to satisfy an obligation that is not fulfilled.

*As holder of a **security interest** in the car, the lender has the right to repossess it and resell it in order to realize funds to pay off an overdue loan.*

See also: Secure, Security

Self defense, *noun*
The right to use reasonable force to defend yourself or protect your family from physical attack by another. In some states this extends to protecting property as well.

*The police concluded that the homeowner was justified in shooting and wounding the armed intruder, saying it was done in reasonable **self defense**.*

Self-employed, *noun, adjective*

A person who owns his or her own business and draws income from it. Also known as a sole proprietor.

*A **self-employed** person must pay both the employee's and the employer's portion of FICA tax.*

See also: Sole proprietorship

Self incrimination, *noun*

Making a statement or producing evidence which tends to prove that you are guilty of a crime. Protections against self incrimination generally do not apply in civil cases.

*The Fifth Amendment of the Constitution protects individuals from being forced to answer questions or otherwise provide testimony that would tend to be viewed as **self incrimination**.*

Seller's agent, *noun*

An agent involved in the sale of property or real property who is acting entirely on behalf of the seller.

*As a **seller's agent**, Jones represents the interests of the owner in any negotiations and preparation of documents.*

See also: Buyer's agent, Agent, Broker

Separation, *noun*

A situation in which married persons are living apart, either under an informal relationship or as the result of a legally binding separation agreement.

*The husband and wife asked an attorney to draw up a **separation** agreement that defined their differing responsibilities and obligations to pay debts, manage finances, and maintain jointly owned property.*

See also: Divorce, Dissolution

Sequester, *noun, verb*

(1) To isolate a jury from outside influences during a trial or deliberations. (2) Also, to place the property of an individual or company that is undergoing bankruptcy proceeding under the control of a trustee.

*(1) The court ordered the jury **sequestered** for the entirety of the trial, arranging for lodging at a nearby hotel and continuous monitoring by sheriff's deputies. (2) The court appointed a trustee to **sequester** the company's assets until the bankruptcy plan was put into place.*

See also: Sequestration

Sequestration (see-kwes-TRAY-shun), *noun*

(1) The act of keeping isolated a jury or a witness for all or part of a trial to avoid outside influences. (2) Also, the act of setting aside assets and putting them in control of a trustee during a bankruptcy proceeding or until a claim has been satisfied.

(1) The judge ordered the **sequestration** *of witnesses for the prosecution so that they would not be influenced by the testimony of others. (2) The trustee took possession of the company's assets during a* **sequestration** *period that will remain in effect until the financial reorganization plan is approved and put into effect.*

See also: Sequester

Servient estate, *noun*

Real property which is subject to an easement or another granted right, called a dominant estate.

Because of the presence in the deed of an easement to allow installation of utility lines across a portion of the land, the property is considered a **servient estate**.

See also: Dominant estate

Set aside, *verb*

To overrule an order or judgment by a court. Other words to the same effect are annul or negate.

The appeals court **set aside** *the lower court ruling and ordered a retrial.*

See also: Annul, Negate, Quash, Vacate

Setback, *noun*

In building codes, the minimum allowable distance between a structure and the lot line that marks one side of the property.

The building code requires homes have a **setback** *of at least twenty-five feet from the front and rear lot lines and fifteen feet from the side lot lines of the property.*

See also: Zoning

Setoff, *noun*

A claim by a defendant that the plaintiff owes money to the defendant, and that the money should be subtracted from any monetary damages claimed by or awarded to the plaintiff.

*The defendant filed papers showing that the plaintiff owed $50,000 to the defendant, and asked the court to subtract that amount from the damage claim as a **setoff**.*

See also: Offset, Recoupment, Counterclaim, Cross claim

Settle, *verb*

To resolve a dispute or lawsuit before the institution or conclusion of a lawsuit.

*At the suggestion of the judge, the parties met with an arbitrator and agreed to **settle** their dispute without going through the full process of a court proceeding.*

Settlement, *noun*

A resolution to a dispute or lawsuit outside of a court proceeding.

*The parties to the dispute reached an out-of-court **settlement** of the lawsuit and petitioned the judge to dismiss the case.*

See also: Settle, Counteroffer

Settlement statement, *noun*

A document that lists all expected costs for an upcoming real estate purchase or the refinancing of a loan. The settlement statement is required by the federal Real Estate Settlement Procedures Act.

*Before a closing, the buyer of real estate is required to receive a **settlement statement** that lists all costs and funds received and provides a final amount for the closing.*

Settlor, *noun*

The person who creates a trust by signing paperwork or making transfer of money or property to a trustee.

*The **settlor** established a family trust to hold assets of the estate.*

See also: Trustee

Severalty, *noun*

The holding of property by an individual, as opposed to joint ownership.

*The building was owned in **severalty** by Beene and not shared with his partner in the business which operated there.*

See also: Joint

Severance, *noun*

(1) A court order to separate two or more defendants charged with the same crime so that they might have individual trials. (2) Also, a division of some of the issues in a trial so that one is decided before the other is considered. This is also called bifurcation. (3) Also, a special payment made to an employee who has been terminated, or made to an employee to encourage a resignation or retirement.

*(1) The judge granted a motion for **severance** so that the attorneys for the two defendants could mount differing legal defenses to the charge. (2) The judge ordered a **severance** of the issues in the trial so that the matter of whether the defendant was guilty of negligence would be decided before the matter of compensation was considered. (3) Consolidated Intergalactic offered a **severance** package that included three months of salary and health insurance to employees who would take early retirement.*

See also: Bifurcation

Sex discrimination, *noun*

Discrimination in hiring, employment, or promotion based on a person's sex.

*The lawsuit claimed that female workers were subject to **sex discrimination** in not being offered available jobs driving trucks; the lawsuit said they were told these jobs were "for the men."*

Sexual harassment (SEK-shew-el he-RASS-mint), *noun*

Unwanted sexual approaches, lewd behavior, or offensive language. Also, a suggestion that employment, promotion, or salary is linked to sexual favors.

*The shop foreman was accused of **sexual harassment** by several employees who said he demanded sex in return for a promotion.*

See also: Harassment

Sexual predator, *noun*

A person identified by the court, or by law, as someone who is considered likely to commit a sexual offense again.

*In many jurisdictions, the law requires any person listed in judicial documents as a **sexual predator** to register their address with local police.*

Share, *noun*

(1) A portion of ownership in or benefit from a business, estate, trust, or claim divided with others. The share may be equally divided or subject to a specific fraction as stated in an agreement. (2) Also, a portion of ownership in a corporation.

> *(1) The three brothers own an equal **share** in the furniture business and all of its assets. (2) Investors in the stock issued by a corporation receive **shares** that can usually be sold or traded with others.*

See also: Stock, Blue chip stock

Shell corporation, *noun*

A corporation that is established and registered with a state but has no current business activities.

> *Sometimes it is easier and quicker to set up a corporation by purchasing an inactive **shell corporation** and adapting its charter to the needs of the new company.*

See also: Dummy corporation

Shop, *noun*

When referring to labor management issues, a shop is a workplace where employees are represented by a union.

> *The collective bargaining agreement between the employer and the union set pay rates as well as working conditions for the **shop**.*

See also: Closed shop, Open shop

Shoplifting, *noun*

The crime of taking items from a store without paying for them, or in some laws the crime of using something from a store without the intention of paying for the item.

> *The **shoplifting** charges against the accused were dismissed after the defense attorney established that the defendant had been detained before he had actually left the store and therefore it could not be proven that he did not intend to pay for the items in his pocket.*

Show cause order, *noun*

A court order directing a party to a lawsuit to appear at a specified date and time to present an argument (show cause) toward which the judge should not make a particular order or finding.

The judge issued a **show cause order** *directing the plaintiff to appear in court to argue against a motion to dismiss the case.*

Sidebar, *noun*

(1) The area to the side or sometimes in front of the judge's bench where attorneys can approach to speak with the judge, usually so that the jury or spectators cannot hear the conversation. (2) Also, an off-the-record or confidential conversation between attorneys and the judge conducted at the side or in front of the bench.

(1) The judge called both attorneys to the **sidebar** *to have a confidential discussion with them. (2) The defense attorney requested a* **sidebar** *to discuss a point of law out of the hearing range of the jury.*

Signatory, *noun*

A party that has signed a contract and is thus bound by its provisions.

As a **signatory** *to the contract, Beecher is required to perform all of the agreed-upon obligations.*

Silent partner, *noun*

An informal term for an investor or partner in a business who takes no part in its management or whose involvement is kept secret.

Barry made a substantial investment in his brother's business, but their agreement called for him to be a **silent partner** *and not involved in day-to-day operations.*

Single-payer, *noun*

A plan for medical insurance where the government pays for health care provided by private providers on the basis of a set fee schedule.

The federal Medicare program is an example of a **single-payer** *health insurance plan.*

See also: HMO, PPO

SIPC (Securities Investor Protection Corporation), *noun*

A nonprofit organization established by Congress to protect assets on deposit with brokerage firms from loss due to insolvency.

Brokers are required to inform their clients about the level of protection afforded by the **SIPC** *for funds on deposit.*

See also: FDIC

Situs (SITE-es), *noun*
A Latin word meaning "site" or "location." In legal terms, it is the place where a crime, accident, or other incident took place.

*The **situs** of a crime is the place where it was committed.*

See also: Premises

Slander, *verb, noun*
A spoken defamation that harms someone's reputation. A written or published defamation is called libel.

*The lawsuit claimed that Mr. Schlein **slandered** the defendant in his commencement speech.*

See also: Defame, Defamation, Libel, Innuendo

Small claims, *noun*
A court that handles claims for damages or money considered to be small; in some jurisdictions the maximum amount of money involved is no more than $5,000.

*The rules of evidence and procedure in a **small claims** court are usually less demanding and make it easier for individuals to represent themselves without hiring an attorney.*

Social Security, *noun*
A federal program, established in 1935, that provides income to most workers after they retire or become disabled. Contributions made over the years are not held in a separate account but are instead disbursed to current recipients.

*Recipients of **Social Security** receive monthly payments that are funded by taxes paid by today's workers and employers.*

See also: FICA

Social Security tax, *noun*
A tax, paid in equal portions by employers and employees, that helps fund the federal government's obligations under the Social Security and Medicare programs.

*Self-employed workers, such as painters or plumbers who run their own business, are responsible for paying both the employer and employee halves of the **Social Security tax**.*

Sodomy (SA-de-mee), *noun*

In general, sexual relations considered "unnatural," including oral or anal intercourse.

> *The definition of* **sodomy** *and its inclusion as a crime has changed over the years as society and lawmakers become more tolerant of consensual sexual acts between adults.*

Sole proprietorship, *noun*

A business owned and operated by one person.

> *Kevin ran his plumbing business as a* **sole proprietorship***, maintaining detailed records so that his accountant can determine profit and loss for tax purposes.*

See also: Self-employed, Partnership, Corporation

Solicitation, *noun*

(1) The crime of offering to engage in sexual activity for money. (2) Also, the crime of encouraging or inducing someone else to engage in the commission of a crime or to commit a crime.

> *(1) The woman was arrested on charges of* **solicitation** *after she approached a plainclothes policeman and offered sex for money. (2) Dylan was charged with* **solicitation** *of others to take part in the robbery of the bank.*

Solvency, *noun*

The state of having sufficient assets to pay all outstanding debts.

> *In order to bid on the government contract, the business had to file a statement that verified its* **solvency** *by showing that its assets were greater than its liabilities.*

Spam, *noun*

In computer terms, spam is a message sent to multiple recipients who did not request its transmission. The term was coined about 1994 and is believed to have come from a sketch by the Monty Python comedy group about a restaurant that served only one dish over and over again—Spam, a canned meat.

> *One of the unpleasant side effects of the e-mail revolution in personal and business use is the uncontrolled growth of* **spam** *sent by mostly unscrupulous individuals or companies.*

Special circumstance, *noun*

(1) A situation, as set forth in law, that allows or requires imposition of a more severe punishment for particularly heinous crimes. (2) Also, a situation, as set forth in law, that allows a judge or jury to impose a lesser punishment because of certain mitigating circumstances.

*(1) In some states, the commission of a crime with the use of a loaded gun is a **special circumstance** that requires the imposition of a longer jail sentence. (2) In the penalty phase of the trial, the judge allowed presentation of testimony about the convicted murderer's abuse as a child as **special circumstances** that would allow a lesser punishment than the death penalty.*

See also: Aggravated, First degree, Mitigation

Special counsel, *noun*

(1) An attorney hired by a prosecutor or appointed by a court because of the need for a special area of expertise or experience. (2) Also, an independent attorney appointed by a government agency to investigate possible wrongdoing by officials.

*(1) The prosecutor added a **special counsel** to his team to assist in the presentation of testimony regarding DNA evidence. (2) The legislature required appointment of a **special counsel** to investigate possible corruption in state agencies.*

See also: Independent counsel

S

Speedy trial, *noun*

As guaranteed by the U.S. Constitution, the right of a criminal defendant to demand a quick trial to avoid being held in jail for an unreasonable amount of time awaiting resolution of charges. An accused person may want to demand a speedy trial to force the hand of the prosecution or may waive the right to a speedy trial in order to gain more time to prepare a defense.

*The defendant's attorney asked the court to demand the prosecution proceed with a **speedy trial** and to not allow further delays.*

Split decision, *noun*

A decision by a jury or a panel of judges that is not unanimous but rather is based on a majority vote.

*The jury indicated its vote for conviction was a **split decision**.*

Squatter, *noun*
An illegal occupant of land or property.

The landowner asked the sheriff's department to assist in evicting **squatters** *from his premises.*

Stale, *adjective*
Made invalid or unenforceable because of a missed deadline or because it was not acted upon within a reasonable period of time.

The judge ruled that the defendant's right to challenge the order had gone **stale** *because five years had passed since the action.*

Standard deduction, *noun*
In taxation, a fixed amount that can be claimed as a deduction as opposed to the preparation of an itemized deduction of a larger amount.

In federal taxation, basic **standard deductions** *are available for individuals, married couples filing jointly, married couples filing separately, a head of household, and a qualifying widow or widower.*

See also: Deduction, Itemized deduction

Standard of proof, *noun*
The type and quality of evidence that a plaintiff (in a civil case) or a prosecutor (in a criminal case) must present in order to win a legal proceeding.

Different types of cases and severity of charges require various **standards of proof** *to be established in order for a plaintiff or prosecutor to prevail.*

Statement, *noun*
(1) A formal account of events given to police or a court by a witness or party in a civil or criminal proceeding. (2) Also, a report of the balance of a loan including amounts paid and amounts due, or a report of the balance of an account from a merchant or service provider that is due for payment.

(1) In his sworn **statement** *to the police, Bean said he was in another city at the time of the crime and was not involved. (2) The monthly* **statement** *from the cable television company showed services provided, the outstanding balance, and recent payments.*

See also: Perjury, Bill of sale

State's attorney, *noun*

An elected or appointed official in a county, city, or other jurisdiction and assigned to oversee the prosecution of crimes. Also known as a district attorney or a prosecutor.

> *The **state's attorney** oversees or personally handles the prosecution of crimes in local jurisdictions; he is generally subject to the supervision of the attorney general in each state.*

See also: District attorney, Prosecutor

State's evidence, *noun*

Evidence including testimony given by a participant or accomplice in a crime against others on trial for the same offense.

> *Hagel gave **state's evidence** against the other defendants after being granted immunity from prosecution.*

See also: Immunity

Statute, *noun*

A law that has been enacted by Congress or a state and ratified as required by the President or a governor or passed over the executive's veto.

> *Federal or state legislatures enact **statutes** that define crimes and civil infractions and set the outlines for regulations that are managed by government agencies.*

S

Statute of limitations, *noun*

A law that sets a maximum amount of time that can elapse between the commission of a particular crime and the filing of charges, or between an event and the filing of a lawsuit.

> *Certain serious crimes, such as murder, are usually exempt from a **statute of limitations**, meaning they can be prosecuted at any time sufficient evidence is found to support a trial.*

Statutory, *adjective*

As enacted, required, or banned by a statute.

> *The **statutory** definition of invasion of privacy has evolved over the year to include various incursions into electronic media and the Internet.*

See also: Statute

Statutory rape, *noun*
The crime of having sex with a person who is younger than the legally defined (statutory) age of consent.

*The teacher was convicted of **statutory rape** for having sexual relations with one of her ninth grade students.*

Stay, *noun, verb*
(1) An action to temporarily stop or delay a judicial proceeding. (2) Also, the order to temporarily stop or delay a judicial proceeding.

*(1) The judge agreed to **stay** the incarceration of the convicted defendant pending the filing of an appeal. (2) The court's **stay** prevented the sheriff from seizing the property included in an earlier order.*

See also: Abeyance

Stock, *noun*
A security that represents a share in the ownership of a corporation.

*The board of directors voted to issue 100,000 new shares of **stock** to raise additional capital for the operations of the company.*

See also: Share, Blue chip stock

Stock certificate, *noun*
A printed document that represents the details of the ownership of a specific number of shares of stock in a corporation.

*Some investors choose to deposit physical copies of **stock certificates** with their broker or other intermediary and to track, sell, and transfer shares electronically or by communication with the broker.*

See also: Share

Stock option, *noun*
The right to purchase or sell a specific number of shares of a particular stock at a certain time in the future.

*As part of his compensation package, the new CEO was granted a **stock option** to purchase 10,000 shares of stock in the company at $20 per share after two years had elapsed; if the chief executive has succeeded in running the company such that the shares are selling for higher than that price the option will be valuable.*

See also: Option

Stockbroker, *noun*

A financial professional who brokers (brings together a buyer and seller) the purchase or sale of shares of stock or bonds.

> Most **stockbrokers** *make a commission on either the purchase or sale of shares of stock.*

See also: Share, Stock

Strict construction, *noun*

A court, judge, or legal expert that applies a very limited view of a law or an element of the Constitution, focusing on the language used and not on circumstances of the time it was drafted or the present day.

> A **strict construction** *interpretation of the century-old law does not allow for the application of the law to modern issues such as electronic privacy.*

See also: Liberal construction, Construction

Sublease, *noun, verb*

(1) A secondary or subsidiary lease to a third party issued by the original lessor of property. (2) Also, the act of producing and executing a secondary lease with a third party.

> (1) *The tenant, forced to move because of a transfer of employment, was able to negotiate a* **sublease** *with a new tenant to cover the remaining six months on the original lease.* (2) *The original lease, as executed by the landlord and the tenant, does not allow the tenant to* **sublease** *the premises to another person without permission from the owner.*

See also: Sublet, Lease

Sublet, *verb*

The act of subleasing to a third party.

> Tessa **sublet** *her apartment to a college student for the summer.*

See also: Sublease, Lease

Subordination, *noun*

Making a debt or claim take secondary (or further back) position behind other debts or claims.

> As part of the bankruptcy reorganization, several lenders had to agree to the **subordination** *of their loans to a lower priority for repayment than the new loan given the company for operating expenses.*

S

Suborn, *verb*
To bribe or induce someone to commit perjury or certain other crimes.

The defense attorney was disbarred after he was convicted of attempting to **suborn** *perjury by a witness against his client.*

Subornation of perjury (se-BOR-nay-shun), *noun*
Encouraging or inducing (persuading) someone else to commit perjury.

The defendant was charged with **subornation of perjury** *for allegedly contacting witnesses in the trial and asking them to testify falsely.*

See also: Perjury

Subpoena, *noun*
A court order demanding a person appear in court as a witness or for other proceedings.

The prosecution asked the court to issue **subpoenas** *to require several associates of the accused to appear as witnesses.*

Sub prime mortgage, *noun*
A mortgage issued to a borrower with a less-than-optimal credit history or someone who would seem to be not certain to be able to repay the loan. Sub-prime borrowers may be charged a higher interest rate than others.

When the economy went into recession, many holders of **sub prime mortgages** *were unable to keep up payments, especially if the loan had a variable rate that increased over time.*

See also: Creditworthiness, Credit report

Subrogor (SUB-row-ger), *noun*
A person or entity that transfers the legal right to collect a claim to another person or entity (a subrogee) in return for payment of expenses, damages, or a debt.

A holder of an insurance policy might enter into an arrangement as a **subrogor** *so that expenses can be paid while the insurance company enters into a lawsuit to collect damages.*

Succession, *noun*
(1) The rules, as set by state law, for the passing of assets in a deceased person's estate when there is no will. (2) Also, in government, the process and order of passing a job title and responsibility from one official to another.

(1) Under most rules of **succession**, *the assets of a person who dies intestate pass first to a surviving spouse and then to any surviving children of that marriage. (2) Upon the death, incapacitation, or resignation of the governor, state law says the power and title is transferred to the lieutenant governor by* **succession**.

See also: Descent, Intestate

Sue, *verb*
To launch a lawsuit or seek legal proceedings against a person or entity.
A key principle of civil law is the right to **sue** *for redress of injury.*

Sufferance, *noun*
The legal status that applies when a tenant continues to occupy property or premises after a lease has expired, also known as a holdover tenancy.
When a tenant continues to occupy a premises after a lease has expired the tenant at **sufferance** *is still bound by the terms of the original lease.*

See also: Holdover tenancy

Suit, *noun*
A lawsuit or any other filing with the court for judicial action.
The owner of the bowling alley filed **suit** *to recover lost revenues caused by the application of the incorrect varnish on the lanes.*

S

Summary, *adjective*
A judgment or order made without a full legal process.
The court issued a **summary** *judgment dismissing the case before it came to trial.*

Summation, *noun*
An attorney's concluding argument to a judge or jury, summing up evidence presented in a case and asking for a particular verdict. The argument can include points of law. Also known as a closing statement.
The attorney's **summation** *won his case.*

See also: Closing statement

Surety (SHUR-e-tee), *noun*
Someone who agrees to guarantee another person's performance of an agreed-upon task or payment of money due. A company can also act as a surety for another business.

William signed the contract as a **surety***, guaranteeing to step in and perform the services if Fred failed to do so.*

See also: Bond, Surety bond

Surety bond (SHUR-e-tee bond), *noun*

A financial instrument sold by a third party to guarantee that a person or business will perform an agreed-upon task or pay money due.

The contract required Consolidated Intergalactic to purchase a **surety bond** *to guarantee that the client would not suffer financial harm if the products were not delivered on time.*

See also: Bond, Surety

Surrogate (SUR-e-gate), *noun*

(1) A person acting on behalf of or instead of a person. (2) Also, a woman who gives birth to a child for another person, using a donated fertilized egg or other fertility methods.

(1) The attorney asked another lawyer to appear in court as his **surrogate***. (2) Donna acted as a* **surrogate** *mother for Louise.*

Survivorship, *noun*

A right that is dependent upon surviving another person.

Under terms of an investment account that is opened under terms of joint right of **survivorship***, the full amount of funds automatically transfers to the control of the other named party if one of the owners dies.*

Suspend, *verb*

To prevent or halt something from happening or going into effect.

The judge said he would **suspend** *issuance of the injunction by twenty-four hours to give the parties an opportunity to seek a settlement out of court.*

See also: Suspended sentence

Suspended sentence, *noun*

A judgment or sentence by a court in which some or all of the penalties are not imposed and are held in suspense for a specified period of time. If the defendant does not follow rules set down by the judge, the penalties will be put into effect.

*The judge decided to impose a **suspended sentence** on the defendant, saying that the prison term would not have to be served if there were no further convictions or infractions in the next five years.*
See also: Suspend

Sustain, *verb*
The action of a court to agree to an objection or other motion.
*The judge **sustained** the defense attorney's objection to the introduction of his client's past criminal record.*

Tacking, *noun*
In regards adverse possession, the combination of time periods during which the property was occupied and used by different persons.
*The plaintiff argued that by **tacking** the periods of adverse possession the total amount of time during which the premises were not under the control of the owner exceeded the statute of limitations for reestablishment of the estate.*
See also: Adverse possession

T

Taking, *noun*
The act of a government to take private property for a public purpose.
*Under provisions of the Fifth Amendment of the U.S. Constitution, in the **taking** of land by the government the owner must be fairly compensated.*
See also: Eminent domain

Taking the Fifth, *noun*
A rightful refusal to testify in a criminal case under the provisions of the Fifth Amendment to the U.S. Constitution that says that no person can be "compelled to be a witness against himself." If a defendant willingly takes the stand in a case, the protection no longer applies.
*Called before the grand jury, Albright told the prosecutor he would be **taking the Fifth** in answer to any question that might tend to incriminate him.*
See also: Self incrimination

Tangible property (TAN-je-bel), *noun*

Physical items—things that can be touched—as opposed to intangible or incorporeal items such as intellectual property.

*The state applies an excise tax on certain types of **tangible property** such as automobiles, boats, and recreational vehicles.*

See also: Intangible

Tariff, *noun*

A tax or duty on a specific type of import or export.

*The government imposed a **tariff** on all imported petroleum products to raise revenue.*

See also: Tax

Tax, *noun*

An amount of money, usually expressed as a percentage, levied by the government on such things as income, property value, or transactions.

*More than half of the states have one form or another of sales **tax** that is collected from buyers by sellers of goods and paid to the government.*

See also: Excise tax, Property tax, Sales tax, Tariff

Tax avoidance, *noun*

An effort, using legal means, to reduce the amount of taxes that are due to be paid.

*Trusts, tax shelters, and investments in tax-exempt bonds are among ways some people plan **tax avoidance** to reduce their obligation to the government.*

See also: Tax evasion

Tax bracket, *noun*

In calculation of income tax, a particular range of incomes.

*The federal income tax applies increasing tax rates to successively higher **tax brackets**.*

See also: Tax rate, Effective tax rate

Tax break, *noun*

A deduction that reduces taxable income. The state or federal government enacts tax breaks or credits to encourage certain social, environmental, or economic goals.

*The President asked Congress to include a **tax break** to benefit employers who add domestic jobs instead of outsourcing work to foreign locations.*

See also: Tax credit, Tax incentive

Tax credit, *noun*

A reduction or rebate given to certain groups of taxpayers.

*As part of an effort to boost sales of fuel-efficient vehicles, the federal government offered a **tax credit** to buyers of hybrid cars.*

See also: Tax break

Tax evasion, *noun*

The crime of intentionally using means to escape payment of taxes that are required to be paid.

*Orzo was indicted on charges of **tax evasion**; the prosecutor alleged the defendant hid the bulk of his income through use of a series of illegal transactions and techniques.*

See also: Tax avoidance

Tax exempt, *noun*

A transaction, item, or certain types of income that are not subject to taxation.

*Interest on certain types of municipal bonds are **tax exempt** on federal returns and the state where they were issued.*

Tax incentive, *noun*

In general, a tax break or tax credit offered individuals or companies to encourage particular societal, environmental, or economic goals.

*The legislature offered the company a significant set of **tax incentives** to convince the manufacturer to build a new factory in the state.*

See also: Tax credit

Taxpayer identification number, *noun*

The unique identification number used for the reporting of income and certain other tax-related transactions. Individuals use a Social Security number, issued by the Social Security Administration; business entities make reports using a taxpayer identification number assigned by the Internal Revenue Service.

T

*The company requires all contractors to provide either a Social Security number or a **Taxpayer identification number** so that income can be properly reported to the IRS.*

Tax rate, *noun*

The percentage of taxable income that must be paid as tax, or the percentage of the assessed value of real property or tangible property that must be paid as tax.

*In some states, tangible real property such as automobiles is subject to a **tax rate** that is applied to its depreciated value.*

See also: Effective tax rate, Tax bracket, Taxable income

Tax sale, *noun*

A court-ordered sale of property to satisfy the state or federal government's claim for unpaid taxes.

*The judge approved the seizure of the defendant's automobile and its **tax sale** to generate funds to pay back taxes.*

Tax shelter, *noun*

A financial arrangement intended to reduce taxes.

*Some **tax shelter** strategies involve investments that yield deductions and credits that offset income that would otherwise be taxable.*

See also: Tax avoidance

Taxable income, *noun*

The portion of income that is subject to income tax.

*The amount of **taxable income** is determined by totaling all nonexempt income and then subtracting any personal exemptions, standard or itemized deductions, and credits.*

See also: Gross income

Technicality (tek-ne-KA-le-tee), *noun*

A very technical or very specific point of law or element of regulations.

*The case was dismissed on a **technicality**, because the arresting officer had failed to note the correct date and time on the traffic citation.*

Temporary injunction, *noun*

A court order barring an action by a party in a lawsuit until later action in a court proceeding or the conclusion of the trial.

> *The judge issued a **temporary injunction** against the defendant, ordering a halt to production, distribution, or sale of any products that use the patented technology that is at issue in the lawsuit.*

See also: Injunction

Tenancy, *noun*

An interest in real property that gives the holder the right to possess and use it.

> *During the **tenancy** granted by the lease, the tenant cannot make any permanent changes to the property without the permission of the landlord.*

Tender (TEN-dur), *verb*

(1) To make a formal offer for an agreement that will be effective immediately or fulfilled immediately. (2) Also, to present payment.

> *(1) The company **tendered** an offer to make the repair immediately. (2) Jones **tendered** payment one day before the final due date.*

Tenure, *noun*

In an employment contract, the guarantee of a job once a probationary period has passed or the worker has achieved certain milestones or requirements. Once a worker has been given tenure, he or she can only be dismissed for misconduct or as part of a reduction in staffing levels applied to an entire class of employees.

> *At many colleges, professors are granted **tenure** once they have been employed for a specific number of years and have been approved by a committee of their peers.*

Term, *noun*

(1) In a contract or a lease, the period of time covered by the agreement. Also, a specific condition or provision of that contract or lease. (2) Also, in government, the period of time in office for elected officials and certain appointed jobs.

> *(1) The contract covers a **term** of twenty-four months. Under terms of the lease, permanent improvements or changes to the premises require prior*

approval from the owner. (2) The commissioner was elected to a five-year **term***. Members of the board are appointed for two-year terms.*

<u>See also: Lease</u>

Territorial, *adjective*

Related to the ownership or governance of a region of land or sea.

In general, federal laws apply to all land within its borders as well as **ter-ritorial** *waters that extend twelve nautical miles out to sea from the coast.*

<u>See also: U.S. Territories</u>

Testacy, *noun*

Dying with a will (testament) in effect.

The court conducted a hearing to determine whether most died in **testacy***.*

<u>See also: Intestate</u>

Testator (TES-ta-tor), *noun*

The person who leaves a will at death.

The probate court examined the will and determined that the **testator** *had properly executed the document.*

<u>See also: Decedent, Estate</u>

Testimony, *noun*

A statement made under oath in a court of law, or as a deposition before attorneys or officers of the court.

Testimony *may be entered as evidence in a trial, but it is up to the judge or jury to decide whether it is proof of a fact in the case.*

<u>See also: Eyewitness, Witness</u>

Theft, *noun*

The crime of intentionally stealing personal property, or taking property through certain types of fraud.

The definition of **theft** *usually includes an intention to convert stolen items to the thief's own use or to sell it to others.*

<u>See also: Grand theft, Petty theft, Burglary, Breaking and entering, Robbery</u>

Theory, *noun*

The body of law and the facts of the case that justify conviction.

*A prosecutor or a plaintiff's attorney develops a **theory** of the case that he presents to the judge or jury in asking for a particular verdict.*

Third degree, *noun*

An informal term meaning the subjection of a witness or accused person to severe pressure to obtain information or to seek a confession. The phrase is said to have been derived from a Masonic ritual.

*The defense counsel accused the detectives of giving the defendant the **third degree** to force him to admit to the crime, and asked the judge to disallow admission of the confession.*

Third party, *noun*

A party not directly involved in a contract or a transaction but has an involvement.

*The **third party** may be a customer or client, a facilitator or witness to the deal, or completely independent.*

Threat, *noun*

A statement of intention to cause pain, injury, or damage to someone, or an action that serves to indicate that same intention.

*The prosecutor called to the stand several witnesses who testified that the defendant had made a clear **threat** to kill Mr. Jones if he did not pay him the money he said was owed.*

See also: Extortion

Three strikes, *noun*

Legislation in some states that add harsh punishment including life imprisonment for criminals convicted of three violent felonies.

*Under the state's **three strikes** law, Rodham faced an automatic sentence of life imprisonment after her third conviction for armed robbery.*

Timeshare, *noun*

Ownership in real property shared with others, with occupancy typically assigned to a specific time period each year. The deed of occupancy for their period can be sold or transferred to others.

***Timeshare** investments are popular in certain vacation destinations where visitors intend to return to the same location year after year.*

Title, *noun*

The legal right of ownership of real property or personal property.

*The sale of real property is concluded with the transfer of **title** to the new owner.*

See also: Deed

Title insurance policy, *noun*

A specialized form of insurance which protects against unknown defects in the title or liens or encumbrances. The policy is purchased before closing by the buyer or by the lender issuing a mortgage.

*The **title insurance policy** provides legal defense and covers losses that might occur if the title is found to be faulty.*

Tort, *noun*

A civil wrong, intentional or accidental, which causes injury or damage to another person, their property, their rights or interests, or other things that are protected by law.

*The plaintiff's claim stated that the failure of the plumber to properly install the pipes was a **tort** and asked for damages.*

See also: Lawsuit, Damages, Injury

Trade name, *noun*

The name that identifies a company.

*A business's **trade name** is a valuable piece of intellectual property that the company will seek to protect against unauthorized use by others.*

See also: Trademark, Infringe

Trademark, *noun*

A symbol, picture, graphic, wording, or similar design that is associated with a product or company. A trademark can be established by a demonstrated use over time, or by registration with the U.S. Patent and Trademark Office, or both.

*The company filed a lawsuit charging that its **trademark** had been infringed upon by a similar product name used by another manufacturer.*

See also: Infringe, Intellectual property, Trade name

Transaction fee, *noun*

A fee charged by the issuer of a credit or debit card for making a transaction outside of their network of merchants, ATMs, or financial institutions. Sometimes called a foreign fee.

*Acme Savings and Loan charges a **transaction fee** of $3 any time one of their cards is used at an automated teller machine belonging to another institution.*

Transfer, *noun, verb*

The passage of title over property, securities, rights, or responsibilities from the owner to another person or entity.

*The **transfer** of title was scheduled to take place at the escrow agent's office after the completion of the closing.*

Transfer tax, *noun*

A form of estate tax, also called a generation-skipping transfer (GST) tax, that is applied to certain transfers that do not go to the next generation down.

*One situation in which a **transfer tax** might be levied is a gift that skips over the children of the donor and goes instead to the grandchildren.*

See also: Estate tax, Generation-skipping transfer

Trespass, *noun*

Unauthorized or illegal entry onto someone else's property.

*The various states have different laws regarding the rights of a property owner to prevent **trespass** or how they may deal with trespassers they encounter.*

See also: Infringe

Trial de novo, *noun*

A retrial of a case as if no previous trial had occurred.

*After the trial ended with a hung jury, the judge ordered a **trial de novo** to consider the same charges.*

See also: Retrial

Trust, *noun*

A legal arrangement under which one person or an entity is made the nominal or actual owner of property but is required to hold or use it for the benefit of one or more other persons.

*The Rehms established a family **trust** to assume ownership of most of their assets and help simplify the passing of their estate to their heirs and deal with some of the tax issues involved.*

Trust deed, *noun*

A form of deed used to transfer property to a trust.

*The **trust deed** includes a description of the property involved in the trust and the conditions and requirements placed on the trustee.*

Trustee, *noun*

The third party (or entity) given control of a trust and responsibilities as outlined in the trust deed.

*As **trustee** for the family estate, Webster is required to act in a reasonable way to maintain or enhance the value of the assets in the trust and to follow the conditions that set it up.*

See also: Trust, Trust deed

U

Uncorroborated, *noun*

A statement or evidence that is not confirmed or supported by other evidence.

*The defense attorney argued that the testimony of the prosecution's principal witness was completely **uncorroborated** by any other evidence introduced and should not be sufficient as the basis for the jury to make its decision.*

Under the influence, *noun*

Being drunk or high as the result of the use of legal or illegal alcohol or drugs.

*The trooper put the man under arrest after conducting a field sobriety test and determining the driver was **under the influence**.*

See also: Driving under the influence, Driving while intoxicated

Understanding, *noun*

(1) A preliminary or informal agreement. (2) Also, one party's expressed interpretation of a term or other element of a contract.

*(1) The two parties reached an **understanding** and intend to produce a formal letter of agreement within the next week. (2) It is our **understanding** that the work specified in the contract is to be accomplished using products made in America wherever possible.*

Underwrite, *verb*
(1) A guarantee to provide payment under the terms of an insurance policy. (2) Also, a guarantee by a financial institution to purchase any unsold shares of stock or bond in a public offering.

*(1) The insurance company agreed to **underwrite** a policy protecting Consolidated Intergalactic against liability claims for its products. (2) The investment bank agreed to **underwrite** the public offering of shares of stock.*

Undue influence, *noun*
Improper or disproportionate pressure placed on someone to induce that person to take a particular action.

*The court found that the financial advisor had exerted **undue influence** on his client and found for the plaintiff, ordering restitution of all losses.*

Unearned income, *noun*
Income that comes from investments or other sources other than as the result of employment in a job.

*The tax code differentiates between earned and **unearned income** in some of its rates and rules.*

Unemployment compensation, *noun*
Payment made by a government agency to workers who lose their jobs.

*Most **unemployment compensation** plans exclude workers who are fired for cause or who quit their jobs.*

See also: Unemployment insurance

Unemployment insurance, *noun*
The underlying government plan that funds unemployment compensation to laid-off workers. In most plans, the program is funded by state and federal taxes paid by employers.

*Employers are generally required to pay **unemployment insurance** taxes on payrolls for all permanent employees.*

See also: Unemployment compensation

Unencumbered, *noun, adjective*

A deed or other legal instrument that has no known burden or impediment that would block its transfer or implementation.

*The company that conducted the title search reported that they had found the deed to be **unencumbered**.*

Unethical, *adjective*

Not in keeping with generally accepted standards for the conduct of business or government affairs.

*The attorney was sanctioned by the state bar association for what it described as **unethical** behavior in preparing witnesses for trial; the report said that no laws appeared to have been violated.*

Unfair competition, *noun*

The conduct of business in such a way as to illegally cause economic damage to a competitor.

*The court found that Transglobal Trucking had intentionally infringed on the trade name and trademark of Transnational Trucking resulting in the tort of **unfair competition**.*

Union, *noun*

An association of workers created for the purpose of collective bargaining with an employer for wages and working conditions.

*The hourly workers are represented by a **union** that deals with the company to negotiate contracts and protect the rights of unionized workers in any dispute with the employer.*

See also: Collective bargaining, Grievance, Closed shop

United States Attorney, *noun*

An attorney that represents the federal government to prosecute or oversee the prosecution of civil or criminal cases.

*The Attorney General appoints a **United States Attorney** for each federal district in the nation.*

USA Patriot Act, *noun*

A broad-reaching statute, passed in the aftermath of the September 11, 2001, terrorist acts, that gave new powers to the Justice Department including the ability to conduct certain domestic and international surveillance.

> *Some of the provisions of the **USA Patriot Act** have been challenged by civil liberties groups on the grounds they may violate some of the protections of the Bill of Rights.*

U.S. Territories, *noun*

Land owned, occupied, or governed by the United States but not granted status as a state. There are a total of fourteen territories claimed by the United States.

> *The best-known **U.S. Territories** are Puerto Rico and the U.S. Virgin Islands in the Caribbean, and Pacific islands including American Samoa, Guam, Midway, and Wake.*

Usury (YOU-zhurr-ee), *noun*

The crime of charging an unreasonably high rate of interest on a loan.

> *In most situations, state laws set the maximum interest rate that can be charged; rates above that level are considered **usury**.*

See also: Loan shark

UTMA custodial account, UGMA, *noun*

A custodial account under the control of a guardian for the benefit of a minor. The governing law is called the Uniform Transfers to Minors Act (UTMA), or in some states the Uniform Gift to Minors Act (UGMA).

> *The grandparents gave a gift of cash to each of their grandchildren, with the parents listed as guardians of a **UTMA** custodial account.*

Utter, *verb*

To put forth a financial instrument as good and negotiable.

> *In the language of the law in some states, it is illegal to **utter** a forged or altered check.*

See also: Forge, Forgery

Vacant, *adjective*
Empty of inhabitants and their possessions, or a property without any structures on it.

*The landlord inspected the apartment to assure it was **vacant** and in proper repair before returning the security deposit to the former tenant.*

Vacate (VAY-kate), *verb*
(1) An action by a court to set aside an order or judgment, an action by a judge. (2) Also, to leave a premises and end occupancy.

*(1) The appeals court justice **vacated** the lower court's order and ordered a new hearing on the matter. (2) The tenant **vacated** the premises one day before the end of the lease.*

See also: Set aside

Variable rate, *noun*
An interest rate on a loan that is subject to change on the basis of a specified index, such as the prime rate or the LIBOR.

*The adjustable rate mortgage is based on a **variable rate** that can be reset once a year based on the current level of the prime rate.*

See also: Adjustable rate mortgage, Prime rate, LIBOR

Variance, *noun*
In zoning regulation, the authorization by a governmental agency of an exception to an applicant.

*The zoning board of appeals approved a **variance** to zoning regulations to permit the applicant to locate the new building ten feet away from the side lot line noting that this would avoid interference with wetlands on the other side of the parcel.*

Vehicular manslaughter (vee-HIH-kyoo-ler), *noun*
The crime of causing a death as the result of negligent or reckless driving, including operating a motor vehicle under the influence of alcohol or drugs.

*After the results of the blood alcohol test was received, Simon was arrested and charged with **vehicular manslaughter** for causing the death of a pedestrian in an automobile accident.*

See also: Manslaughter, Involuntary manslaughter

Vendor, *noun*

The seller of an item, including real and personal property.

*In general, state law requires the solicitation of bids from at least three capable **vendors** before a contract for the purchase of property is awarded.*

Venue (VEN-yu), *noun*

The jurisdiction where a trial is ordinarily expected to take place, generally because it has a connection to the crime or lawsuit.

*The defense attorney filed a motion for a change of **venue** because the widespread publicity about the case would make it very difficult to obtain an impartial jury.*

Verdict, *noun*

A jury's decision in a civil or criminal trial.

*The jury reached its **verdict** after three days of deliberation.*

See also: Guilty, Not guilty, Convict, Acquit, Finding of fact

Versus, *preposition*

Against. A legal dispute is usually expressed as one side versus another. Versus is often abbreviated as vs. or v., as in Dred Scott v. Sandford.

*In the case of the Commonwealth of Massachusetts **vs.** Lizzie A. Borden, Miss Borden was found innocent of the charges of murder.*

Vested, *adjective*

(1) An interest in property that takes effect at a certain time or after certain events occur. (2) Also, rights that are protected under the Constitution and cannot be arbitrarily taken away by the action of a court or a legislature.

*(1) Ownership in the property is transferred and becomes **vested** upon the death of the donor. (2) The freedom of assembly is a right that is **vested** in the Constitution and courts have struck down certain laws that have sought to unreasonably limit that right.*

Vexatious, *noun, adjective*

A lawsuit deemed to be without merit and filed only to harass another party.

*The court dismissed the lawsuit, ruling that it had been filed for **vexa-tious** purposes, only to embarrass the defendant.*

See also: Frivolous suit, Abuse of Process

Visa, *noun*

A special form of official permission required to enter or to live and work in a country.

*Tourists seeking to visit certain countries must file for a **visa** in advance of their trip and receive permission from the foreign government.*

Visitation, *noun*

In family court matters, the right of a parent, family member, or guardian to visit or spend time with a child who is in the custody of someone else.

*The judge ordered that the boy's natural father be granted **visitation** rights of two weekends per month.*

Void, *noun, adjective*

A law, contract, or order that has been made null or invalid.

*Noting that a subsequent law had made the previous statute **void**, the court directed the prosecutor to dismiss charges brought under the nullified law.*

See also: Null, Abrogate, Vacate

Voir dire (VWAHR-deer), *noun*

The questioning of potential jurors by attorneys or a judge before selection of a panel. Also, a preliminary examination of a witness by attorneys or a judge before testimony is given before a jury.

*During the **voir dire** of prospective jurors it was determined that very few people in the community were unaware of most of the details of the murder case.*

W-2, *noun*

An annual statement of taxable wages earned and taxes withheld, given to an employee by an employer.

*The **W-2** form is an essential piece of information needed to file federal taxes, proving wages earned in the previous calendar year.*

W-4, *noun*

The IRS W-4 form is the Employee's Withholding Allowance Certificate, submitted by an employee to an employer to indicate the number of personal exemptions claimed.

*An employer uses the **W-4** form prepared by each employee in calculating the amount of tax withheld from each paycheck in anticipation of taxes that will be due state and federal governments.*

W-9, *noun*

An IRS form, also known as a Request for Taxpayer Identification Number and Certification. It is used by companies to verify the taxpayer identification number (TIN) of a business or the Social Security number of a U.S. citizen or resident alien for tax purposes.

*In most situations, a company entering into a contract with another business or an individual will require submission of a **W-9** form to verify information.*

See also: Taxpayer identification number

Waiver (WAY-vur), *noun*

A voluntary relinquishment of a right or claim. Someone can grant a waiver, or fail to exercise a right and lose the opportunity to do so at a later time.

*The agreement included a **waiver** of the right to sue for damages caused as the result of any errors in the agreed-upon specifications.*

W

Ward, *noun*

A person who, under a court order, has a guardian to manage affairs. In most cases, wards are minors although the term can also be applied to someone who needs assistance because of mental or medical incapacity. A person who is in need of protection but does not have an appointed guardian is called a ward of the court.

*Tanya Gross signed the papers as guardian for Sammy Artem, her **ward**.*

See also: Guardian, Guardian ad litem, Custodial parent, Conservator

Warrant, *noun*

(1) An order from a court authorizing a law enforcement official to take a specific action, including making an arrest or searching a premises. (2) Also, a right granted to someone to purchase a financial security at a specific price within a particular time period.

*(1) The judge issued a **warrant** for the arrest of Klein on charges that he had amassed more than $3,000 in unpaid parking tickets. (2) To entice new investors in a bond issue, the corporation also included a **warrant** for the purchase of stock at today's price any time within the next twelve months.*

See also: Search warrant

Warrantless search, *noun*

Search of private property without a court-issued warrant. There are certain exceptions that permit such a search, including "hot pursuit" of a suspect into a building or probable cause to believe that a serious crime was taking place at the time law enforcement authorities are at a location.

*The prosecutor argued that the **warrantless search** of the building was justified because police officers had followed the gunman to the location in hot pursuit.*

See also: Search warrant

Warranty, *noun*

(1) A written guarantee to the purchaser of an item to repair or replace the product if necessary, within the specified time period and subject to the conditions that are included. (2) Also, in contract law, a promise by the seller that the item being sold is as promised or described.

*(1) The **warranty** on the tire covers all problems caused by the failure of materials or improper workmanship for a period of three years; the warranty does not cover any damage caused by use of the car on unpaved roads. (2) The contract included a warranty by the seller that the products would meet all applicable state and federal regulations and would be merchantable.*

Waste, *noun*

Damage to real property caused by a tenant.

*The lease allows the landlord to subtract the loss of value to the apartment caused by **waste**, including neglect or damage to appliances.*

Whistleblower, *noun*

An employee who reports illegal or wrongful actions by an employer.

*Most states and the federal government have enacted legislation to protect **whistleblowers** who expose dangerous or illegal activities in the public or private sector.*

Will, *noun*

A written document that contains legally acceptable instructions regarding the distributions of assets and performance of other acts after the death of the person making the will.

> *Harrison's **will** included the appointment of a legal guardian to look after the financial and other affairs of his minor children as well as bequests to his children and other family members.*

See also: Estate, Testacy, Intestate

Willful, *adjective*

Something done deliberately and sometimes with disregard for the consequences.

> *The indictment charges that the defendants engaged in **willful** disregard for the law and of the effect their actions would have on others.*

Withholding, *noun*

Money held back from wages and paid directly to the government by an employer as an advance against income tax and FICA obligations.

> *Employees can change the amount of **withholding** from their paychecks by adjusting the information included on their W-4 form.*

See also: W-4

Witness, *noun*

A person who has firsthand knowledge about a crime or a particular event related to a criminal or civil trial.

> *The prosecution called Malone as a **witness** to the events leading up to the assault.*

See also: Eyewitness, Hearsay, Hostile witness

Work for hire, *noun*

An agreement in which a writer, designer, or other creator of a work sells all rights to another party, such as a publisher.

> *In a **work for hire** agreement, an author does not retain the right to resell or reuse a manuscript or other document.*

Work release, *noun*

A program that allows prisoners to perform work outside of prison while serving their sentences.

*The state's **work release** program is intended to allow convicts to gradually re-integrate into the outside world before their prison term is finished.*

Workers' compensation, *noun*

A state program that provides payment to workers injured on the job. Plans are funded by taxes levied on employers.

*Most state **workers' compensation** plans cover medical expenses, rehabilitation, and some or all of lost wages.*

Writ, *noun*

A written order from a court demanding specific action by a person or entity.

*The judge issued a **writ** requiring the sheriff to close down the noncomplying business that had been opened in the storefront.*

See also: Court order, Decree, Habeas corpus

Wrongful, *adjective*

Something that is illegal, unfair, or contrary to judicial equity.

*The basis of a civil suit is that a **wrongful** act has been committed and must be remedied.*

Wrongful death, *noun*

The death of another person as the result of a wrongful act.

*The family filed a civil suit against the pharmacist, alleging that a mistake in preparation of a prescription resulted in the **wrongful death** of the child.*

Zone, *noun*

A defined area or district within a municipality or county that comes under the regulations of a zoning plan.

*The parcel of land was entirely within the **zone** that is reserved for single-family residences, with no commercial use permitted.*

See also: Zoning

Zoning, *noun*

A plan to control development of a municipality by establishing specific zones that are to be used only for particular purposes.

> *The town's **zoning** plan is intended to maintain the character of the historic downtown and to maintain a separation between industrial and commercial enterprises and residential districts.*

See also: Zone

Z

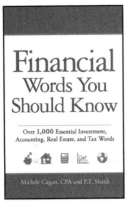
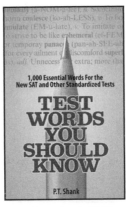
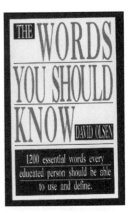
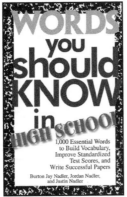